T3-BUW-376

CELEBRATION OF
GRACE

Godly Character
Through Grace Alone

by Jeff Harkin

Applied Grace Publications
P.O. Box 1055, Mundelein, IL 60060-1055

Dedication

To my precious children, Stephen, Joe and Arricka,
that the crucial message of God's grace
be most available to you who are
my most vital responsibility here on earth.

Table of Contents

Bookmark

CELEBRATION OF
GRACE

by Jeff Harkin

For I am confident of this very thing, that He who began a good work in you will perfect it until the day of Christ Jesus.
Philippians 1:6 NASB

How you can make a **big** difference — see other side.

Applied Grace Publications
P.O. Box 1055
Mundelein, IL 60060

How you can make a

BIG

difference:

If you like this book and if you see its value to the rest of the Body of Christ, will you help us distribute it? At this point, you are the key. We are a new, small publishing company with no national network for distribution.

SIMPLE STEPS you can take:

1) In recommending *Celebration of Grace* to your friends, ask your local Christian bookstore to order, stock and display a few copies. This will save you and your friends packaging and postage costs **and** it will get this book out to major distribution points. Tell bookstore owners that Applied Grace Publications will give them excellent terms.

2) Perhaps you would like to form a small study group and go over *Celebration* together. If you want to order books direct from us for your group, volume discounts are available on orders of six or more. Please send self-addressed envelope for price list.

Thank You Thank You Thank You

Preface

Thank God for failure! Why? Because if I had not failed miserably as a legalistic Christian, I could never have known the transforming power of the grace of God. Oh yes, I **became** a Christian totally on the basis of God's grace. But I had no knowledge that the Lord intends for me to continue growing in my walk with Him on the basis of grace alone. Therefore, as happens with scores of Christians, it wasn't long before I let go of grace and fell into the abyss of legalism as my basis for relating to God. And then came failure…upon failure. Christ had taken away my sin and guilt, but legalism amplified both! As a result, I quit on Christianity for five years (in the mid-1960's), and lapsed into worse condition than I had been in as an unbeliever, until I began to understand grace.

Many Christians (especially those like myself who are from dysfunctional backgrounds) constantly doubt the premise that God's will for them is to continue to relate to Him on the basis of grace alone. Is this biblical? Is it orthodox? Can it produce Christian maturity? Of course, most blood-bought, born-again believers in Jesus Christ realize that they came to God initially as nothing more than lost sinners and the Lord reconciled them to Himself on the singular basis of the blood of Christ. In other words, they **began** with grace alone. But does God intend to produce Christian maturity in us through exactly the same grace whereby He saved us to begin with? The answer to this question is an emphatic YES!

It has been my observation throughout 20 years of Christian ministry as both a counselor and a teacher that a surprisingly high percentage of true believers in Jesus Christ are hindered or crippled in many vital areas of their Christian growth, worship and witness because they lack understanding of how to appropriate the grace of God on a daily basis. This lack of understanding causes multitudes of Christians to become disillusioned and frustrated. Some have given up the faith, while many more are merely treading water, having been robbed of the joyful, intimate relationship with the Lord which He Himself deeply desires.

Church history demonstrates that believers in **every** generation become enslaved to legalism. It is a constant temptation for all who desire to please God.

Celebration Of Grace is offered as a tool to help eradicate legalism from your life and to establish you in the grace of God as a way of life. **Celebration** is a book aimed at dealing with guilt and shame PERMANENTLY, God's way. And in this context I will speak to crucial issues such as developing forgiveness, commitment, a consistent devotional life, and learning to pray with confidence. **Celebration** is organized as a series of daily readings which define both legalism and grace and continually encourage the reader to learn to stand in the **grace** of God and to live in **His** righteousness.

The series is designed to be read slowly and meditatively in much the same way as one would use a book of daily devotions. The articles are in a logical sequence. Most of them build upon those preceding. The emphasis is not merely informational, but it is on **applying** the truth of grace in one's life day after day.

Purposeful redundancy has been placed into this work because it seems so difficult for most Christians to learn to habitually relate to God on the basis of grace. If you read this book through in one sitting this redundancy might bother you, but if you use these grace studies on a more or less one-a-day basis, the redundancy will greatly help and reinforce you.

Acknowledgement: I owe the origins of my understanding of "in Christ" and "in Adam" to James S. Stewart, *A Man In Christ,* and to Watchman Nee, *The Normal Christian Life.* My readings named, "In", "Suicide By Crucifixion?", "Count the 'I's'" and "Satisfied With Jesus" originated, either in concept or in terminology, in *The Normal Christian Life.* While I certainly don't agree with everything Watchman Nee taught (which should become obvious as you read the other 117 articles in *Celebration*), nevertheless he had some important things to say.

It is my hope that (in addition to the original concepts in this book) I can assemble important concepts from diverse sources, carefully maintain the integrity of the Gospel itself, and somehow avoid getting cubbyholed into the theological "camps" of most of my sources. Impossible you say? Perhaps, but I've given it my best shot!

The bottom line in this book is this: It must bring you to Jesus Himself, again and again, for *that* is your real need.

Introduction

I publish a monthly devotional letter called "Grace Plus Nothing," the title of which, no doubt, at first glance appears to be imbalanced. Therefore I always head "Grace Plus Nothing" with the following introductory statement:

> Every Christian should be aware that Jesus Christ is "full of grace **and** truth," not just grace. (John 1:14). Therefore, what I mean by "Grace Plus Nothing" is NOT some sort of cheap grace without truth. But my intent in naming this letter "Grace Plus Nothing" is to EMPHASIZE the biblical truth that, in the formation of Christian character, God's truth works ONLY through His grace, and not apart from it.
>
> I emphasize "Grace Plus Nothing" because there has always been a tendency in the body of Christ to preach salvation by grace through faith, but then to proceed to attempt sanctification and holiness through every imaginable form of legalism. Certainly the Lord calls every Christian to press into sanctification and holiness, but neither happens apart from grace. Legalism (works righteousness) can never satisfy God. Therefore, sanctification is by grace:

> For sin shall not be master over you, for you are not under law, but under grace.

> ...those who receive the abundance of grace and of the gift of righteousness will reign in life through the One, Jesus Christ.
>
> *Romans 6:14, 5:17*

This introduction from "Grace Plus Nothing" (including the Scripture) expresses the exact thrust of **Celebration of Grace**. Christians need to be taught to completely forsake the self-righteous performance basis for relating to God, and to forever embrace the grace basis, carefully avoiding the error of cheap grace in the process.

There have always been **two** dangerous tendencies in the Body of Christ, one toward the error of legalism and the other toward the error of cheap grace. But the grace of God is neither legalistic nor cheap.

One of my most important objectives in **Celebration of Grace** is to help you to define and to avoid both legalism and cheap grace. In a nutshell, legalism means works righteousness while cheap grace refers to the all too common misconception that we can ''accept Jesus'' as our Savior and yet somehow simultaneously avoid His Lordship. Cheap grace is also inherent in the belief that mere church attendance or church membership somehow conveys the forgiveness of sins and eternal life.

In our generation many Christians fear cheap grace so much that they have rejected grace preaching completely. Thus, in many circles, even sincere believers are not secure in their salvation. Legalism is usually substituted for grace. Clearly, the baby has been thrown out with the dirty bath water. The cure is worse than the disease.

Celebration of Grace asserts that, without grace, all preaching is just wasted hot air. Sin cannot be removed apart from grace. Hearts and minds cannot be transformed apart from grace. Grace is God's program. Grace is God's design. We have celebrated virtually everything else; NOW, LET US CELEBRATE GRACE! My central objective in **Celebration of Grace** is to glorify God through definition and application of His grace.

I do not address this book to people who want to play games with God and therefore attempt to abuse grace. God Himself will have to deal with you some other way. But I dedicate this book to all of you grace-starved Christians who have a genuine hunger for God. Grace is for you! You will be liberated as you read.

I have included a lot of my own personal testimony in **Celebration of Grace** because I have found it to be helpful for illustrating grace. I hope none of it offends you in any way. I think you will discover that it ministers to you and encourages you. Besides, I have treated the written Word of God itself as authority far superior to any personal testimony.

May the Lord bless you as you read, and may this book provide a springboard for you to study these things for yourself.

Our Righteousness Can't Do It

This is the issue every Christian must face: Our righteousness can't do it.

What do I mean by this? Let me explain.

The Body of Christ in the United States has had access to more teaching and preaching than any church in history. Technology has made an overabundance of Christian tapes, books and TV available to us. All of these are the blessing of God. But, for many of us, our knowledge has outstripped our ability. If we are honest, most of us must admit that we're not applying all that we've learned. We're not living up to God's expectations. We're striving too much. Our righteousness is falling short of the mark.

This book on grace applies to every Christian, but many of you are in an **especially** good place to receive it: Perhaps you yourself have gradually realized that the majority of your attempts at righteousness are falling short of the mark, and perhaps you are feeling quite confused and condemned about it. Perhaps you came to this realization many years ago and your zeal for the Lord gradually cooled, and you became a more or less nominal Christian, because you lost hope that you could learn to live the victorious Christian life. Perhaps you gave up completely. You may think God gave up on you.

But something good is about to happen to you even if you don't expect it: You have finally come to a place where the Lord Himself can intervene powerfully in your life.

While the Lord has not **caused** you to fail, He has **allowed** you to fail in order to reveal **to you** that your righteousness can't do it. He usually accomplishes this through a process (familiar to every generation of God's people) where He allows you to struggle for years and years trying to be spiritual, trying to be holy, reading everybody's exhortations and formulas, and zealously applying new keys to true spirituality, or learning new principles which apply to the deeper life, or to healing, or to prosperity; and then, after all those years of striving, you discover that many of the standard formulas don't seem to

1

work and, worse yet, your righteousness still has blemishes all over it.

Or, on the other hand, perhaps you are the sort of person who usually **succeeds** at your own righteousness. Then the Lord reveals your own sriritual inadequacy in quite another fashion, in that, even though you usually **do** manage to sustain your spiritual performance, nevertheless there remains a deep hunger for more holiness and power in your soul. And there is a recognition that, with all your success, the true spirituality and the abiding peace and the lasting satisfaction which you expected haven't been realized. Where are they? I thought Christians were supposed to have them!

You have them sometimes, maybe in worship or praise, but they are all too fleeting. You have tried to obey the biblical injunction to be holy as your Heavenly Father is holy and you have usually tried to respond zealously to preaching which exhorted you to aim at perfection. But you are becoming discouraged, and exhausted!

Face it: **Your** righteousness and spiritual activity can't do it. God wants you to be totally convinced of this biblical and practical reality. Totally convinced. Why? Because the requirement of God is nothing less than **His righteousness** and **His holiness**! Always. The Lord expects and accepts nothing less than His Own righteousness and His Own holiness. The peace which you seek cannot be found in your own righteousness. The only sort of peace which can ever satisfy your soul is peace with God.

The standard in the Gospel is **always** God's righteousness. But HOW DO WE GET THIS? The Bible tells us how:

> But now apart from the Law *the* righteousness of God has been manifested, being witnessed by the Law and the Prophets, even *the* righteousness of God through faith in Jesus Christ for all those who believe; for there is no distinction, for all have sinned and fall short of the glory of God, being justified as a gift by His grace through the redemption which is in Christ Jesus;
>
> *Romans 3:21-24*

See, God's standard is always God's righteousness, and **that** is where you must find your peace, through faith in Jesus Christ and **HIS** righteousness:

2

> Therefore having been justified by faith, we have peace with God through our Lord Jesus Christ
>
> *Romans 5:1*

Perhaps you are a new Christian, or perhaps, up until now, you have not hit the brick wall which I have described in this article. Thank God, because, if you will learn grace **now**, you **can** avoid a lot of the pain and confusion which the rest of us have suffered. Begin **now** to allow the Lord to show you how to live in His righteousness rather than your own.

Finally, perhaps you have been plagued by some kind of addiction, or maybe you have done some other horribly unacceptable or sinful things. READ ON, READ ON, for it is those who are most desperate who most need this book.

Imprisoned For Mercy

We have said, "Our righteousness can't do it." It can't satisfy God and it seldom satisfies us. Those who **are** satisfied with their own righteousness are actually in a world of trouble, but they don't know it.

Today I want to expand our understanding of why our righteousness can't do it. The Bible says that the entire world is under **the penalty** of sin, death:

> For the wages of sin is death . . .
>
> *Romans 6:23a*

We already know this — it's why most of us became Christians. Death is obvious and we want eternal life.   But the Bible also constantly declares that all humanity is imprisoned not only under the penalty for sin, death, but also under **the power** of sin, enslavement; not just the penalty, but also the power. That is, we human beings are unable to extricate ourselves from sin. Sin has power over us. The **penalty** and the **power** — both are undeniable reality. Humanity struggles to free itself from its prison of sin, and from death, as if some human cure is possible, but sin and death continue unabated.

> ...for all have sinned and fall short of the glory of God...
> ...God gave them over in the lusts of their hearts...
>
> *Romans 3:23; 1:24a*

Both of these verses refer to **all** humanity. See here that **God gave us over** in our lusts. In other words, He gave us over to the power of sin. Thus we are **unable to free ourselves** from the power of sin. We are imprisoned by sin so that the Apostle Paul cried,

> Wretched man that I am! Who will set me free from the body of this death?
>
> *Romans 7:24*

Perhaps it is not so difficult to see why the Lord ordained that the penalty for sin should be death. Clearly sin cannot give life. Nor can the Lord allow the universe to become filled with **eternal** sinners. No, sin must have an end. Therefore there must be death. All this makes sense. But why would a **good** God turn us over to the **power** of sin so that we are unable to free ourselves? Is it all a cruel hoax? No, it is the wisdom of God:

> For God has shut up all in disobedience that He might show mercy to all.
>
> *Romans 11:32*

Here is God's program: All of us are "shut up," (imprisoned) in disobedience (under **the power** of sin), so that God can have mercy on us. Our imprisonment is effective because it leaves us with only one alternative: If we want to be forgiven and freed from the penalty and power of sin we **must** accept God's mercy. In other words, we have been imprisoned for mercy. That is what the Word of God says. God's will is mercy. It makes sense, and it is God's will, that we have been unable to free ourselves from sin so that we must put our hope **totally** in God's mercy. Note, **totally**. Not **partly** in God's mercy and **partly** in human ability. That is why Peter told us,

> ...fix your hope completely on the grace to be brought to you at the revelation of Jesus Christ.
>
> *I Peter 1:13b*

The primary issue is placing our hope **completely** in the grace of God. This means that the primary issue is trusting Christ and His finished work at the cross, **plus nothing**! This sounds radical, and it is. But it is also biblical. The Gospel of Jesus Christ is radical because nothing less can accomplish His purposes in us. Works righteousness is dead! The performance basis for right standing before God is dead!

I plan to demonstrate many times **from the Scriptures** and from experience that, even **after** you become a Christian, the **only** way to maintain freedom from the power of sin is to **continue** to receive God's mercy. And, don't kid yourself, if you persist in works righteousness then the Lord will allow you to fail in order to drive you back to trusting totally in His mercy. Even as a Christian, sin will seem to prevail until you forsake works righteousness and begin trusting God's mercy as a way of life

Someone will question this and say that the Bible teaches us that God has transferred us from the kingdom of darkness to the kingdom of His dear Son (Colossians 1:13), so how can sin still have power over us? Of course, this transfer is complete, but it happened **totally** on the basis of grace. Many Christians forget this, and they return again to works righteousness. So I intend to demonstrate that the Lord allows sin to continue to have limited power over them until they acknowledge that their freedom is **totally** on the basis of grace, not works. This happened to me, and it may be happening to you. I repeat, the Lord **never** causes us to sin, but He may allow us some painful struggles and defeats until we acknowledge His grace more fully.

Most Christians say they know grace, but their struggles and defeats indicate quite the opposite.

Don't depend upon your own human ability to grasp and apply grace. Rather, repent of that, and right now, ask the Lord Himself to begin to reveal His grace to you — what it really means and how it really works.

"O Lord, have mercy upon us and grant that we may see and know and accept your grace. Grant that we may learn to fix our hope totally in Jesus Christ and His shed blood."

Imputed Righteousness

The first essential point we have made is that our righteousness can't satisfy God. And furthermore, because we are so imperfect, our own righteousness seldom satisfies **us** either. Christians who **are** somehow satisfied with works righteousness are in for trouble.

God's requirement is nothing less than **His** righteousness and **His** holiness. Our righteousness cannot earn for us RIGHT STANDING before God. Such RIGHT STANDING before God must be **imputed** to us, as a gift, by God Himself.

How many people have you talked to who will say, "Hey, I'm a good person. I haven't murdered anybody. I try to keep the rules. I try to help my neighbors," and so on and so forth?

But the issue in the Gospel is **God's** righteousness. So the issue in the Gospel is this: Who does **God** recognize as righteous? To whom does **God** impute RIGHT STANDING? What is **God's** criterion for RIGHT STANDING before Him? The Bible clearly announces that there are people to whom **God** imputes righteousness. Who are they? In Romans 4:3 Paul quoted Genesis 15:6 which says,

"AND ABRAHAM BELIEVED GOD, AND IT WAS RECKONED TO HIM AS RIGHTEOUSNESS."

Here's what Paul said about how this applies **to you**:

What then shall we say that Abraham, our forefather according to the flesh, has found?

For if Abraham was justified by works, he has something to boast about; but not before God.

For what does the Scripture say? "AND ABRAHAM BELIEVED GOD, AND IT WAS RECKONED TO HIM AS RIGHTEOUSNESS."

Now to the one who works, his wage is not reckoned as a favor but as what is due.

7

> But to the one who does not work, but believes in Him
> who justifies the ungodly, his faith is reckoned as
> righteousness.
>
> *Romans 4:1-5*

Here is what happened between Abraham and God: God made a promise to Abraham, Abraham believed it, and the Lord reckoned Abraham's simple faith to Abraham as righteousness. In other words, God reckoned Abraham righteous on the basis of faith alone. This, then, is how God "justifies the ungodly."

According to Paul, the Gospel works exactly this way for us. The Lord has promised right standing before Him (righteousness) to **anyone** who will put their faith in the finished work of Christ for forgiveness of sins and eternal life. Therefore, like Abraham, when we simply **believe** this promise of God, the Lord reckons (imputes) righteousness to us.

Anyone qualifies for this grace — every day! You can simply believe God and receive the gift of imputed (reckoned) righteousness. And the best part is that this imputed righteousness is **God's** righteousness, nothing less. Furthermore, understand that this salvation is the **only** salvation. And it is God's **best**, not some lukewarm compromise. Then, and **only** then:

> . . . much more those who receive the abundance of
> grace and of the gift of righteousness will reign in life
> through the One, Jesus Christ.
>
> *Romans 5:17*

It's that simple: The grace of God is primarily the gift of God's righteousness (through the blood of Jesus Christ) and, as a believer, you have it.

How I Lost My Devotional Life
or
If It Ain't Broke, Don't Fix It

I include this story because it provides an excellent example of the difference between grace righteousness and works righteousness.

I turned my life over to Christ while I was stationed on an Army Base. I was alone in my decision. As far as I knew there were no other Christians in my barracks. I had been taught the Gospel years before in Sunday School, thank the Lord, and that's the only reason I understood how to receive Him.

Immediately, when I received Him, I **wanted** to get a Bible, and I **wanted** to study it. I **wanted** time with God. I **wanted** to pray. I didn't know this practice was called "devotions" by most Christians. But I was so full of joy: I had been a wicked sinner, always in trouble, who had been reconciled to God and saved totally as a gift, because Jesus died for me. My **response** was a strong desire to know God. And I wanted to learn to share Him with others. My **response** was genuine hunger for the Lord.

I found a chaplain on the Army base who gave me the key to his office, and every evening I eagerly spent hours **literally** with God. My Bible lived; prayers I prayed got answered; God showed me **so** much then. This continued for months.

After I was discharged from the Army I began to associate with more and more Christians. They were very sincere, and they immediately began to teach me that I **had** to have a devotional life. Not just, "Hey, the Lord really wants time with you, and it will be good for you" (which would be the correct approach) but, "You **have** to do this if you want God's blessing and direction on your life day by day." And, in addition, "Devotional time **early** in the morning is best." Thus, my evening devotions, though powerful, were inferior to morning devotions. Christians who rose early in the morning were considered more spiritual. I had best hasten to add that the Christians who said these things to me may not have meant such statements as strongly as I took them. I may well have jumped to the wrong conclusions totally on my own.

Unbeknownst to me, I moved from devotions as **a response** to grace to devotions as **a law**. I already **had** God's blessing and direction on my life, as gifts, but now I had to try to **earn** these gifts. I already **had** a healthy relationship with God, as a gift, but now I had to try to **earn** it.

What do you suppose happened to my devotional life after that? Right! It died. It became drudgery after that, and much less edifying.

All legalism bears similar fruit: DEATH. As soon as I shifted from the grace basis of relating to God (being a simple sinner saved by grace) to the works basis (developing my own righteousness), sin revived and my spiritual life died. Bang! Like I was shot! Whenever I succeeded at keeping my devotions religiously I felt righteous (self-righteous), and whenever I failed I felt that God had withdrawn His presence from me.

> . . . for the letter [law] kills, but the Spirit gives life.
> *II Corinthians 3:6b*

I encourage you, by the mercies of God, to put all of your confidence in the Lord to bless you and to direct you, even if your devotional life presently **stinks**! He can **create** devotion in you through grace. "Devotions," by definition, should spring from devotion, rather than from self-justification.

And may He help us all to learn that since the power of grace ain't "broke," we don't need to "fix it" with legalism.

As time goes on we shall observe how faithfulness and self-control (both of which are "fruit of the Spirit" according to Galatians 5:22,23) play a definite role in building a stable devotional life, but suffice to say for now that the fruit of the Spirit is utterly opposed to legalism. Legalism is any systematic attempt to **earn** right standing before God. Whereas, by contrast, true obedience to the Lord is never an attempt to earn right standing before Him, rather it is a response to **the gift** of righteousness which we have received from Him in Christ.

Legalism Arouses and Aggravates Sinful Passions

Does the "honeymoon" have to end? Mine did. I had months and months of powerful times with God, but it all ended.

However, remember that **God** didn't end the "honeymoon," **I** did, with legalism. I suspect this happens to most Christians. We begin totally by grace, the gift of righteousness. But then we can't rest there, and grow there. Grace is too radical: It is diametrically opposed to the world system in which we are immersed. Our world system defines human worth mainly in terms of production, beauty, power and wealth. Thus, we feel insecure with grace, and we grasp again at a legalistic, production basis for acceptance. Legalism is any attempt on our part to establish legal righteousness for ourselves before God. Legalism is essentially self-righteousness.

But God uses our thickness of skull! Because the pain and the pride of our legalism ultimately drive us back to justification by faith. Beginning with Romans 3:20 here are the basics of this process:

> . . . because by the works of the Law no flesh will be justified in His sight; for through the Law comes the knowledge of sin.

See, ultimately, instead of perfecting us, our legalism exposes our sinfulness simply because we always fail to keep the law perfectly. Here is a fact worth remembering: **Any** spiritual principle, no matter how biblical, which is used legalistically (i.e., which is made into a law for righteousness) will do one thing for sure: It will show us that we are sinners, **because we are sinners**! So we get forced back to justification by faith. Romans 3:20 is pure and simple truth: Through the law comes, not righteousness, but the knowledge of sin.

If you are a sinner (I could as easily say, If you are a human being . . .), legalism will actually make you **worse**:

> For while we were in the flesh, the sinful passions, which were *aroused* by the Law, were at work in the members of our body to bear fruit for death.
>
> *Romans 7:5*

11

You see, God's laws relating to morality (primarily the Ten Commandments) can actually **arouse** our sinful passions. This is not because God's Law is evil but because we are sinners and God's Law diagnoses the problem for us. To illustrate how well this works, I will fabricate an imaginary, tongue-in-cheek law for you. Here is your Law; keep it diligently: Do **not** think of a red flag. Do **not** think of a red flag. Do **not** think of a red flag. Now, if you **know** what red is, and if you **know** what a flag is, then this law actually arouses you to think of the **forbidden** red flag. This fact seems obvious enough. Well, pretty much the same thing happens when sinners are forbidden to sin. This is part of the purpose of the Law of God: "through the Law comes the knowledge of sin." The Law defines sin and brings sin into dramatic relief. Thus, any legalism, **especially** when it is based on biblical principles, will **aggravate** rather than alleviate your sinful desires.

Externally, law can control sinful passions, even as a prison can contain criminals. Thus, civil law can **externally** control society. Galatians 3:23 enunciates this principle clearly, speaking of being, "kept in custody under the law," and, "being shut up" (as in Romans 11:32). This terminology is normally used to refer to incarceration, imprisonment. But incarceration is not transformation. It is external, not internal. It is prison, not freedom. And God Himself tells us this. He **never** implies that the Law by itself transforms anyone.

Well, if God's Law used legalistically arouses sinful passions, and if the Law merely incarcerates, does it have any value beyond revealing or exposing sin? Yes, the Law has great value **beyond** diagnosing sin, but only if we use it lawfully. That is, we must use the Law properly, not attempting to establish legal righteousness. Once you know this you will learn to love God's Law.

The Psalmist said,

> Those who love Thy law have great peace,
> And nothing causes them to stumble.
>
> *Psalm 119:165*

All of Psalm 119 sounds like this. The Law can be a dear friend. But if you try to use it to establish legal righteousness, the Law automatically turns against you. God doesn't want His Law to be your enemy and that's why He,

...cancelled out the certificate of debt consisting of decrees against us *and* which was hostile to us; and He has taken it out of the way, having nailed it to the cross.

Colossians 2:14

The Lord wants His entire Word to be **for** you, not against you. Let no one deceive you: Even the Psalmist knew grace and mercy, or else he could not have loved the Law. Grace and mercy were available in the Old Testament too.

Celebration of Grace will have much more to say concerning how the entire Bible, including the moral Law, can work as your dear friend. But you can't get **there** until you've been **here**: The Law of God itself militates against legalism because it constantly reveals our sin and our need for grace.

Thus, just in case you've fled back to legalism because grace was too simple and therefore too difficult, the Law of God works on your sin, even arousing and aggravating it, to bring you back to grace. If per chance you have temporarily succeeded in legal righteousness, then the Word of God will ultimately reveal spiritual pride and self-righteousness in you, to bring you back to grace, and to **His** righteousness and obedience.

Will you return to grace today? Jesus is calling you now. Once again you can be just a sinner saved by grace. You can begin a **new** honeymoon with the Lord today. You can experience, afresh and anew, the joy of your salvation. You can experience the security and power of imputed righteousness and forsake the insecurity of legal righteousness.

Satisfied With Jesus

Isaiah 53 begins this way: "Who has believed our message? And to whom has the arm of the Lord been revealed?" Then Isaiah went on to describe the crucifixion of Jesus Christ hundreds of years before it happened, even to the details of His burial ("with a rich man in his death").

Verses 5 and 6 in Isaiah 53 are specific as to what Jesus accomplished for us:

> But He was pierced through for our transgressions, He was crushed for our iniquities; The chastening for our peace *fell* upon Him, And by His scourging we are healed. All of us like sheep have gone astray, Each of us has turned to his own way; But the Lord has caused the iniquity of us all To fall on Him.

Then, in verse 11, Isaiah went on to make an exceedingly relevant, but often overlooked statement:

> As a result of the anguish of His [Jesus'] soul, He [God the Father] will see *it* and be satisfied.

This Scripture asserts unequivocally that God the Father **is satisfied** with Jesus' work at Calvary. The question is, are we? Are you? Will you believe it? Specifically regarding your right standing before God? Will you be satisfied with Jesus? The rest of this verse 11 says:

> By His knowledge the Righteous One, My Servant, will justify the many, As He will bear their iniquities.

According to God, what Jesus did at Calvary is enough. It is total and complete. You can't add a thing to it. And not a demon in hell can take anything away from it. **God** is satisfied. So Jesus declared

14

from the cross, "It is finished." If it is finished, it is finished! The major problem in the Body of Christ today is that Christians have not learned to be totally and completely satisfied with Jesus in the same way that Our Father is completely satisfied with Jesus.

You can be satisfied with Jesus plus nothing: His righteousness; His sin offering; all that He is **for** you. God the Father is satisfied. You can be satisfied also. Jesus plus nothing! **His** righteousness is the basis for your relationship with Him.

What Is Grace?

Most Christians "say grace" before meals. I must regretfully admit that for many years that's about all grace meant to me: prayers before meals. Hopefully, having read even the first few pages of **Celebration of Grace**, grace already means a whole lot more to you than that.

The grace of God is essentially the gift of righteousness (right standing before God) and the gift of the Holy Spirit. Not only are these **gifts**, but they are also **unmerited** gifts. We will speak much more concerning the gift of the Holy Spirit in a couple of weeks, but for now we must understand that Paul tied grace to the gift of righteousness:

> . . . those who receive the abundance of grace and of the gift of righteousness will reign in life through the One, Jesus Christ.
>
> *Romans 5:17*

This understanding is foundational to Christianity. And furthermore, **grace alone has the power to free you** from sin:

> For sin shall not be master over you, for you are not under law, but under grace.
>
> *Romans 6:14*

Remember that the Lord imprisoned the entire world under the penalty and power of sin in order to induce all of us to receive His mercy (Romans 11:32). Therefore the **only** way **you** will ever get free from sin is to get under grace, **and stay there**. Paul said sin shall not be master over you **because** you are not under law, but under grace. It makes sense then that the opposite is also true: To put a Christian under legalism is to bind him under sin! Remember that legalism has the power to actually arouse sinful passions.

In I Corinthians 1:30 Paul said that Jesus, "became to us wisdom from God, and righteousness and sanctification, and redemption." The word "became" is past tense. What Jesus has become for you is a finished work. You needn't add a thing to Paul's list in I Corinthians 1:30 in order to gain right standing before God. Jesus became all of this **for you** and He continues to be all of this **for you**, as a gift. This is imputed righteousness, the true essence of the grace of God. Remember Isaiah 53:11, God the Father is totally satisfied with Jesus. Grace means that, together with the Father, you must be satisfied with Jesus, and thus you can rest in Him and abide in Him, in all that He is **for you**. Romans 1:16 and 17 says,

> For I am not ashamed of the gospel, for it is the power of God for salvation to every one who believes, to the Jew first and also to the Greek.
> For in it *the* righteousness of God is revealed from faith to faith; as it is written, "BUT THE RIGHTEOUS *man* SHALL LIVE BY FAITH."

We will be looking at this many times and in many different ways until it is your way of life.

But **today**: Be totally satisfied with Jesus plus nothing. That is, put all your faith in Jesus Christ Himself to be all that you need for right standing before God, and begin to move from faith to faith. Relax. Stop striving to justify yourself. To be legalistic is to lock yourself under the power of sin because sin **shall** be master over you as long as you are "under law."

> But if it is by grace, it is no longer on the basis of works, otherwise grace is no longer grace.
> *Romans 11:6*

> "I do not nullify the grace of God; for if righteousness *comes* through the Law, then Christ died needlessly."
> *Galatians 2:21*

The Actual Source Of All Teaching And Doctrine Is Revealed In Whom It Glorifies

Works righteousness glorifies man. Grace righteousness glorifies God. God's gift of righteousness to us is unmerited: We did not earn it. In the Bible grace means literally unmerited favor. Thus, grace people boast in the Lord rather than in themselves.

I Corinthians 1:30, 31 describes God's gift of righteousness, then hammers home one immediate and unavoidable ramification:

> But by His doing you are in Christ Jesus, who became to us wisdom from God, and righteousness and sanctification, and redemption, that, just as it is written, "LET HIM WHO BOASTS, BOAST IN THE LORD."

It is clear that grace eliminates boasting, except in the Lord. Here's a simple rule of thumb for discerning teaching: The actual source of all teaching and doctrine is revealed in whom it glorifies. Undoubtedly you will observe that teaching which emphasizes success through **your** great discipline, or even success through **your** great faith, also tends to aim the glory **at you**. Thus, it is frequently true that faith in faith glorifies your faith and faith in self-discipline glorifies your self-discipline. But faith in God's grace and in the gift of His righteousness glorifies God, because a gift cannot be bought or earned: It can only be received. This seems obvious enough.

The Apostle Paul had myriads of magnificent accomplishments to boast about (lots more than most of us have), but he lived by grace. Therefore, he exclaimed,

> But may it never be that I should boast, except in the
> cross of our Lord Jesus Christ, through which the world
> has been crucified to me, and I to the world.
>
> *Galatians 6:14*

God's grace working in us will ultimately cause all of us to accomplish much for Christ's Kingdom. But our accomplishments will be the **result**, not the cause, of a healthy relationship with the Lord. And because our failures have shown us graphically that our own righteousness stinks, both our hearts and our lips will boast only in the Lord.

Sound too good to be true? It is the Gospel. Discernment begins here, in the humility of all people who must hope completely in the grace which is in Jesus Christ. Their hope in grace glorifies God and no one else.

The spirit of antichrist is inextricably bound to the spirit of spiritual pride, but we are the exact opposite:

> ...for we are the *true* circumcision, who worship in
> the Spirit of God and glory in Christ Jesus and put no
> confidence in the flesh...
>
> *Philippians 3:3*

Feelings of Perishing

In I Corinthians 1:18 Paul said,

> For the word of the cross is to those who are perishing foolishness, but to us who are being saved it is the power of God.

This statement concerning those who are perishing, of course, refers to unbelievers. Yet I have talked with thousands of committed **Christians** who felt as if they were perishing spiritually. They were committed to Christ, yet they still had feelings of perishing.

I felt exactly that way myself for several years. I was quite certain that God had saved me out of the world to let me die in the Church! (Remind you of Israel at the Red Sea?)

Perhaps you feel, or have felt, that you are perishing spiritually. The most common reason is that, even though you are saved by grace, you still do not take the word of the cross totally seriously.

It is most likely that, to whatever extent you feel you are perishing, that is the extent to which you are unknowingly counting the word of the cross as foolishness, rather than as the power of God.

I am writing this book to cause you to totally trust Jesus Christ and His grace. That is how you will come to know that you are not perishing, but instead you will walk in the power of God.

One time a young lady came up to me after a meeting and explained that even though she had been a Christian for several months, she still felt like she wasn't right with God. I asked, "Do you understand the cross?" She said, "The cross? What's that?" In order for her to know that she was right with God, she had to **know** that Jesus Christ died on the cross in HER place, for HER sin, and that she could be accepted by Him totally on that basis. Do YOU see how this works? If we understand the work of the cross, then we can appropriate grace.

Daily Filling

Do you feel like a failure because you can't seem to get fixed and **stay** fixed, or because you can't seem to get filled with the Holy Spirit, and **stay** filled? —because you sometimes need to start over?

There is nothing wrong with needing to be filled with the Holy Spirit again today even if you just got filled yesterday. This **daily** need you have is legitimate and understandable. God's gift to you is **daily** inward renewal: Paul said,

> . . . though our outer man is decaying, yet our inner
> man is being renewed day by day.
> *II Corinthians 4:16b*

Over the years people have asked me many times, "Jeff, do you believe in a second experience?" My answer is, "Absolutely! I believe in a **second** experience, and a **third**, and a **tenth**, and a **hundredth** and a **thousandth** and so on, no limit." The "Charismatic Renewal," which has powerfully touched so many of us, is more correctly termed the "Charismatic Renewals," **plural**, or else it may be nothing more than a mere cosmetic renewal! We need many renewals and many fillings. Paul says we can have this "day by day."

In Acts 2:1-4, one hundred and twenty people got "filled" with the Holy Spirit. **Then**, in Acts 4:32, many of these same people got filled **again**. They were locked in constant spiritual warfare. The Lord knew they needed a fresh infilling.

So, the Lord isn't upset if, like the early Christians, you need many fillings. Hey, He designed things to work this way so that you can never become independent of Him. You are not some kind of wind-up toy which the Lord mechanically winds up once and then leaves. The Bible teaches that you can be renewed each day, without condemnation. That's why,

> *It is of* the Lord's mercies that we are not consumed, because His compassions fail not. *They are* new every morning: great *is* thy faithfulness.
>
> *Lamentations 3:22,23 KJV*

Amen and Amen! The restoration you seek is a daily one. It is scriptural.

No problem.

What Is Forgiveness?

If grace means the gift of God's righteousness through the blood of Christ, what is forgiveness? You may think you know this, but listen to Jesus' definition of forgiveness:

> "For this reason the kingdom of heaven may be compared to a certain king who wished to settle accounts with his slaves.
> "And when he had begun to settle *them*, there was brought to him one who owed him ten thousand talents [millions and millions of dollars by our standards].
> "But since he did not have *the means* to repay, his lord commanded him to be sold, along with his wife and children and all that he had, and repayment be made.
> "The slave therefore falling down, prostrated himself before him, saying, 'Have patience with me, and I will repay you everything!'
> "And the lord of that slave felt compassion and released him and forgave him the debt."
>
> *Matthew 18:23-27*

Here is a slave in an impossible situation, just as we were in sin. The slave stupidly promised to repay the millions, but the debt was hopelessly more than any slave could repay. His lord was moved with compassion and cancelled the debt.

Thus, this Scripture gives us Jesus' working definition of forgiveness: cancelled debt. Cancelled debt!

Get this: Once you owed overwhelming debt, now you don't. Your debt has been suddenly cancelled through the blood of Jesus. The balance is zero. That's it, just like that. Once you owed everything. Now you owe nothing. The debt is cancelled as a gift. Period.

That is Jesus' working definition of forgiveness, not mine.

According to Jesus, when He forgives you, your total debt is marked

"Cancelled, Paid In Full," by the Savior with nail scars in His hands.

You must appropriate this forgiveness **as often as you need it**, or else you can't grow as a Christian. In a few days we will see how repentance ties into this picture. Then you will understand that even repentance is a gift of grace, yet your volition is not excluded. What a magnificent God we have!

The Up-And-Outer Versus
The Down-And-Outer or
The *How* Of Justification

And He [Jesus] also told this parable to certain ones who trusted in themselves that they were righteous, and viewed others with contempt:

"Two men went up into the temple to pray, one a Pharisee, and the other a tax-gatherer.

"The Pharisee stood and was praying thus to himself, 'God, I thank Thee that I am not like other people: swindlers, unjust, adulterers, or even like this tax-gatherer.

'I fast twice a week; I pay tithes of all that I get.'

"But the tax-gatherer, standing some distance away, was even unwilling to lift his eyes to heaven, but was beating his breast, saying, 'God, be merciful to me, the sinner!'

"I tell you, this man went down to his house justified rather than the other; for everyone who exalts himself shall be humbled, but he who humbles himself shall be exalted."

Luke 18:9-14

First, it is obvious that those who trust in their own righteousness are very far from God's justification. This is not primarily because the Lord doesn't **want** to justify them, but rather because, in their own self-righteous minds, they don't need it! Second, those who trust in their own righteousness tend to judge others who seem less spiritual, and thus they themselves get judged.

That's why, if you have come to a deep sense of humility through your personal failure to become righteous, you actually have an

advantage over those who have had no such experience. The Lord can do more with your life now than ever before.

However it is **not** essential for you to suffer through years of failure. Just believe the Word of God today.

This story which Jesus told concerning the Pharisee and the tax-gatherer unquestionably offended many Pharisees, not only because it rebuked their self-righteousness, but also because of the **apparent** ease with which Jesus justified the tax-gatherer. I say **apparent** ease because it is, in fact, **not easy** for the Lord to justify sinners; it cost Him His life on the cross to do it. Therefore, perhaps it is more accurate to speak of the **simplicity** with which Jesus justified and accepted the tax-gatherer. In any case, this tax-gatherer prayed a simple prayer with no claims to righteousness, calling sin sin, not proud of his sin, asking God for mercy, and he received mercy: Jesus said that he went down to his house justified. In this passage, justification obviously means to be **reckoned** just. Justification was **imputed** to the tax- gatherer. The tax-gatherer was still far from perfect.

This is terribly offensive to those who are proud of their own righteousness: How can God justify some sinner who hasn't **done** anything except humble himself and ask for mercy? That's why I'm so glad that **Jesus** Himself told this story. He is our authority. His statement concerning the justification of this tax-gatherer is foundational for every person who wants right standing before God. If Jesus Himself had not made such clear statements concerning mercy and justification, then most of us sincere believers would have to spend the rest of our lives here on earth under the condemnation of a few Pharisees.

Remember this: Mercy is one point at which you can touch God and **always** find acceptance.

And let me add one more vital truth today — may it penetrate your heart and become part of your daily faith: The rules for justification **never** change. The Bible doesn't teach that you are supposed to **grow out of** justification by faith, but rather that you are to grow **in** it! Justification before God works the same way for the rest of your life, regardless of your level of maturity. Never let anyone scare you or otherwise persuade you to return to a religion of self-justification.

Pharisees

Yesterday we read the parable which Jesus directed, "to certain ones who trusted in themselves, that they were righteous, and viewed others with contempt." The Lord **always** wants to correct our tendencies toward Pharisaism because such tendencies are so deadly.

Legalists compulsively judge others. Jesus warned, "Do not judge lest you be judged yourselves." (Matthew 7:1) Grace works wonders on judgmental attitudes and critical spirits. Once we realize the enormity and the gravity of our own sin, and once it dawns on us what a miracle it is that God forgives all our sin, **then** it becomes much more difficult for us to judge others.

Nobody is tougher to live with than a super-critical pharisaical person.

But let me hasten to get to a rather hilarious story I need to tell you. Years ago, in a church which I attended, most of the men had quit smoking. But there were a few men who hadn't quit. Sometimes two or three of these remaining smokers would light up their cigarettes right outside the church building after Sunday services.

One of the brothers who had quit smoking began to poke fun at these smokers. He called them "the nicotine squad". He made a big deal out of it. Certainly it would have been best for all the men to quit smoking, but it was not love or concern for them which was at work here.

Time went by. The judgmental joker didn't seem to change his attitude. Then, one day, the joker was at an automobile dealership waiting for his car to be serviced, and someone offered him a smoke. For some reason he took it! He went in, sat down in the waiting room, and lit up.

Unbeknownst to anyone, gasoline fumes had crept under the wall of the waiting room from the service area. The joker's cigarette ignited the fumes. No one was injured, but quite a fire ensued. Worse yet, the **whole** story was covered in our local newspaper. His name was prominent in the article. God made the incident famous. I have never forgotten it.

The Lord has ways of chastening critical spirits, but if we will listen to grace, no further chastening is necessary, at least not on this issue.

Critical **thinking** is essential in the Body of Christ: It means the ability to examine preaching, teaching, prophecy, or opinion, in light of God's Word. But a critical **spirit** is destructive.

Grace and Truth

Yesterday we saw how grace can cure Pharisaical, judgmental, critical attitudes. Thus, we need not judge others.

But, if we do not judge others, does that mean we must flatly accept anything and everything that people do? All sin? All rebellion? All perversion? No way. Jesus certainly didn't. Real love can't, and neither can real grace.

For example, say you see your best friend sitting on a railroad track and you know there is a train coming. Because you love him, you do not judge him. You don't say to yourself, "Look at that stupid jerk sitting on those tracks. He deserves to die!" You do not have a critical spirit toward him. However, you certainly are not going to let him rest there either, and fail to warn him about the train that's coming. He is your best friend. You are **not** going to say, "Hey, you do your thing and I'll do mine." Or, "Be cool, I know you must express yourself." No, but instead, although you **do** accept him, you would warn him: "There's a train coming!"

Grace is like that. It will speak the truth in love.

We know that, "grace and truth were realized through Jesus Christ." (John 1:17b) Both grace **and** truth! These two work together to transform lives. Neither works apart from the other.

God's transformation, once you are born again, works because you are under grace: God's transformation works from acceptance, not from rejection...and **never** from conditional love. The Lord loves you unconditionally. Thus, He **cannot** leave you in sin. Therefore He speaks the truth in love and He disciplines in love, for your good. That is the confidence you have toward Him. That's how grace and truth work together.

Together, grace and truth express the very nature of Jesus Christ.

Anti-Nomian Accusations

The term anti-nomian means anti-law. There is an anti-nomian heresy which has repeated itself many times in the Body of Christ. In this heresy, grace is interpreted to mean anti-law, and thus grace would mean that anything goes (including sin). Thus law itself is rejected, as if law somehow contradicts grace.

No, it is not **law** that contradicts God's grace. It is **legalism** that contradicts God's grace. Works righteousness is diametrically opposed to grace.

What we saw yesterday was that grace works together with truth and neither works without the other.

The grace of God does not contradict God's moral law: rather God's grace establishes His moral law because His grace ultimately produces obedience in us:

> Do we then nullify the Law through faith? May it never
> be! On the contrary, we establish the Law.
> *Romans 3:31*

Study the context in Romans 3. The emphasis is salvation by grace, not works, with this conclusion:

> For we maintain that a man is justified by faith apart
> from the works of the Law.
> *Romans 3:28*

Observe: The justification by faith in verse 28 leads to the **establishment** of law in verse 31. Thus, God's grace is not anti-law. Obviously the Apostle Paul, who wrote these important verses, was not anti-law — no way — for, "we establish the Law through faith." Yet he was clearly anti-legalism: "a man is justified by faith apart from works of the Law."

Paul, the grace preacher, was frequently misunderstood by legalists in his time. This is because legalists are unable to distinguish between anti-legalism and anti-law. They automatically jump to the conclusion that anyone who is an anti-legalism is anti-law. Therefore, Paul was frequently accused by legalists of being anti-law.

Historically, balanced grace preachers are never immune from anti-nomian accusations. Therefore I must include this article. Paul himself answered some heavy anti-nomian accusations.

Interestingly, one of Paul's most stinging references to anti-nomian accusations against him is right here in Romans 3, sort of introducing the verses we've already read for today:

> And why not *say* (as we are slanderously reported and as some affirm that we say), "Let us do evil that good may come"? Their condemnation is just.
>
> *Romans 3:8*

Because grace preaching contradicts legalism it **appears** to encourage, or to be soft on, sin. So Paul's grace message was misrepresented in the extreme by Paul's legalist enemies as "Let us do evil that good may come."

I have never yet been accused or misrepresented as severely as Paul, but I have had people warn me, "Jeff, if you continue to emphasize grace, no one will obey God." Many of these people who were giving me these warnings were sincere Christians, but apparently they did not know either the Scripture or the power of God. The fact is, I have seen this grace message producing obedience for nearly twenty years now.

It is possible to encourage obedience, and to see beautiful obedience develop in people's lives through the message of grace, **without** being legalistic, coercive or manipulative. We can preach convicting messages, seasoned with ample grace.

I hope it is clear in **Celebration of Grace** that right standing before God by faith does **not** mean that we have no further need for spiritual growth or sanctification. No way. However, the way the sanctification process works is like this: Right standing before God is prerequisite to sanctification. Right standing before God is essential in order to **facilitate** continued spiritual growth and sanctification. In other words, justification is prerequisite to sanctification. Therefore, obedience must always be preached IN THE CONTEXT OF GRACE if true obedience is to be developed in believers. True obedience is no mere performance of mechanical laws (to obtain a blessing or to avoid punishment), but true obedience is a **response** to God's grace, **empowered** by His Spirit. This way, we learn obedience, and Jesus receives the glory.

"Sinless Perfection"

The other day I read a Christian book in which the author strongly asserted that Christians need not sin every day. This, of course, is true, but don't attempt to apply it apart from grace.

Apart from grace, this truth that Christians need not sin every day can bear some very bad fruit in your life. Here's what happened to me: Not long after I became a Christian I picked up on the truth that, now that the Holy Spirit lives in me, I have power over sin, and thus I have power **not** to sin. Okay, but at this point I departed from the truth, because my automatic "logical" conclusion was that I should therefore be able to achieve sinless perfection.

I began striving for sinless perfection!

There are several serious problems with the concept of sinless perfection. For one thing, sinless perfection focuses too much attention on **us**, rather than on the One Who Is Sinless and Holy, Jesus Christ of Nazareth.

Secondly, you may not realize this yet, but the longer a Christian walks with God, the more he or she becomes aware of what sin really is, and of what the sin nature is. **And** mature Christians develop a high degree of sensitivity to sin. Thus, to the mature Christian, even though sinful passions are substantially defeated, sinless perfection often seems more distant than at the beginning of the Christian life.

The Apostle Paul himself (obviously an excellent example of a mature Christian) described his walk with God as follows:

> Not that I have already obtained *it*, or have already become perfect, but I press on in order that I may lay hold of that for which also I was laid hold of by Christ Jesus.
>
> *Philippians 3:12*

Let us all, by the mercies of God, consecrate ourselves as Paul did, and let us press on to that for which Christ Jesus laid hold of us. Yet you see that even Paul had quite apparently not achieved sinless perfection (or, as some might read this, perfect maturity). It is important to remember that he did not allow himself to become preoccupied or sidetracked by his failure. I am convinced that Paul hated sin and loved God. But his occupation and focus were not on his failure to achieve sinless perfection, but rather on fulfilling the call and the commission which God had given him, and in this latter endeavor he succeeded, far beyond all that he could ask or think.

So be it in our own lives and ministries. Let us aim at perfection, yet let us abide in this grace which encourages us to continue to serve God and to press on, even though we may seem no closer to sinless perfection than when we first began.

Sinless perfection puts the focus constantly on you. But true godliness puts the focus constantly on Christ.

Be Yourself With God

In a preceding article I said that becoming legalistic about my devotional life destroyed it. But now think about this: Even **with** such legalism there might have been a way to save my devotional life.

We know that grace and truth came through Jesus Christ. Well, grace and truth could have saved my devotional life and my walk in the Spirit back then. Here's how:

The **truth** was, I hated getting up at 5:30 in the morning for a devotional time, and I wasn't getting anything out of it! But I didn't tell the Lord that. I was still a new Christian and I wanted to be spiritual for my Lord. I had much zeal. So, instead of telling the Lord the truth that **I wished I was asleep** at 5:30 AM, I began my devotional time praying, "Lord, I thank You for the privilege of coming to You this morning . . ." and so on. Without knowing it, I was putting on a front for God, as if He couldn't see through it. I was lying to my Lord. I was play-acting, posturing. And that is one major reason why my devotional life died. Fronts and lies don't build real friendships. This is obvious.

When we are immature, most of us put on fronts for people whom we most want to impress. Yet these people are usually the very people with whom we most desire to build meaningful relationships! How can meaningful relationships develop with fronts? Impossible.

I dated a lot in my teens and twenties. I hesitate to mention this part of my past, but it provides a perfect illustration concerning fronts, so I think I'll take the risk. In those days I'd put on my best front (and put my best foot forward) for the girls I cared most about, and **only** for the girls I cared most about. With the rest, I'd take them to cheap restaurants, burp at the table, and go to drive-in movies instead of walk-ins. I was a real loser in those days. Sounds horrible, but such behavior is common. During my years as a counselor, wives who came in for counseling often told me that, during courtship, their husbands-to-be "lied" to them, that the person they married "changed" radically after the wedding. What actually happened was that the husband-to-be had put on his best face and he had put his best foot forward **during courting**. He had put on a front! After marriage, he quit his front and became himself. But because of his front, no solid relationship had been built during courting.

I sometimes heard similar tales from husbands. Many people would say that the person they married is not the person they now know as husband or wife. That isn't fair. It isn't right. It is a fraud. It hurts. Real friends don't do this to each other.

Yet, I have done the same thing thousands of times to my Friend Jesus.

So, a few years ago, the Lord said to me (not in an audible voice, but in my mind), "Jeff, if only you had been honest with me during your devotions at 5:30 AM, and said, 'Lord, you know I don't want to be up at 5:30, even for You. But as long as it's the rules, please forgive me and accept me, and make this time productive,' I would have had mercy on you and we could have made good use of the time. But instead you put on a front and our relationship suffered as a result."

Grace and truth: The combination works. If we know grace, we can tell God the truth. In the future you may face many situations (far more serious than devotional time) where you are being sorely tempted to do some sin (and you may really **want** to do it!). Tell God the truth. Tell Him all about it. **Tell Him** you want to sin. Come clean. Confess. He can handle this, and your chances for coming through the temptation will be much improved. Tomorrow we will see more reasons why this is true.

It is very difficult to get truthful with the Lord until you know His grace. But once you **do** know grace:

> Behold, Thou dost desire truth in the innermost being,
> And in the hidden part Thou wilt make me know
> wisdom. Purify me with hyssop, and I shall be clean;
> Wash me, and I shall be whiter than snow.
> *Psalm 51:6, 7*

See how beautifully self-disclosure fits with God's grace. You might want to study **the occasion** for Psalm 51.

Transparency

Yesterday we saw how grace and truth can save you specifically in terms of being honest before the Lord. You can't be honest before the Lord until you believe in His grace. Why? Because until you believe in His grace, you will always fear His rejection.

Jesus often rebuked religious fronts. This is obvious in the many confrontations He had with Scribes, Pharisees and Sadducees. But perhaps Jesus' most revealing rebuke of religious fronts concerns false prophets. In Matthew 7, speaking of false prophets, Jesus described them in this way: "who come to you in sheep's clothing, but inwardly are ravenous wolves." (verse 15) So first, these false prophets put on spiritual fronts (sheep's clothing) to impress **you**. They look like sheep but inside they are wolves. Then Jesus went on to say that you would "know them by their fruits" (**not their gifts**). (verse 16)

Then, still in this context, Jesus emphasized that it is not those who **appear** to do the will of the Father, but rather those who actually **do** it, who are accepted:

> "Not everyone who says to Me, 'Lord, Lord,' will enter the kingdom of heaven; but he who does the will of My Father who is in heaven.
>
> "Many will say to Me on that day, 'Lord, Lord, did we not prophesy in Your name, and in Your name cast out demons, and in Your name perform many miracles?'
>
> "And then I will declare to them, 'I never knew you; DEPART FROM ME, YOU WHO PRACTICE LAWLESSNESS.'"
>
> *(verses 21-23)*

You see, these false prophets **do** all sorts of spiritual work in Jesus' Name. But they aren't actually obeying God! They are lawless, but they **appear** spiritual. Jesus' discussion of this issue is quite comprehensible to most of us.

However, Jesus said one thing here which might seem incomprehensible: "I never knew you." What? God knows everything about everyone. Therefore, what does this statement mean, "I never knew you"? Put as simply as possible, it means this: These false prophets are doers, but they have no **relationship** with Jesus. In the context of the sheep's clothing which the false prophets wear, their claims to works righteousness (prophesying, casting out demons, performing miracles in His Name) may well be interpreted as **fronts** put on for **God's** benefit, not just for man's benefit. Can you see that? Sure, God knows everything about everyone, but in **a relationship** there are no fronts. It is clear that these false prophets wear fronts (sheep's clothing) and it is also clear that they never open up to God in honesty, confessing their sins before God; thus, no relationship exists. **Everyone who knows God lets God know them!** The false prophets never open up to the Lord at all. They may pray or even "worship," as the Pharisees did, but they never come to worship, "in spirit and truth" (John 4:24). Thus, they never allow the Lord to know them intimately, as in a marriage (which is the biblical implication of the word "know" as Jesus used it here in Matthew 7:23). So Jesus said, "I never knew you."

Grace and truth go to work, not just when we know truth, but when we tell God the truth. Look how grace and truth and transparency work together:

> . . . but if we walk in the light as He Himself is in the light, we have fellowship with one another, and the blood of Jesus His Son cleanses us from all sin.
> *I John 1:7*

God is light. He is Truth. So when we walk in the light, when we open up to Him, we are totally exposed, and we are penetrated by His light. All is open to the light of His Truth. This can be painful and threatening to us. But, don't forget, His blood is there so that we can be forgiven immediately. Once we learn to open up **voluntarily**, it may hurt, but it feels so good! We walk in the light **and His blood cleanses us from all our sin.** And that creates fellowship, fellowship with God and fellowship with one another.

Much of our society tries to accomplish this truthfulness and transparency amongst themselves without Jesus, and therefore without His blood and without His acceptance. If you've ever tried truthfulness and transparency without the blood (I have), you know how brutal it can be. So-called truth therapy groups often cut their members to pieces.

So, don't try truthfulness and transparency, even before the Lord, without the blood. But **with** the blood you can let Him know you. You can be transparent. You are the Lord's sheep because He declares it so. If sometimes you don't look or act like a sheep, remember, do not merely put on sheep's clothing as if to **masquerade** as a sheep. Can you imagine sheep masquerading as sheep? Nonsense! Go to the Lord without the mask and let the Shepherd take care of your need:

> For God sent not his Son into the world to condemn the world; but that the world through him might be saved.
>
> He that believeth on him is not condemned: but he that believeth not is condemned already, because he hath not believed in the name of the only begotten Son of God.
>
> And this is the condemnation, that light is come into the world, and men loved darkness rather than light, because their deeds were evil.
>
> For everyone that doeth evil hateth the light, neither cometh to the light, lest his deeds should be discovered [NASB, exposed].
>
> But he that doeth truth cometh to the light, that his deeds may be made manifest, that they are wrought in God.
>
> *John 3:17-21 KJV*

This way, you receive all things pertaining to life and godliness, and Jesus receives the glory.

Five and Five

One of my objectives in this book is to demonstrate how your devotional life can be built or rebuilt by the Lord Himself, without legalism, as you respond to grace. Thus, my approach is exactly the opposite from what most of you are accustomed to. The Lord will bless and guide your life even if so far you haven't been able to maintain consistent devotional time. Or, on the other hand, if you have been in bondage to legalism concerning devotional time, it is probably a good idea to quit for a while. But, if you do quit, you will discover something beautiful after you have been out from under legalistic bondage for a few weeks or months: You **do** hunger for the presence of God and His Word. And an hour at church on Sunday mornings won't be enough to satisfy this hunger.

When you **do** get this hunger, eat! — just like when you get physically hungry. But this time, do not set idealistic or perfectionistic goals for your devotional time. Even if you read five verses a day and sit and worship for five minutes, fine. You will probably find that you often hunger for more than five verses and five minutes. And you will no doubt discover the benefit of a regular "Five and Five," just like regular breakfast or lunch or dinner. Keep in mind that, while the Lord loves this special time with you, it doesn't make "points" with God in terms of works righteousness. It is normal, and it is healthy, like eating. But **Jesus** already has all the "points," so you don't need to try to get any.

Notice, your motive is now hunger rather than spiritual pride or trying to make points. Thus, you have quit attempting to manipulate God.

Your hunger may develop into a disciplined habit of five chapters and an hour of prayer and worship per day; maybe even three or four hours. Fine! Wonderful! Healthy! But you do not **have** to do this. You will never learn to "pray without ceasing" until you know God's grace, the only thing that can produce such hunger.

> . . . like newborn babes, long for the pure milk of the
> word, that by it you may grow in respect to salvation,
> if you have tasted the kindness of the Lord.
>
> *I Peter 2:2:3*

What Peter says here makes perfect sense: When you taste something good, you want more. The goodness (or kindness) of the Lord is God's grace, and **tasting** this, according to Peter, is **prerequisite** to longing for God and His Word, as newborns hunger for milk: "If you have tasted the kindness of the Lord." The "if" is essential: That is, tasting of God's kindness is the Lord's way of making you hungry, and this is the primary emphasis of **Celebration of Grace**. Recognize and respect the fact that Peter related spiritual growth to hunger developed through tasting of **God's kindness**. This is radical new motivation which multitudes of Christians can receive if they will submit to grace.

I know you will understand what I'm about to say: Experience has taught me that it is often the **most** committed Christians who are also the **most** vulnerable to condemnation and depression when they fail the Lord. The zeal of their commitment means that they have high expectations for themselves. Therefore they are more likely than other Christians to get down on themselves when they fail.

Perhaps this applies to you. Remember, you can't have a powerful walk in the Spirit if you spend a lot of time kicking yourself because your prayer life (for example) isn't as good as you think it should be!

TASTE GRACE; IT'S YOUR LAST AND BEST HOPE. God says GRACE IS YOUR **ONLY** HOPE.

That way, you get the hunger, and Jesus gets the glory.

Guilt-Free Living
Part I

There is no way to live guilt-free under our present world system which is for the most part Godless and powered by selfishness and guilt. But guilt-free living is **exactly** what God's will is for you as a man or a woman of God.

You can't walk in the Spirit with joy and effectiveness while dragging a load of guilt and condemnation. There is no way you can please God while kicking yourself for your failures, sins and short-sightedness. The Lord knows this.

So the Lord's intent at Calvary, for one thing, is a guilt-free conscience. This is the awesome power of the shed blood of Jesus Christ:

> For if the blood of goats and bulls and the ashes of a
> heifer sprinkling those who have been defiled, sanctify
> for the cleansing of the flesh, how much more will the
> blood of Christ, who through the eternal Spirit offered
> Himself without blemish to God, cleanse your conscience
> from dead works to serve the Living God?
> *Hebrews 9:13,14*

The only thing needed for this TOTAL CLEANSING OF CONSCIENCE to work in you, as you repent, and as you confess past sins which pain your conscience, is that you BELIEVE IT! Period! That's it.

Here is another crucial issue: This Scripture clearly links this cleansing of conscience to serving God. It is clear that the Lord is neither pleased nor adequately served when Christians are motivated to serve Him by guilt and condemnation.

False guilt: To those of you who suffer from false guilt it is important to say that the shed blood of Christ has the power to cleanse both real guilt **and** false guilt.

Shame: If you had an alcoholic parent or if you are from an otherwise dysfunctional family then it is probable that you are plagued by a deep sense of shame. Such deep shame is common among children of dysfunctional households. Here again, even though your shame is certainly not a direct result of your own sin, Calvary is the place where healing begins for you because Christ died to cleanse **your** conscience completely!

Whatever the source of your guilt and shame, God's will for you through Jesus' blood is a clean conscience, and **this** releases you to serve Him.

Guilt-Free Living
Part II

What Jesus did at Calvary goes even further than all of your sin; it goes as far as the curse is found:

> "Comfort, O comfort My people," says your God. "Speak kindly to Jerusalem; And call out to her, that her warfare has ended, that her iniquity has been removed, That she has received of the Lord's hand Double for all her sins."
>
> *Isaiah 40:1,2*

God says that He has provided "double" for **all your sins**. As a born-again Christian, you are part of New Jerusalem, the bride of Christ. So Isaiah 40:1, 2 definitely applies to you.

I have three children. I was present when each was born. As I looked upon each of them for the first time, there is one question I never asked: I never said, "I wonder what kind of filthy, sinful past this new-born baby has?" Why not?

Obviously, my babies had no sinful past. My babies were brand new.

The same thing can be said of you, hour by hour, minute by minute. It is exactly what the Lord wants for you: No guilt, no shame, always new, always cleansed...even if you still don't know how to fix yourself!

Note also, in Isaiah 40:1,2, that this is a **finished** work. It has **already** been accomplished for you: Past tense. Your "warfare has ended." Your "iniquity has been removed."

There is so much written and said about how to get victory in your Christian life. But this Scripture teaches something very different concerning victorious Christian living: Not that you are to **seek** victory, but rather that the victory has already been won. Therefore you need not **seek** victory, but rather you are TO PROCEED FROM VICTORY.

You are to learn to walk in Jesus' victory, victory which is total, victory which has been **imputed** to you through your faith and trust in the finished work of Calvary.

Guilt-Free Living
Part III

From 1966 to 1968 I went to a psychiatrist with all sorts of emotional pain and insecurity. But the bottom line turned out to be guilt.

Humanistic psychology's weapons against real guilt are like squirt guns against a forest fire. Humanistic psychology's arsenal includes, "Hey, everyone has faults." Or, "Hey, there is no absolute truth." Or, "Just tell yourself you are okay, and that everyone else is okay too." Or, "This is your parents' fault."

Let me tell you, it doesn't work! But you probably already know this. Humanistic psychology is essentially unarmed when it comes to removing guilt. The New Age movement is even worse. It says, in so many words, "You are God. Therefore, as you realize and experience your own divinity you will escape all guilt and all finite existence." This is the sin of Satan to try to ascend and be as God, and it will end in Hell! Obviously, such deception holds no permanent cure for guilt. The New Age Movement is the very essence of how guilt entered creation to begin with. But, more on that later.

The Bible says, "without shedding of blood there is no forgiveness." (Hebrews 9:22b) This is the same chapter we looked at the other day, which speaks clearly of cleansing your conscience. Again, in the same chapter, we read:

> For where a covenant is, there must of necessity be the death of the one who made it.
> For a covenant is valid *only* when men are dead, for it is never in force while the one who made it lives.
> *(verses 16 and 17)*

It is obvious that the definition of "covenant," as this word is being used here, is a will, that is, a last will and testament, which never comes into force until the one who made it dies. Then and **only** then, the heirs inherit. This analogy describes exactly how the Gospel works: The Lord has a **will** for you which includes direction for your life, an inheritance with Himself, and a guilt-free conscience. The writer of Hebrews is emphasizing that it is **impossible** for you to inherit God's will for your life apart from the death of the One who made the will. You'll need to apply the atonement frequently, perhaps hour by hour, in order to experience your inheritance. It is perfectly all right with God if you do this.

Even God's creation teaches us that there is no life without death. Each day, as you eat your meals, many things are dying so that you can live. It is your most frequent and vivid reminder that, for each of us, all life comes out of death. Why, then, is it so difficult to allow our spiritual lives to flow continuously out of Christ's death? The Lord intended that His entire creation should teach us His ways:

> For since the creation of the world His invisible attributes, His eternal power and divine nature, have been clearly seen, being understood through what has been made . . .
>
> *Romans 1:20 a,b*

Thus, all life on earth shouts the Gospel to all mankind, for nothing lives unless something dies. Always. This is an unalterable law of nature, established by the Lord in love, to teach us that, "without the shedding of blood there is no forgiveness."

The Gospel of Christ may seem offensive and exclusive to New Agers. But the fact remains, there is only ONE WAY, JESUS.

We receive Him. Amen!

Coming To Jesus
With Mixed Motives

Jesus said,

> "All that the Father gives Me shall come to Me; and the
> one who comes to Me I will certainly not cast out."
> *John 6:37*

Think of all the sick, all the demon-possessed, all the lame and all the blind who came to Jesus. Do you think all those people had perfectly pure motives for coming to Jesus? Did they all come purely because they loved Jesus? Or do you think most of them had mixed motives for coming to Jesus? It seems likely (you can disagree if you like) that most of them had mixed motives. It seems likely that most of them were at least partially, if not primarily, motivated by the desperate needs in their lives.

They came to Jesus driven by pain and suffering and fear rather than pure love for God, but Jesus never cast **any** of them out. Matthew records,

> And when evening had come, they brought to Him
> many who were demon-possessed; and He cast out the
> spirits with a word, and healed all who were ill . . .
> *Matthew 8:16*

He healed **all** who were ill. All. He cast out no one. Only the demons got cast out. He **never** rebuked a blind person saying, "You are selfish. You just want your eyesight. You are just trying to use me. Go away and produce pure motives, and then I will accept you and heal you."

No, no hurting person was ever cast out for being selfish. **The only issue was** that these hurting people came to the right Person.

In our Scripture for today, John 6:37, Jesus said that He will

certainly not cast you out if you will only come to Him. Certainly means certainly! The only issue is that you COME TO THE RIGHT PERSON. Your motives for coming to Him are probably mixed (mine usually are too), but His invitation is, ''Come to Me.'' (Matthew 11:28)

The Lord will purify our motives, sure enough. But it will be through acceptance, not rejection. The issue is, **always** begin by coming to the right Person.

Transformation In Motives

Yesterday we saw how the primary issue is that we come to the right Person, Jesus, even if our motives are mixed. We saw no instance where Jesus ever attacked the motives of hurting people who came to Him for help.

Yet we know that the Lord cares about our motives. What follows in today's reading is an example of how grace can transform your motives where nothing else can.

This book, **Celebration of Grace**, is not my first book, it's my second. My first book never got published.

I think it was 1974, and I had just finished that first book, and I was out walking, praying as I walked. And I began praying for my book, not conscious of my motives for wanting it published. I was saying things like, "Lord, the Body of Christ needs this book." And, "Glorify Yourself through it, Lord." And, "Please get my book published, Lord."

For years and years, prior to this moment, the Lord had been teaching me to be honest with Him through the blood of Jesus. So, after listening politely to me for a while, He spoke inside me and asked me one burning question, "Why are you praying for your book?" I knew He was looking for **motives**. His question shocked me. But He had also sacrificed His own Son for moments like this.

I knew my true motives. I took a deep breath. Then I said, "Well Lord, I want to be rich and famous. Forgive me, please, and help me repent."

Instantly — no, even less — in a split second —He said, "Okay, **now** you can pray for your book." In that moment I **knew** total acceptance by my Lord. I **knew** forgiveness and cleansing and repentance. And I became filled with thanksgiving and great joy. He approved of me. He pronounced me okay! Even my prayer became okay! God reckoned righteousness to me.

I was awestruck, but I knew it was the Gospel, GOOD NEWS! I became so filled with love there on the sidewalk that it took a long time to get back to praying for the book: The book was too mundane. Worship was far more thrilling. But when I finally did get back to praying for my book, guess what? I had been cleansed in my motives. I was responding to grace, with love. I couldn't even find any fleshly motives. I looked, but they were gone. I cared instead for the glory of God, and for helping His people. **That's** how the Gospel works.

See how it works?

> If we confess our sins, He is faithful and righteous to forgive us our sins and to cleanse us from all unrighteousness.
>
> *I John 1:9*

Frankly, I'm thankful that my first book never got published. I said some things in there which I wouldn't say today. God is good.

Finally, I don't know about you, but my own selfish motives reassert themselves so often that I'm forced to repeat the process I've described in this article almost daily. Nevertheless, it works as well for me now as when the Lord first showed it to me. The Lord will cleanse your motives as well as He does mine, on a daily basis if you need it.

Inferior Motives: Fear of Punishment and Desire for Reward

We've seen how God's grace deals with selfish motives in general, but we need to talk more about these two Behemoths: fear of punishment and desire for reward. First, let's talk about fear: Because grace works from acceptance rather than from rejection, it eliminates the fear that Christ will reject us. Instead we know we have been accepted through His grace (Heb. 4:16). Thus, fear of punishment is out the window! Second, let's talk about desire for reward: Grace begins immediately to transform our desires for reward from **primary** motivations into **secondary** motivations. No one can legitimately deny that there **are** definite rewards for obedience, but suffice it to say that to mature in grace is to be freed from reward **as a primary motivation** to obey God.

Both fear **and** desire for reward are basic **human** motives. They have enormous power. They are the primary motivating forces behind **all** worldly economic systems and behind **all** worldly religion. But neither fear nor desire for reward contain anything inherently supernatural. Both are very human motivations.

Legalism works primarily through fear of punishment and desire for reward. That is why legalism can never break the mastery of sin. The Lord often uses fear of punishment or desire for reward as **starting** points with us. And, of course, if you are not a Christian, then fear of punishment has a legitimate place in your life. But ultimately the Kingdom of God must rest on motives superior to those which are merely human and selfish, partly because such motives also lend themselves to satanic influence. The Bible says that Satan dominates the world through fear of death (see Hebrews 2:14,15) and through love of money (see I Timothy 6:10). It's easy to see how fear of punishment and desire for reward fit insidiously into Satan's program.

Grace renders these inferior motives of fear of punishment and desire for reward either impotent or irrelevant. **And** grace engenders the ultimate motive for obedience: Love. The Bible says, "We love, because He first loved us." (I John 4:19) Thus, love flows as **a response** to grace. And true love fulfills the Law. (Romans 13:8-10)

You may be far from such maturity. Or perhaps near. In any case, the **unconditional** love of God in Jesus Christ is the only place where worldly motives can be superseded by godly motivation.

Fixing Unbelief

All the time I see Christians trying to believe the Lord for healing, or for the salvation of a family member, or to move a mountain. Praise God for this! We need to learn to believe God for great things.

I refer to these dear people as **trying** to believe the Lord because, by their own admission, their faith is often far from perfect. Why? And how can faith be perfected?

The bottom line in this struggle (and often the end of this struggle) is God's **imputed** righteousness. Many of these struggling Christians aren't actually appropriating the Gospel itself, and thus their faith is failing in other areas as well.

No doubt you have wrestled with this problem yourself from time to time. The most commonly recommended remedy for unbelief these days, especially in faith teaching, is to pump up your faith through quoting, verbalizing, and repeating Bible verses. Okay, there is truth to that. But if you have a problem with unbelief, does God call you **first** to try to hype up your faith by repeating Bible verses? No, not first. Why not? Because quoting Bible verses can't take away sin. And unbelief is sin! Jesus identified unbelief as sin when He said that the Holy Spirit would convict the world of, "sin, because they do not believe in Me." (John 16:9) So **first**, take your sin of unbelief to the finished work of Calvary. That is God's **only** provision for sin. Confess it, and be totally cleansed and forgiven. Unbelief is a horrible sin. Don't add insult to injury by trying to fix it yourself through merely quoting Bible verses and trying to hype up your faith.

Put **all** your confidence in grace, in the gift of God's righteousness. Be reckoned righteous by His work alone. Believe this. You see, when the Lord **imputes** righteousness to you, faith is part of that package. And, since imputed righteousness through Christ is nothing less than God's righteousness, the faith you receive as a gift is **God's faith**, imputed to you, whether you **feel** it or not.

Now, faith for anything else will come much more easily because of your faith in Jesus' righteousness. You can go back to quoting verses

54

and building faith as a vital aspect of your walk in the Spirit (assuming that you bear in mind that such Bible knowledge does not give you manipulative control over the Lord).

See how this works.

Sanctification Does Not Precede or Cause Justification

This is a crucial issue in the Body of Christ today. Why? Because there is so much teaching out there which either asserts or implies that if you are not sanctified then you cannot continue to be justified! The Bible teaches the exact opposite, that without justification you can **never** be sanctified.

We have already seen how the Lord justified Abraham through faith, **reckoning** him righteous on the basis of his faith in God's promise to him. And in Romans 4 the Apostle Paul used God's justification of Abraham as exemplary of how God "justifies the ungodly." (verse 5)

More extensive study of Romans 4 and of the rest of Paul's writings will make it obvious to you that God's justification of Abraham through faith became Paul's model for saving faith for all of us. And Paul didn't stop there — he took the example of Abraham's life even further, using even the subsequent **sequence** of events in God's dealings with Abraham to teach us the **necessary** sequence of events in God's dealings with us. Let's examine this sequence of events in terms of justification and sanctification.

First, we know that Abraham was **justified** by faith. Second, it is of utmost importance to understand that any outworking of God's **sanctification** in Abraham's life was **subsequent to**, and therefore did not cause, Abraham's justification by faith. Look at the sequence of events as recounted by Paul:

> Is this blessing then upon the circumcised, or upon the uncircumcised also? For we say, "FAITH WAS RECKONED TO ABRAHAM AS RIGHTEOUSNESS."
>
> How then was it reckoned? While he was circumcised, or uncircumcised? Not while circumcised, but while uncircumcised;

> and he received the sign of circumcision, a seal of the
> righteousness of the faith which he had while
> uncircumcised...
>
> For the promise to Abraham or to his descendants that
> he would be heir of the world was not through the Law,
> but through the righteousness of faith.
>
> *Romans 4:9-11a, 13*

In Paul's mind, to understand the Gospel, it is extremely important for you to see **first of all** that Abraham did not have the circumcision and he did not have the Law (not even the Ten Commandments) when he was reckoned righteous (justified). The Law (including the Ten Commandments) was not given until hundreds of years later through Moses, one of Abraham's descendants. **Therefore**, right standing before God did **not** come through the Law, **even in the Old Testament**. Please let this fact sink into you.

And regarding circumcision, Abraham did not receive the "sign" of circumcision until AFTER he was reckoned righteous (justified). Then he was circumcised as, "a seal of the righteousness of the faith which he had while uncircumcised." This is the crucial sequence of events which becomes our model. Circumcision, the cutting off of the male foreskin, had significance beyond its use as a sign of the covenant between God and Abraham, and beyond its practical health and hygiene considerations, because it was also intended by God to foreshadow or to prefigure for us the removal of our carnal flesh, "by the circumcision of Christ." Therefore, circumcision prefigured and presently symbolizes a very important aspect of sanctification:

> and in Him you were also circumcised with a circumcision made without hands [i.e., not physical], in the removal of the body of the flesh by the circumcision of Christ.
>
> *Colossians 2:11*

Note carefully what circumcision symbolizes to every Christian: The removal of the flesh, which is a very important aspect of our sanctification. Now, we know that Abraham received circumcision as a sign and a seal, as a result, if you will, of justification by faith. **Never, never** is it taught that Abraham's circumcision preceded or caused his right standing before God. Just the opposite is true: Abraham's circumcision was a "sign" of his right standing before God.

Abraham could not have been justified either by the Law or by his own circumcision because both events occurred after he was **reckoned** righteous through faith.

Likewise, the circumcision which you have in Christ, that is the removal of your flesh, the defeat of your carnal, sinful, fleshly nature, is always and only the **result**, never the **cause** of right standing before God. Thus, sanctification is a result, not a cause, of right standing before God. Never, never is it taught that the removal of the carnal nature precedes or causes justification by faith. Exactly the reverse is true.

The "rules" never change: Justification, then sanctification. It always works that way. Getting your cart before your horse (trying to justify yourself through your sanctification) can only lead to vexation and frustration. Remember, the Bible does not teach that you are supposed to **grow out of** justification by faith, but rather that you are to grow **in** it.

The Bible teaches clearly that in order to be sanctified it is necessary to be justified, that apart from justification by faith sanctification is impossible. Teaching to the contrary contradicts Scripture and brings much condemnation and confusion in the Body of Christ.

Fixing Your Flesh?
Part I

> For I know that nothing good dwells in me, that is,
> in my flesh; for the wishing is present in me, but the
> doing of the good *is* not...
> I find then the principle that evil is present in me, the
> one who wishes to do good...
> Who will set me free from the body of this death?
>
> *Romans 7:18, 21, 24b*

Here is a horrible problem for those of us who would follow God: Our flesh compulsively cleaves to the dust; it is a spiritual pig. For years we have begged God to deliver us from it, but it still rears its ugly head all too often. It seems like, even though we constantly rededicate ourselves to the Lord, there is a Judas in us which keeps trying to betray the Lord.

Many of us have experienced deliverance from deadly demonic forces and compulsions. Praise God, I myself am free today because of this miracle. But, alas, my flesh, my filthy nature, still wrestles against the Holy Spirit Who is also at work in me.

Our Scripture reading today makes it obvious that Paul grieved over this. But he knew the answer.

First, we need to understand what Paul meant by the term "flesh" in Romans. We know that in his use of the term "flesh" Paul was not usually referring to the human body itself. Paul had a very different attitude toward the human body than he did toward the flesh. For example, in Romans 6:13, referring to the **human body** itself, he said that our **bodies** can be **either** servants of God or servants of sin. But, concerning **the flesh**, Paul said exactly the opposite. In Romans 7:18, the Scripture which opened today's article, Paul said that **nothing** good dwelt in his flesh. Therefore, in Paul's usage of these terms, the human body **can** be a servant of God, whereas clearly "the flesh" can **never** be a servant of God.

So, what did Paul mean by his use of the word flesh in this passage? Not the human body, but rather our fallen, self-centered, sin-filled, Adamic nature; i.e., that part of us which was born "in Adam," and therefore is **always** in rebellion against God. It is rotten to the core.

Now, and only now, we can embrace a critical truth concerning our flesh which many Christians fail to understand: God puts no hope whatsoever in **fixing** our fleshly, fallen, self-centered Adamic nature. Rather He puts all His confidence in a whole new creation in Christ Jesus. That's why we, "must be born again." (John 3:7)

Thus, it is unnecessary and counterproductive for you to waste time and effort trying to fix your flesh. Strangely, much of Christianity is preoccupied in an endless struggle to fix the flesh. But since the Holy Spirit won't try to fix the flesh, this endless struggle in Christians to fix the flesh **can only be** the flesh trying to fix the flesh. No way can this work! It's like trying to purify sewage with sewage. It's like expecting a dead woman to conceive a child. It is time to return to the Gospel. The flesh is hopelessly dead. Redemption and new life are in the resurrection power of the Spirit.

> For as in Adam all die, so also in Christ all shall be made alive.
>
> *I Corinthians 15:22*

> Who will set me free from the body of this death?
> Thanks be to God through Jesus Christ our Lord!
> There is therefore now no condemnation for those who are in Christ Jesus.
> For the mind set on the flesh is death, but the mind set on the Spirit is life and peace...
>
> *Romans 7:24b; 7:25a; 8:1,6*

These verses explain how Paul resolved his conflict concerning his flesh in which dwelt no good thing: Not a fixing of his flesh ("the body of this death"), but totally through Christ's redemption: A new creation in Christ where all are made alive.

Furthermore, the Lord accomplishes this new creation in Christ Jesus **without**, I repeat, **without** obliterating human identity and personality. Sounds incredible, but it is true, and scriptural.

Shocking Confession

In Romans 7:25 Paul made what appears to be a shocking confession:

> ...So then, on the one hand I myself with my mind
> am serving the law of God, but on the other, with my
> flesh the law of sin.

We might expect any preacher to give us the first half of this confession, "I myself with my mind am serving the Law of God." But the second half, "with my flesh the law of sin," is a horrible thing for a preacher to admit, right? Wrong.

On the contrary, it is exactly what we have learned about the flesh: It is a pig, compulsively given to sin. Your flesh will **always** serve the law of sin. And God never tries to fix it. It is dead. So Paul said his flesh was serving sin; he could not fix his flesh anymore than you can.

We put our hope in Christ and put no further confidence in the flesh. And the promise gets better: In the very next verse (8:1) Paul went on to say,

> There is therefore now no condemnation for those who
> are in Christ Jesus.

Thus, the Lord wants us feeling no condemnation for our flesh. Rather, we can have a new focus and a new life in the power of the Spirit. We can stop trying to fix ourselves and rest in what Christ has done, completely redeeming us at Calvary. Now we can set our minds on Him and His purposes for us without being constantly preoccupied with the limitations and imperfections of our flesh.

Have you been afraid of your flesh, like David facing Goliath? David won, you'll recall. The Lord wants you set free from wasting time worrying about your filthy flesh:

> For the mind set on the flesh is death, but the mind set on the Spirit is life and peace...
>
> *Romans 8:6*

You tend to become what you look at. If you look at your flesh all day, what sort of results do you expect?

Fixing Your Flesh?
Part II

If God NEVER intends to **fix** your flesh, what can you do with it? For one thing you can stop worrying and feeling condemned over it.

The Bible says that God puts all His hope and confidence in the new creation in Christ. At the Cross, Jesus, the last Adam (I Corinthians 15:45), took the flesh (all that is "in Adam") to judgement[1]; all sin was judged then and there. Your flesh is identified with Jesus at Calvary. Golgotha is God's answer to the flesh.

The cross is the Lord's proclamation that He puts no hope in the flesh.[1] Yet the flesh is the source of discouragement for many Christians. Why? Because most of us foolishly continue to put some hope in our flesh: That we can fix it; or that God will fix it; or that somehow it will be wondrously transformed from a pig into a lamb. But, if we examine our flesh twenty-five years from now it will still look the same: full of lust and jealousy, and too lazy to pray! It will never change. So we **can't** put our hope there. Misplaced hope in the flesh is the major source of discouragement for many Christians.

For years I was angry at God. I claimed He had not changed my life because my flesh had not disappeared. I thought that II Corinthians 5:17 was a lie:

> Therefore if any man is in Christ, *he is* a new creature; the old things passed away; behold, new things have come.

I used to tell the Lord, "That's not true because my flesh still has too much power." You see, I expected God to fix my flesh. I quit my Christian life for five years — years wasted, I might add — because my flesh wasn't fixed.

---

[1] While not exact quotes, I derived these sentences from *The Normal Christian Life*, pp.43 and 81 respectively.

You know His answer? "Jeff, I said **in Christ** all things are new." Here's the point: **In Jeff**, that is, in my flesh, dwells no good thing. So, "in Jeff," that is, in my flesh, all things are old. But in Christ (and all that He is for me) all things are new. Now I can abide in Him.

Therefore, do not be discouraged that **in you**, that is, in your flesh, all things are old. That state of affairs is scriptural. The object is to learn to abide in Christ, and **all that He is for you**, and learn to **ignore** the flesh, and let it atrophy, and don't worry about it, and begin to put all your trust in the power of the Holy Spirit. In Christ, in the Holy Spirit, in the new creation in Christ, all things **are** new.

Your discouragement usually comes from putting some kind of hope in your Adamic nature.

The Apostle Peter said to fix your hope **completely** on Jesus Christ, specifically on His grace:

> Therefore, gird your minds for action, keep sober *in spirit*, fix your hope completely on the grace to be brought to you at the revelation of Jesus Christ.
> *I Peter 1:13*

The implication here is that this hope, only in the grace which Jesus brings, will gird your mind for action. It will give you stability of mind. Instability of mind is often characterized by hopelessness and discouragement (i.e., hope in the flesh!).

The Apostle Peter, if you know his story, had known hopelessness, and he had known the hope which only Jesus brings. He was teaching from experience.

Trust Jesus plus nothing, especially when it comes to your flesh. Jesus is your rock. Your flesh is quicksand; it can never be trusted.

> My flesh and my heart faileth: *but* God *is* the strength of my heart, and my portion for ever.
> *Psalm 73:26 KJV*

If My Old Man Is Dead,
Why Is He Making So Much Noise?

We have said that the source of discouragement in your Christian life may be due to putting some sort of hope in your old man, that is, in your flesh. **No wonder** you have been discouraged.

The problem is that, even though the flesh is identified with Christ's death at Calvary, it still **seems** very much alive. I once preached a sermon called, "If My Old Man Is Dead, Why Is He Making So Much Noise?" The answer to that question is in Colossians:

> For in Him all the fullness of Deity dwells in bodily form, and in Him you have been made complete, and He is the head over all rule and authority; and in Him you were also circumcised with a circumcision made without hands, in the removal of the body of the flesh by the circumcision of Christ...
>
> *Colossians 2:9-11*

Back to circumcision again: We know that physical circumcision is the removal of the male foreskin with a sharp cutting instrument. In Christ we have been spiritually circumcised: "The body of the flesh" has been literally cut off, "by the circumcision of Christ."

Then why does our flesh seem so alive? Here is an analogy which the Lord used to help me understand the answer to this question: Have you ever pruned an evergreen tree?

I used to live on the seacoast where the climate could stay damp for weeks. Once during such a period I pruned some evergreens. I tossed all the severed branches in a pile. Several weeks later, because the air was cool and moist, those severed branches still looked lush and alive. But they were dead, having been cut off from their source of life.

They died when they were cut off, but they still looked alive. So it is with your flesh. It has been cut off "by the circumcision of Christ," even if it still looks alive and well. **You** are complete in Jesus, and, "your life is hidden with Christ in God." (Colossians 3:3) And **that** is where you must place all your hope.

Your flesh is in an environment (this world) which is favorable to sort of preserve it (like the evergreen branches) for awhile. But it has been cut off.

Suicide By Crucifixion?

No way. Common sense tells us that no one ever committed suicide by crucifixion.[1] One hand may get nailed down, but after that, forget it!

The body of Christ has been plagued with myriads of misconceptions concerning the "crucified life" (as it is often called). For example, I have heard some Christians say that they have developed such a closeness to the Lord that their whole existence is now a continual process of repentance, that they find themselves in constant repentance hour by hour.

This sounds deeply spiritual, but it is in fact a sin-centered, self-centered existence where the mind is set constantly on the flesh, concerned with fixing it, or killing it.

While repentance itself is essential whenever the Holy Spirit is convicting of sin, it is important to remember that no one ever committed suicide by crucifixion. Day after tomorrow we will take a close look at true repentance.

Paul himself called us to the "crucified life":

> Now those who belong to Christ Jesus have crucified
> the flesh with its passions and desires.
> *Galatians 5:24*

But this is not suicide by crucifixion because, in the same letter, Paul also said, "I have been crucified with Christ. . ." (2:20) The crucifixion is past tense. The emphasis here is not on **do**, but rather on **done**. So what did Paul mean when he said that "those who belong to Christ have crucified the flesh"? The crucified life means that we have **already** been crucified with Christ and we are learning to **reckon** ourselves dead (even as God **reckons** us righteous). The flesh is dead, let us reckon it so:

---

[1] Concept and terminology are from Nee, *The Normal Christian Life*, p.41.

> Likewise reckon ye also yourselves to be dead indeed unto sin, but alive unto God through Jesus Christ our Lord.
>
> *Romans 6:11 KJV*

We already understand that the Lord has reckoned us righteous through faith, and that our flesh is identified with Jesus at Calvary. Now we see that the Lord calls us to reckon **ourselves** dead to sin. But reckoning ourselves dead is not the same thing as this self-centered process of constant repentance. It seems to me that the enjoyment of constant repentance is probably a product of some sort of compulsive perfectionism, or compulsive introspection, not of the Holy Spirit, since Paul also said, "The mind set on the flesh is death." (Romans 8:6)

Thus, you do not need to be constantly mindful of sin in order to be repentant. In fact, that is death. You need not worry about your flesh so much.

What you **can** do hour by hour is to enjoy the powerful acceptance that flows from Calvary; and let those rivers of living water (also a gift) flow from your innermost being. You can focus on Christ and worship Him. Romans 6:11 says not only that you are to reckon yourself dead unto sin, but even more importantly, to reckon yourself "alive unto God through Jesus Christ." This emphasis on life will deliver you from constant, compulsive introspection. For, "the mind set on the Spirit is life and peace." (Romans 8:6b)

The Bible is full of examples of how to do this. Here's one: "The joy of the Lord is your strength." (Nehemiah 8:10c) If you will read the context of this verse in Nehemiah 8, you will discover that the people spoken of there had been deeply convicted of their sin through the reading of the Law. They were repenting, and, of course, this is essential.

But, then, they continued to mourn and weep over their sin. They remained focused on it. So Nehemiah and Ezra and the Levites began to exhort them,

> "This day is holy to the Lord your God; do not mourn or weep."
>
> Then he said to them, "Go, eat the fat, drink the sweet, and send portions to him who has nothing prepared; for this day is holy to our Lord. Do not be

grieved, for the joy of the Lord is your strength."
...And all the people went away to eat, to drink, to
send portions and to celebrate a great festival, because
they had understood the words which had been made
known to them.

Nehemiah 8:9a,10,12

Do you see where the Lord wants your focus? Certainly not on suicide by crucifixion! Not on the negative DON'T, but on the positive DO. These people were to replace their mourning over their sins with the joy of the Lord. Sanctification works by replacement. You cannot become a vacuum, merely emptied of sin and dead to self. Thus, for instance, the Lord said He would give us "the garment of praise for [in place of] the spirit of heaviness." (Isaiah 61:3b KJV) He works by replacement: The fruit of the Spirit in place of the works of the flesh. In Christianity "dying to self" always means "living to God." No vacuum!

Therefore the "crucified life" flows out from the completed work at Calvary, and the infilling and power of the Holy Spirit, and it is lived out in us as we place increasing emphasis on "living to God." So I have said that repentance works, not as a constant minding of sin, but rather primarily as a REPLACEMENT of sin.

One of the ways the Lord frees us from sin is that He shows us His specific replacements for sin: The gifts and the fruit of the Holy Spirit working together with His Word. Remember that joy is a fruit of the Spirit (Galatians 5:22). The joy of the Lord (not introspection) is your strength. Constant repentance leads simply to constant introspection. Too much introspection is a bad thing, not a positive spiritual practice. People who are overly introspective are seldom filled with the joy of the Lord. This is because their focus is on themselves, not on Him.

Spiritual Hypochondria

What I dealt with yesterday is this tendency of many Christians to be introspective, trying to be repentant and trying to fix their flesh. Many people are just naturally introspective, and the pain is even greater for them.

This habit of introspection could be labeled **spiritual hypochondria.** Believe me, I know what hypochondria is. I used to suffer from it.

When I was a hypochondriac I was constantly checking my pulse, maybe forty times a day, because I was afraid of a heart attack. And somehow I could develop lots of heart attack symptoms.

Many Christians suffer similar anxiety over their spiritual health.

Normal people go about their business all day and seldom think about their heart or their immediate health (except perhaps to exercise, etc.). They simply **assume** that their heart is beating, and they don't worry about it. That is exactly how I had to learn to think in order to be free from my hypochondria: I had to learn to **assume** that everything is working okay and to quit checking my pulse.

That is also exactly what has to happen to Christians who suffer from spiritual hypochondria. Spiritual hypochondria is a plaguing insecurity about our spiritual health. We have to learn that introspection can be destructive, and we have to learn to **assume** that spiritual health questions are settled in Christ.

You have to learn not to worry by trusting Christ. Certainly, there will be times for self-examination before God, like visiting the doctor for a check-up, but constant checking of your spiritual pulse is not in the Bible. You are called to worship, not to hypochondria. You are called to focus on the Lord and to appropriate His power. You are called to the sort of confidence before God that only grace people know. (Hebrews 4:16) The Holy Spirit is perfectly capable of convicting you of sin without your excessive introspection.

You have to learn to **assume** you are okay because you have trusted Christ. Then you are free to fix your attention on living, not dying:

For the law of the Spirit of Life in Christ Jesus has set you free from the law of sin and of death.

Romans 8:2

Repentance Is A Gift

If true repentance is not a **constant** minding of sin, what is it?

It is obvious that the Lord calls us to repent. He is, "now declaring to men that all everywhere should repent." (Acts 17:30b)

Why become a Christian if you don't want to repent, if you don't want to be set free from sin to serve God? Anyone who doesn't want to repent would automatically **hate** Heaven because, in Heaven, obedience to God is the only option available. This book is dedicated to all of us sinners saved by grace who **desire** to be free from sin to serve the Lord.

It will delight all such people to know that repentance is as much a part of God's grace as anything else in the Gospel.

Repentance, in its simplest biblical application, means to turn around. Beyond that, repentance is typically understood in terms of turning **away** from sin. I fear that most Christians' understanding of repentance stops right there. But turning away **from** sin **is not the focal point of repentance: The focal point** of biblical repentance **is the Lord** Himself. We turn from sin **to the Lord**. II Chronicles 7:14 provides a good example of what I'm saying:

> If my people, which are called by my name, shall humble themselves, and pray, and seek my face, and turn from their wicked ways; then I will hear from heaven, and will forgive there sin, and will heal their land.
>
> *(KJV)*

See, turning from our wicked ways is certainly an important part of biblical repentance, but note the focus: "Seek my face," God says. Turning **from** sin cannot save us from sin. Only turning from sin **to the Lord**, "the Lamb of God who takes away the sin of the world," can save us from sin. (See John 1:29.)

Therefore, total repentance would be a total change in orientation from sin **to trusting Christ**. Our focus cannot remain sin-centered.

That would not be true repentance. True repentance is obviously no mere turning over of the proverbial new leaf.

True repentance will call sin sin. For example, bitterness and unforgiveness are often caused because someone else injures us, perhaps through rejecting us, or some other sort of abuse. Thus, on one level, bitterness and unforgiveness are inner wounds needing healing. But bitterness and unforgiveness are also sins, regardless of origins, and they must ultimately be dealt with as sin, through the Gospel, if we are to be healed and made whole. Likewise, unbelief is not just some sort of negative mental attitude resulting from a poor self-image. It is primarily sin.

But don't let that scare you. Remember that the blood of Christ deals totally and effectively with **real** sin, in **real** sinners. While it is often important to know how sin got planted in us, such knowledge alone cannot heal us. It is grace which heals **real** sinners, **and** it is grace which restores our self-images.

Psychological counselors may be able to help sort out problems, they may be able to teach relational skills and coping skills, they may be able to provide a practical environment for learning to relate to others, but if they do not know how to call sin sin, and how to deal with sin God's way, they cannot facilitate permanent emotional healing. The Gospel heals.

Healing and repentance seem interrelated in some way in the mind of The Great Physician,

> And Jesus answered and said to them, "*It is* not those who are well who need a physician, but those who are sick.
>
> "I have not come to call righteous men but sinners to repentance."
>
> *Luke 5:31, 32*

In context, Jesus was explaining why He spent so much time with sinners. He was not commenting specifically on a link between healing and repentance. Nevertheless, Jesus never selected an analogy arbitrarily. A link between healing and repentance seems to be there.

As a pastor, I also did counseling for ten years. During that period my consistent observation was that every person suffering with a broken personality suffered also with the agony of an **unbroken will**. Their healing processes always included the link Jesus saw between healing and repentance: When their will began to break before God (repentance), their personality began to heal, and this process of the healing of the person and the breaking of the will continued hand in hand, ultimately culminating in wholeness of person and brokenness of will. Thus, the healing was a breaking, in the most positive sense of the word. For it is the Lordship of Jesus (i.e., our will yields to His will) which brings wholeness in our souls and spirits. Do you see the connection? Repentance is a wonderful miracle of healing of spirit and emotions. Caution! Not all **physical** healing can be linked so directly to an unbroken will.

You often need deeper repentance. As always, the Lord is your source, not you. Did you know that repentance is a gift? II Timothy 2:25 talks about God "granting" repentance. That is, God GIVES repentance. I have often asked the Lord to grant me repentance, and He has become my source for true repentance. Thus, my volition and choice are involved, but I am **not** the source of repentance (or of anything else for that matter).

Trust the Father to draw you to Jesus. Jesus said,

> "No one can come to Me, unless the Father who sent Me draws him; and I will raise him up on the last day ...
> "All that the Father gives Me shall come to Me; and the one who comes to Me I will certainly not cast out...
> *John 6:44, 37*

Note the emphasis on God's initiative. This is what grace is all about. Then observe that His action is **totally** effective in that you **will** be drawn to Jesus, and not cast out. You will partake in His resurrection.

Begin to call out to Him, asking Him to grant you true repentance. Let Him become your source for repentance the same way you are learning to look to Him for all righteousness. Patience is needed; this may take time; it is usually more of a process than an event.

Repentance
Part II

If we say that we have no sin, we are deceiving ourselves, and the truth is not in us.

If we confess our sins, He is faithful and righteous to forgive us our sins and to cleanse us from all unrighteousness.

If we say that we have not sinned, we make Him a liar, and His word is not is us.

My little children, I am writing these things to you that you may not sin. And if anyone sins, we have an Advocate with the Father, Jesus Christ the righteous;

and He Himself is the propitiation for our sins; and not for ours only, but also for *those of* the whole world.

I John 1:8--2:2

First, IT IS VERY IMPORTANT TO EXAMINE **WHO** THIS POWERFUL SCRIPTURE WAS WRITTEN TO. This Scripture, especially the startling assertion, "If we confess our sins, He is faithful and righteous to forgive us our sins and to cleanse us," was not written primarily to a bunch of unregenerate sinners, but rather, John wrote this Scripture **to Christians**, for he called the recipients of this letter his "children," and he consistently included himself, "we," "us," "our," "ours."

Thus, you need not feel like a second-class Christian if **you** need to appropriate I John 1:9: it is for you! Recognize that the total forgiveness and cleansing which you have through your Advocate (your defense Lawyer) covers **real** sin, as you become willing to call sin sin. This is how conscience is cleansed. If you have sin, even if it was planted in you by the injuries of others, blaming others can never free your conscience. It is only as you call sin sin, regardless of its origin, that you are totally forgiven, and your debt of sin is cancelled because of the Advocate, Who became your propitiation (your mercy seat).

It says God is "faithful and righteous" in forgiving and cleansing you. He is "faithful," i.e., He **always** does this without fail on the basis described in these verses. And He is "righteous," i.e., sin is not accepted or tolerated, but sin's wages (death) have been paid in full through the blood of your Advocate, "Jesus Christ the righteous." God is JUST because the death sentence has been executed. Thus, He can be, "just and the justifier of the one who has faith in Jesus." (Romans 3:2b)

Repentance is a gift, and it means to appropriate the shed blood and the resurrection power of God. It means to call sin sin, to turn from sin as best you can, and to trust Christ.

Repentance
Part III

It is clear in the Bible that the Lord wants you to be able to **forget** sin. It is clear that you are not able to walk freely in the Spirit while dragging loads of guilt. God wants past sin gone: completely, totally, permanently! Eradication of **past** sin is crucial in obtaining victory over **future** sin. Obviously it takes an act of God to eradicate either past or future sin.

Most Christians don't seem to realize that true repentance includes not only turning from sin to God, but repentance also means disassociation from sin. Thus, repentance is complete when that sin has been forgotten: Not forgotten in the sense that you would be unable to testify later to the power and mercy of God which saved you from it, but forgotten in terms of guilt and condemnation. Repentance is complete when guilt is gone and you are walking freely in the Spirit before God. Thus, there are many Christians walking around with only partial repentance because they are trying to repent by constantly rehashing old sins.

So the Lord Says,

> As far as the east is from the west,
> So far has He removed our transgressions from us.
> *Psalm 103:12*

God did not say, "as far as the **north** is from the **south**," but rather, "as far as the east is from the west." This distinction may at first seem like hairsplitting, but, in fact, it is incredibly important. Here's why. Picture yourself in an airplane circling the earth from pole to pole. As you fly north and pass the North Pole, circling the earth, what direction will you then be going? South. As you fly south, continuing to circle the earth, and finally pass the South Pole, what direction will you then be going? North. Now picture yourself circling the earth at the equator. If you circle the earth traveling east, you will **always** be going east, and if you circle the earth traveling west, you will **always** be going west. So God said, "As far as the east is from the west": That distance is infinite. As far as the north is from the south would be finite. The Bible is a wonderful book; the Lord is a wonderful God. He has placed your sins an infinite distance from you. He is infinite. He wants you totally disassociated from your sins.

So, you can walk totally unburdened: Paul said,

> One thing *I do:* forgetting what *lies* behind and reaching forward to what *lies* ahead,
> I press on toward the goal...
>
> *Philippians 3:13b, 14a*

The Lord forgives and forgets your sin, and He will grant this freedom **to you** as well, to forgive and forget your sin. He **wants** this for you so you can "press on" with Him, **and to Him**. The day must come when you stop grieving and stop kicking yourself over past sins and past mistakes. Then you can forget. Then healing can come. Then freedom. Then new beginnings. Then, the possibilities are endless. This process of forgetting takes time (not for the Lord, of course, He can do it instantly), but you have to begin someplace: That someplace is simply to agree with God and start over, every day.

The Holy Spirit

In Greek, the word **grace** is closely related to the word **gift**. Total grace is two gifts: The gift of righteousness through the finished work of the cross, **and** the gift of righteousness through the gift of the indwelling Holy Spirit in every born-again believer. The Bible says that the Holy Spirit Himself is a gift to you, and that He is what the promise of the Father:

> . . . . He commanded them not to leave Jerusalem, but to wait for what the Father had promised. [Jesus speaking]
> . . . and you shall receive the gift of the Holy Spirit. [Peter speaking]
>
> *Acts 1:4 and 2:38b*

In Acts 1, Jesus explained that "the promise of the Father" is the Holy Spirit. Then, in Acts 2:38, Peter explained that the Holy Spirit is a gift.

You got "in Adam" by being born. Now you have come to be "in Christ" by being born again.

Do you see that this new birth in the Spirit is **all** grace? Each aspect of God's program is a gift which you could never earn. But you have received both the gift of justification by faith and the gift of the Holy Spirit. Anyone can receive. Many of the least worthy people in the world have received. **Whosoever will** may come and take the water of life freely. (Revelation 22:17)

You cannot earn the Holy Spirit today, but He is eager to fill you. You need not convince God that you are finally spiritual enough to be filled, but He is willing to **give** you His fullness based on the finished work at Calvary. The Holy Spirit moves gladly in conjunction with, and in response to, the blood of Christ.

The Holy Spirit Works Through Grace

If a man has been shot dead and you remove the cause of death, the bullet, will that bring him back to life? No way. You would also have to resurrect him. That's why grace is **two** gifts: The shed blood **and** the gift of the Holy Spirit. The blood of Jesus Christ removes the cause of death (sin) completely. Then, the outpouring of the Holy Spirit creates a new life in Christ.

The Cross **and** the Resurrection: You can't have one without the other. You need to understand that the Holy Spirit does nothing apart from the blood which Jesus shed for us: The cause of death **must always** be removed first. But it is also true that the blood alone doesn't impart life. The work of the Holy Spirit is essential:

> . . . if anyone does not have the Spirit of Christ, he does not belong to Him.
>
> *Romans 8:9b*

Thus, every born-again person has become a partaker of divine nature. (See II Peter 1:4) And this Person, the Holy Spirit, is a gift of grace as we saw yesterday. God has literally given Himself to us. Now it is very important for you to understand something: The Holy Spirit does not work apart from the blood. He does not work apart from the removal of the cause of death. Therefore, I can correctly say that the Holy Spirit does not work apart from grace. Therefore, the Holy Spirit works in you **as you receive grace**, and no other way!

Thus, the move of the Holy Spirit upon **you** is directly related to receiving grace. Anyone who will receive God's grace in Jesus Christ can begin immediately to expect the Holy Spirit to go to work in them. There is no need to somehow ''get spiritual'' first.

The Holy Spirit will fill **you** today, totally on the basis of grace plus nothing. Our next article will examine a clear biblical example of this.

You Are Ready

Yesterday we said that the move of the Holy Spirit **in you** is direct-ly related to you receiving grace: That's **all**, nothing more, nothing less. Let us examine a clear biblical example of this.

In Acts 10:39-46, the scene is the house of Cornelius, a Gentile. Cor-nelius and his household are hearing the Gospel for the FIRST time. The apostle Peter is speaking:

> "And we are witnesses of all the things He [Jesus] did both in the land of the Jews and in Jerusalem. And they also put Him to death by hanging Him on a cross.
>
> "God raised him up on the third day, and granted that He should become visible, not to all the people, but to witnesses who were chosen beforehand by God, *that is*, to us, who ate and drank with Him after He arose from the dead.
>
> "And He ordered us to preach to the people, and solemnly to testify that this is the One who has been appointed by God as Judge of the living and the dead.
>
> "Of Him all the prophets bear witness that through His name every one who believes in Him receives forgiveness of sins."
>
> While Peter was still speaking these words, the Holy Spirit fell upon all those who were listening to the message.
>
> And all the circumcised believers who had come with Peter were amazed, because the gift of the Holy Spirit had been poured out upon the Gentiles also.
>
> For they were hearing them speaking with tongues and exalting God . . .

Here is the point: When Peter reached the place in his message where he said, "everyone who believes in Him receives forgiveness of sins," the Holy Spirit fell upon them. Period. We know they **believed** Peter's words because Acts 11 says that they had received the word of God, but they never even had time to verbalize their faith or to be baptized in water before the Holy Spirit fell upon them.

This is central: The Holy Spirit was responding to simple faith in the forgiveness of sins through Christ, **plus nothing**! So, as these people received Christ and the forgiveness of sins, the Holy Spirit fell upon them. We know therefore that the move of the Spirit upon these people was directly related to their receiving grace.

If you have ever been taught against any important biblical aspect of the present work of the Holy Spirit then, to some extent, His work has probably been hindered or quenched in your life. The impact of such wrong teaching has done damage, but it is not irreversible, as many of us have discovered.

You are ready right now for a fresh move of God in your life, based entirely on right standing before Him through grace, exactly as Cornelius' household was ready.

YOU ARE READY. Go ahead and begin to believe Him to do this in you.

Receiving grace is simply believing the gospel and asking Jesus to redeem you. You have already done this. And you also understand that it is the Lord's will for you to continue to respond to His grace on a daily basis for the rest of your life. On this basis alone you might as well begin to expect the Holy Spirit to work powerfully in you.

I used to make a big mistake concerning the power of the Holy Spirit. I used to think that I had to really "get spiritual" first, **before** the Holy Spirit would work powerfully in me. Just the opposite is true: His powerful work in us is prerequisite to getting spiritual.

Therefore, you are ready! You cannot "get spiritual," or get sanctified, BEFORE the Holy Spirit moves powerfully in you. Opening your heart to grace is opening your heart to the Holy Spirit: He wants to become your source of life.

Prophetic Hunger

I have not referred specifically to this particular verse before, but Jesus emphasized a point which I have attempted to emphasize over and over again in **Celebration of Grace:**

"Blessed are the poor in spirit, for theirs is the kingdom
of heaven . . .

Matthew 5:3

Since the Lord never encourages spiritual poverty, this verse is correctly interpreted, "Blessed are those who **recognize** their own spiritual poverty apart from the righteousness of Christ, for theirs is the kingdom of heaven." My book has emphasized our own spiritual poverty apart from the righteousness of Christ, **and** I have stressed that the Lord has allowed the failure of our self-effort in order to teach us this lesson. According to Jesus, this understanding is essential in order to inherit the Kingdom, "for theirs is the kingdom." Reread Romans 5:17 again. Reigning in life with Jesus, i.e., inheriting the Kingdom, results from receiving the abundance of grace and the gift of righteousness. And none of us ask for grace apart from our own personal recognition of our own spiritual poverty. Thus, the Lord causes even our failures to birth success.

You probably realize your spiritual poverty apart from Christ or you wouldn't have read this far in this book; and you probably also experience deep hunger for lasting holiness in your soul.

For **you**, Jesus went on to make another promise in Matthew 5. Take a look at verse 6:

"Blessed *are* they which do hunger and thirst after
righteousness: for they shall be filled. (KJV)

Thus, Jesus said unequivocally that **everyone** who hungers and thirsts for righteousness WILL be "filled" with righteousness. The

Holy Spirit Himself is the fulfillment of this promise since, like Jesus and the Father, He Himself is the very definition of righteousness; and He comes to fill you.

If Jesus' word is true, and He never lies, then the **hunger** of your heart (the hunger and thirst for righteousness) is the **prophecy** of its fulfillment. Your hunger invites and assures God's filling.

Be encouraged: Jesus said that your spiritual hunger itself is an unusual state of blessedness: "Blessed are those who hunger and thirst for righteousness..." Be thankful that the Lord has **blessed** you with hunger and thirst, even if you feel frustrated at times. Worldly people don't have such desire for the Lord. The majority of the world's population apparently has no such hunger. Thus, even your hungry frustration is unique, and it demonstrates that God has **already** done a powerful work in your life even if you don't seem "filled" yet. Your hunger itself is strong confirmation of the transformation which the Lord has already worked within you. Praise His excellent Name!

Perspective On Gifts Of The Holy Spirit

There are believers who are worried or who feel inferior because they don't speak in tongues. Then also, there are other believers who say that every Christian should or must speak in tongues, and that tongues is **the** sign of the infilling of the Holy Spirit. One thing I want to do in this book is correct such false impressions. Don't feel inferior if you don't speak in tongues. Jesus is your righteousness! He is your defense.

Speaking in tongues is not **the** sign of spirituality, nor should tongues be exalted as a standard for fellowship. The blood of Jesus is our standard for fellowship. What tongues is, when properly used, is a wonderful instrument for worship, and for communion with God. I encourage it, and practice it; but you are neither "in" nor "out" based on whether or not you speak in tongues.

Speaking in tongues is one among many "gifts" or "manifestations" of the Holy Spirit. Read I Corinthians 12:4-11, taking special note that all these "manifestations" of the Spirit are "gifts," just as He Himself is a gift. And we know that, in Greek, the word gift is closely related to the word grace.

Jesus said you could have rivers of living water flowing from your innermost being, totally on the basis of grace:

> "He who believes in Me, as the Scripture said, 'From his innermost being shall flow rivers of living water.'"
> But this He spoke of the Spirit, whom those who believed in Him were to receive...
> *John 7:38: 39a*

See: THOSE WHO BELIEVE IN HIM will receive. It's that simple. Tongues and other gifts of the Holy Spirit are valuable tools to facilitate release of these promised rivers of living water from your innermost being. Recognize also that, even though some spiritual gifts **are** more important than others (See I Corinthians 14), **none** of these gifts of the Holy Spirit are worthless. **All** manifestations of the Holy Spirit have enormous value and power. Therefore, never let anyone convince you that even the least of these gifts of the Spirit is worthless and therefore not worth seeking.

Instead, the Bible says, "desire earnestly spiritual **gifts**." (I Corinthians 14:1) This desire is related to hunger and thirst after righteousness.

Find a quiet place, alone. Or, better yet, find some Christians who are not afraid of manifestations of the Holy Spirit, and ask them to lay hands on you. Then, trust the Holy Spirit to move powerfully in you whether you **see** immediate manifestations or not!

Worshippers Or Workers

Let me introduce this subject by saying that the liberating truth contained in this article certainly did not originate with me; it has been circulating for many many years. I only wish I could have learned this earlier in my Christian experience.

I spent years laboring under the false impression that, above all else, the Lord is seeking workers. You may be laboring under the same impression. There is much emphasis in the Body of Christ on training workers, and on production. I am still committed to fulfilling the Great Commission in our generation. God **does** want production (in the form of fruit). But God has no inordinate emphasis on production.

Inordinate emphasis on workers and on production places the cart before the horse. Such imbalanced emphasis caused me severe burnout. I lost my zeal and, worse yet, I nearly lost my First Love, Jesus! Emphasis on work and production can do this to anyone. Including you.

The Gospel does not base acceptance upon production even though production is important.

I did not realize that God's work (when it's done God's way) flows out of **supply**, and not merely in response to needs or commands.

Now here is my point: It is the Lord's will that all of His workers be worshippers FIRST. The Lord is seeking worshippers first (John 4:23, 24), workers second. He puts much more emphasis on relationship than He does on production. So Jesus taught us,

> "I am the vine, you are the branches; he who abides
> in Me, and I in him, he bears much fruit; for apart from
> Me you can do nothing.
>
> *John 15:5*

See, the **relationship** is always prerequisite to the production. The production comes out of supply from the vine.

Thus, the Lord values **you** more than He values your ministry.

It is the tendency in much of the Body of Christ to build Marthas rather than Marys. But look,

> Now as they were traveling along, He entered a certain village; and a woman named Martha welcomed Him into her home.
>
> And she had a sister called Mary, who moreover was listening to the Lord's word, seated at His feet.
>
> But Martha was distracted with all her preparations; and she came up *to Him,* and said, "Lord, do You not care that my sister has left me to do all the serving alone? Then tell her to help me."
>
> But the Lord answered and said to her, "Martha, Martha, you are worried and bothered about so many things; but *only* a few things are necessary, really *only* one: for Mary has chosen the good part, which shall not be taken away from her."
>
> *Luke 10:38-42*

Martha had been busy serving, and she was upset with Mary who had been sitting at Jesus' feet, and not helping. But Jesus affirmed Mary's priorities, didn't He.

See, the relationship is valued more than the production. God's production comes out of supply from the vine. The Lord values **you** more than He values your ministry. He builds worshippers, then workers. By grace you abide in Him, and so you can receive supply, and ultimately bear much fruit. That's God's design: worshippers, then workers. If you have somehow been sent out with your cart before your horse, my heart goes out to you, believe me. But it's never too late to become a worshipper.

The Fruit Of The Spirit In
An Environment For Growth

It is important to understand that Christianity does not come down **primarily** to what you do for God, but rather it comes down primarily to what He does for you, and in you. Thus, biblical Christianity is understood best in terms of fruit bearing. When Christianity is working properly, with grace and truth, you wind up bearing much fruit: thirty, sixty and a hundredfold. (Mark 4:20) The fruit is the "fruit of the Spirit."

No vine or tree can be beaten into bearing fruit, but instead, every good farmer feeds, cultivates and waters his plants. He drives off pests and parasites. Essentially, he helps create a favorable environment for growth; then he must wait patiently. Harvest time will come, but he cannot **cause** growth. He can only facilitate it.

You can learn to provide a favorable environment for growth in your own life, and your church is an important part of this.

This means you need to stay exposed to the moving of the Holy Spirit and to the teaching and preaching of God's Word. This is because the fruit of the Holy Spirit is not a product of human striving, but rather it is the work of the Spirit. Fruit will be in you as a product of the rivers of living water (the Holy Spirit) flowing in you. We have already emphasized that Jesus said that **you** can have these rivers:

> "He who believes in Me, as the Scripture said, 'From his innermost being shall flow rivers of living water.'"
> But this He spoke of the Spirit, whom those who believed in Him were to receive; for the Spirit was not yet *given*, because Jesus was not yet glorified.
> *John 7:38, 39*

Thus, it makes sense that an environment where the Holy Spirit is quenched is not the best environment for growth. Conversely, you cannot grow in an environment where there is disorder and unbridled freedom. Sometimes such unbridled freedom is mistaken for the freedom of the Spirit.

The best environment is where the leadership knows how to, "let all things be done properly and in an orderly manner." (I Corinthians 14:40 — the context here is gifts of the Holy Spirit) This verse says two things: First, "Let all things be done." In other words, "Do not quench the Spirit." (I Thess. 5:19) Honor His presence. Allow His manifestations to work in the Church.

And second, I Corinthians 14:40 says to let all things be done "in an orderly manner." Freedom for the Holy Spirit to move does not mean unbridled freedom and disorder. When the Holy Spirit moves, there is a powerful, orderly flow and direction in the meeting. People need to be instructed in these matters by their pastors and spiritual leaders.

My comments thus far apply mainly to "manifestations," "gifts" of the Holy Spirit (see I Cor. 12:4-11), but what is the "fruit" of the Spirit?

> But the fruit of the Spirit is love, joy, peace, patience, kindness, goodness, faithfulness, gentleness, self-control; against such things there is no law.
>
> *Galatians 5:22-23*

This fruit of the Spirit is a product of the power of the Holy Spirit working in us **together with** the grace of God itself. For example, we already know that joy flows from the joy of our salvation (Psalm 51:12-13), and that peace flows from peace with God through faith in the Gospel (Romans 5:1), and that, "We love, because He first loved us." (I John 4:19) Thus, the fruit of the Spirit rests in the Gospel itself.

The fruit of the Spirit is not born in some euphoric vacuum or spiritual high, apart from the word of the Cross. No, grace and the Spirit work together. The fruit of the Spirit is born as a direct response to the word of the Cross. Any spiritual high not rooted in Calvary is dangerous.

All of the fruit of the Spirit is God's work in you IN THE CONTEXT OF GRACE. Therefore **grace needs be the primary ingredient in your environment for growth**.

Tiny Faith, Enormous Results

Just to show you what the tiniest amount of faith in Jesus can do, let me tell you another story from my own life. In 1968 my life was nearly snuffed out, and God did an incredible thing. I had spent five years full of anger against God (because He seemingly had not fulfilled His promises to me), full of anger against myself (for not being what I felt God wanted me to be), and, of course, full of anger against others (because I blamed others for most of my problems). This anger caused me ultimately to carry a gun, and to think often of murder and suicide.

Anyhow, in 1968, I became deathly ill and I had to be hospitalized for over three months. I went from 165 to 104 pounds. My death became so certain that one day my doctor called my parents (who lived 200 miles away) and told them that if they wanted to see me alive they needed to be at the hospital before 5 o'clock that afternoon.

The Lord did **not**, repeat, did NOT put me in that hospital! But I didn't know that at the time. I thought God was punishing me for all my sin and failure.

Obviously, I didn't die, but I got out of the hospital and returned to my flea-infested apartment; I weighed about 112 pounds. My return home was a return to depression and hopelessness and marijuana! The only way I can describe it is that my total environment was dark all the time, no light at the end of any tunnel. Just more tunnel! The only **friends** I had who I felt totally comfortable with were my two cats; I was $10,000 in debt with medical bills; no work, psychedelic music, paperback books — this was my total environment. What a horrible fate, what agony, especially for a person whose entire self-worth had been totally based on his productivity! Life was over for me, even though I had not yet quit breathing. I still hated everyone.

Something incredible happened. I know that the Lord did it. One day when the darkness became so thick that I couldn't stand it anymore, an idea came to me: I decided to pretend, to PRETEND mind you, that somehow God could still save me. I figured such pretending might bring welcome temporary relief from my darkness. I would pretend that there was a make-believe God in whom there was hope, even for me! Perhaps this little game could ease the hopelessness for a day or two.

I dug out my Bible. I knew my Bible well; I had been a Christian for many years. I turned to Romans 8:28 and 29:

> And we know that God causes all things to work together for good to those who love God, to those who are called according to *His* purpose.
>
> For whom He foreknew, He also predestined *to become* conformed to the image of His Son, that He might be the first-born among many brethren...

Then, for relief from the darkness, I began to pretend that those verses were true **for me**. I didn't believe this, mind you. I knew I didn't love God. But I **pretended** that the Lord could accept me as I was. I pretended that He could **use** every tragedy and every disaster in my life, and every terrible thing that I had ever done to anyone, and even my present physical, mental and financial condition, and that He would work all this together for good, to conform me to the image of His Son. I pretended that I was called of God and predestined (**whatever** that meant; this was no time for theological gymnastics!). I pretended that God was in control, **and** that He had included me in His plans.

I knew there was no hope in trying to change myself because I had tried unsuccessfully to change myself in the early years of my Christian life. **Nothing** worked. So, I pretended not only that God **could** change me, but also that He **would** change me! I pretended that He could and would bring me into a powerful ministry. I took the psychedelic music off my turntable and put on an old Mahalia Jackson album I had. She sang, ''All Hail The Power of Jesus' Name, let angels prostrate fall.''

I started out pretending. But **God** intervened within 24 hours by giving me a measure of **actual** hope in Romans 8:28 and 29. Somehow during that 24 hour period He assured me that Romans 8:28, 29 was true for me because I was still His. He had **never** forsaken me. He showed me that I was pretending the truth! What happened next astounded me: I believed Him! Then, everything began to change. I changed. Within one year I was preaching and teaching, and many were coming to Christ. I was filled with the Holy Spirit. My bills were all paid. I had gained weight. The Lord had taught me to forgive everyone, including myself. By mid-1970 I was ordained, and married.

This permanent transformation could happen only **after** the Lord showed me His grace plus nothing, and I simply received it, first by pretending, then by believing.

The grace of God is radical, more radical than any love you have ever imagined. Believe it. Or just pretend, as I did, just act as if it's true.

If you will **act** on God's **grace**, it will work; I don't care whether you initially "believe" it or not.

Do not attempt to dictate to God what He is supposed to change, or when. Just accept His acceptance. Something will happen, if not outside you, at least inside, you'll see.

Those of us who are becoming grace people can learn to capitalize on everything we have ever done to ourselves, using everything for God's glory, through grace. And then we can learn to take **everything** that the devil has ever done to us and, in effect, cram it right back down his filthy throat! All the evil, all the suffering, all the tragedy: We can cram it all back down the devil's throat because of Romans 8:28 and 29. God causes **all things** to work together for our good. Thus, defeat is transformed into victory. Thus, "DEATH IS SWOLLOWED UP IN VICTORY." (I Corinthians 15:54b) This book is a good example of what I mean.

God wants to use everything in your past for His glory, and for your good, now and in your future.

You can appropriate this. The Lord will show you how. It's all a reasonable and biblical response to His radical love.

Defending Ourselves
Part I

A good litmus test to see whether or not you are abiding in grace is to notice how quickly you jump to defend yourself (or to blame others) when you are accused, caught, or suspected of error. The reason this is such a good litmus test is that the need for self-justification stops at Calvary. You don't need self-justification if you trust Christ for your righteousness. You are totally justified because Jesus became your sin offering.

> ...being justified as a gift by His grace through the redemption which is in Christ Jesus...
>
> *Romans 3:24*

What a relief when you can relax and let down your walls of defense! You are okay, not because some psychologist realizes that it will help you to believe that you are okay, but rather because God Himself declares that you are okay. And He has the authority to say that. His declaration took effect for you the instant you repented and put your faith in Christ.

> Who will bring a charge against God's elect? God is the one who justifies; who is the one who condemns? Christ Jesus is He who died, yes, rather who was raised, who is at the right hand of God, who also intercedes for us.
>
> *Romans 8:33, 34*

This took effect for you the instant you put your faith in Christ, and the rules for justification never change. You never need to grow out of justification by faith, because you can't! Day by day, year by year, the grace of God is the narrow way that leads to life. Fifty years from now you will still be appropriating grace.

Self-defense **is** sometimes necessary, on your job, or in court. But usually, self-defense is self-righteousness, an awesome burden which you were never created to bear: It means you have to be right, **always**, or it means you have to have an excuse, **always**, or, worse yet, it means you have to find someone else to blame, **always**! But if Jesus is your righteousness, you can forget all that, stop defending yourself, and simply flee to Calvary whenever necessary. Thus, self-justification stops at Calvary. What a relief!

Defending Ourselves
Part II

One of the significant indications that a person is healing and/or maturing in Christ is a lack of defensiveness.

Remember, I'm not saying there is **never** an occasion to answer critics or to make a defense. Paul did this from time to time where the Gospel or someone else's well-being was at stake. But **for himself** he had nothing to defend:

> For I am the least of the apostles, who am not fit to
> be called an apostle, because I persecuted the church
> of God. But by the grace of God I am what I am...
> *I Corinthians 15:9, 10a*

So you couldn't hurt Paul's feelings by telling him that he wasn't fit to be called an apostle because of his past. He always admitted that. He did not defend himself. His only qualification to be an apostle was grace.

A man came to me a few years ago, sat at my desk, looked me in the eye, and told me (based on my distant past) that I was totally unqualified to be an elder in the body of Christ. You know what? He was right. He had me. He wanted me to stop winning souls and to sit down and shut up. "The letter [law] kills." (II Cor. 3:6)

It felt so good to relax, and to let him talk, and to hear it all, and to have no defense, and to know that he was right, **and** to know that he was wrong: To know that my only qualification for ministry was, and continues to be, the grace of God. Thus, I did **not** defend myself to Him. He knew the Bible so well that he could kill me with it. But apparently he didn't know Jesus because he had no sense of His grace. Jesus is, "full of grace and truth." (John 1:14)

I am convinced that some people (like the Pharisees of old) are going to go to hell with a Bible hanging out of every pocket. Their problem is that they are steeped in self-righteousness, experts on the letter, dead in the spirit. The Bible is God's book to us. He anointed every word. But men can twist it so that God's emphasis on **grace** becomes obscure.

Jesus is our strong defense:

> Blotting out the handwriting of ordinances that was
> against us, which was contrary to us, and took it out
> of the way, nailing it to his cross.
>
> *Colossians 2:14 KJV*

The Word of God itself is clear; Jesus has done all to reconcile us to Himself. He knew that we could never rightfully defend ourselves anyhow. He Himself has provided righteousness. It is time to allow our defensive walls to come down, and trust Him.

Defending Ourselves
Part III

The need to defend ourselves is a major indication of alienation, from the Lord and from each other.

Adam and Eve became instant experts at self-defense when they sinned:

> Then the eyes of both of them were opened, and they knew that they were naked; and they sewed fig leaves together and made themselves loin coverings.
>
> And they heard the sound of the Lord God walking in the garden in the cool of the day, and the man and his wife hid themselves from the presence of the Lord God among the trees of the garden.
>
> Then the Lord God called to the man, and said to him, "Where are you?"
>
> And he said, "I heard the sound of Thee in the garden, and I was afraid because I was naked; so I hid myself."
>
> And He said, "Who told you that you were naked? Have you eaten from the tree of which I commanded you not to eat?"
>
> And the man said, "The woman whom Thou gavest *to be* with me, she gave me from the tree, and I ate."
>
> Then the Lord God said to the woman, "What is this you have done?" And the woman said, "The serpent deceived me, and I ate."
>
> *Genesis 3:7-13*

You see, we have great fear that our own lack of righteousness (i.e., our nakedness) will be uncovered by others, or by the Lord, so we stitch together our own fig leaf garments (usually psychological walls and defense mechanisms) similar to the fig leaf garments of Adam and

Eve.

However, when we do get exposed, we defend ourselves, and often we find someone else to blame. Sometimes we blame God. Adam ultimately blamed God and implied that his sin was **God's** fault! He blamed his sin on the woman **whom God had given him**!

Blaming others, blaming God: We are alienated and alone, defending our sin! And, if we try to punish ourselves, we are alienated from ourselves. What a painful way to exist!

> Therefore having been justified by faith, we have peace with God through our Lord Jesus Christ.
>
> *Romans 5:1*

That quickly, the need to defend ourselves can cease. Justified: Just-as-if-I'd never sinned! That is a good way to remember what justified means.

The Lord's will is, through Calvary and the power of the Holy Spirit, that you be totally free from psychological defense mechanisms, and from a lousy self-image. God wants you free from psychological walls, and from the pain of blaming others, and from self-punishment. As you can see by implication through the Scripture we read today, many psychological walls do **not** have psychological origins. Rather they are walls which we use to attempt to hide from our own sins and imperfections.

Therefore, many psychological walls do not yield to psychological solutions.

Simply call sin sin, and do not fear your nakedness. Instead, accept the pure justification and peace with God which are in Christ Jesus. **Put on** the Lord Jesus Christ. (Romans 13:14)

When You Sin, Run *To* Me

After Adam and Eve sinned the Lord went searching for them, and they hid from Him! I think we all have the same tendency when we sin: We want to hide from God for a while, and we hope that He doesn't come looking for us, and we hope that time will make our sin seem less sinful.

But the Lord **did** go searching for Adam and Eve. You see, He values His relationship with us.

If God is going to come after fallen Christians anyhow, why run? Besides, when we get snake-bit, He is the **only** one with the cure.

What do you suppose God would like to say to us when we fall? If we could **hear** God when we fall, what would He be saying? Part of our problem is that we become hard of hearing when we fall. But if we could hear, there is little doubt in my mind what the Lord would be saying: "Don't make me chase you! When you sin, run to me. There is no time to lose. Satan can hurt you while you're down."

Here is God's expressed attitude:

"For the Son of Man has come to seek and to save that which was lost."

Luke 19:10

And the Spirit and the bride say, "Come." And let the one who hears say, "Come." And let the one who is thirsty come; let the one who wishes take the water of life without cost.

Revelation 22:17

The Lord wants to teach you, when you sin, to flee to Calvary im-**mediately**. Don't hide, because Satan can beat you while you are down. Instant restoration is a simple matter of instantaneous depend-ence on Calvary and on the Holy Spirit. Run to Him.

Legalism or Faith

You did not put yourself **in Christ**. **You** responded to the Gospel, but God Himself put you **in Christ** when you received Jesus Christ as your Savior and Lord:

> But by His doing are you in Christ Jesus, who became to us wisdom from God, and righteousness and sanctification, and redemption...
>
> *I Corinthians 1:30*

Note: It is by His doing. If you check verse 29 it is clear that "His" refers to God Himself. So **He** put you in Christ. And at that point Jesus became **to you** wisdom, righteousness, sanctification and redemption **from God**. This is true for you from the first breath you draw as a Christian. Faith is reckoned (imputed) to you as righteousness, as it was to Abraham. (Gen. 15:6 and Rom. 4:3) This is the only way to a holy and obedient life: Through faith, continually appropriate God's righteousness.

Obviously, you need add nothing to the Lord's gifts of wisdom, righteousness, sanctification and redemption as your basis for relating to Him, or as your basis for spiritual growth. Jesus Christ is all you need. Nothing needs to be added. But legalism would have you try!

How does legalism do this? By persuading you to attempt to establish your own self-righteousness. Here is an excellent example, written by Paul, which contrasts how the Israelites zealously sought to establish their own righteousness, and failed, whereas the Gentiles attained righteousness by simply receiving imputed righteousness through faith:

> What shall we say then? That Gentiles, who did not pursue righteousness, attained righteousness, even the righteousness which is by faith;

but Israel, pursuing a law of righteousness, did not arrive at *that* law.

Why? Because *they did* not *pursue it* by faith, but as though *it were* by works...

For I bear them witness that they have a zeal for God, but not in accordance with knowledge.

For not knowing about God's righteousness, and seeking to establish their own, they did not subject themselves to the righteousness of God.

Romans 9:30-32, 10:2,3

This Scripture is an exact description, not just of Israel, but also of many Christians today: They have a zeal for God, but they are seeking to establish their own righteousness. They do not know about, or do not submit to, God's righteousness. Thus, they never attain it. They pursue a law of righteousness (works righteousness) rather than the righteousness of faith.

You don't want to be in that place. It will always fail to satisfy the Lord. Israel, pursuing a law for righteousness, seeking to establish their own righteousness, did not attain it. What they experienced is written for your benefit. One Way: Jesus!

Legalism:
Becoming Like The Most High

God Himself put you **in** Christ when you received Jesus Christ as your Savior and Lord:

> But by His doing are you in Christ Jesus, who became to us wisdom from God, and righteousness and sanctification, and redemption...
>
> *I Corinthians 1:30*

You need add nothing to these gifts as a basis for relating to God. But legalism would have you try!

Where did Adam and Eve get their righteousness? As a gift from God. Adam was nothing but a pile of dust before the Lord breathed life into him. Obviously dust can't **earn** anything. Adam and Eve were **created** in right standing with God. They did not earn this. They were created according to God's image and likeness:

> Then God said, "Let Us make man in Our image, according to Our likeness..."
> in His own image, in the image of God He created him; male and female He created them.
>
> *Genesis 1:26a,27b*

Adam and Eve did not need to try **to make themselves** like God because they **already were** like God, created by God Himself, in His image. (Please note: They were **like** God, but they were not God! This is obviously a crucial distinction.)   Therefore, any attempt on their part to make themselves **like** God (beyond having been created in God's likeness) would be both unnecessary and illegitimate. They could be what God made them to be, but any attempt to **improve** on that condition would actually be an attempt to supplant God and to **be** God!

Do you see that?

That is exactly how Satan fell: Lucifer said, "I will make myself like the Most High." (Isaiah 14:14)

And that is precisely how Satan approached Eve: "You will be like God." (Genesis 3:5) Eve could have correctly answered Satan thusly: "I already **am** like God, **He** made me this way. If I try to **make myself** like God I'll be in sin." But she didn't say that. She couldn't become more like God. She and Adam needed simply to walk in what the Lord had already made them to be.

Examine legalism and you will discover something startling. All legalistic pressure in your life is trying to force you to do one thing: To make yourself like God! I am speaking of legalism in this manner so that you can contrast legalism with true obedience. True obedience is always a **response** to God's grace and acceptance. It is never an attempt to make yourself like God, it is just simple obedience to God.

Legalism wants you to strive every day to try to become what God has already made you to be in Christ: Wisdom from God, and righteousness and sanctification, and redemption. Thus, legalism pressures you to repeat Eve's error. What deception!

In I Corinthians 1:30, **God** says **He** put you "in Christ" and declared you righteous. Henceforth, you can spend every day trying to make yourself like the Most High, or you can repent and accept your acceptance moment by moment, and spend every day growing in what God has already declared you to be in Christ. (Ephesians 2:8-10) Then, the Lord can **impart** into your life what He has already **imputed** to you. This is a **gradual**, but powerful, inexorable process. Here is something new to observe in this old, familiar Scripture:

> And we know that God causes all things to work together for good to those who love God, to those who are called according to *His* purpose.
> For whom He foreknew, He also predestined *to become* conformed to the image of His Son, that He might be the first-born among many brethren;
> *Romans 8:28,29*

Note what it means that God causes all things to work together for our good: The definition of all things working together for good is in verse 29: It means God causes all things to work together to conform us to the image of His Son. "For," the first word in verse 29, ties back to verse 28. Most Christians don't understand Romans 8:28 in its context. God causes **all things** to work together to conform us to the image of His Son.

It is important to see how the Lord intends to **impart** His righteousness (which He has already **imputed** to you) into your daily walk. It is a process in which you participate fully, but not Satan's way. You can grow in what you already are, like a child becoming an adult, but you can never improve upon what you already are **right now** in Jesus Christ. In other words, you cannot increase your present right standing before God any more than you can become more of a human being. You may be able to become a better human being, but you cannot become more of a human being. The same is true in the spiritual realm in Christ. Does that make sense to you?

There Is Nothing New In The New Age Deception

Legalism and the New Age Movement may not sound alike, but they are cut from the same mold:

> 'I will ascend...
> I will make myself
> like the Most High.'
>
> *Isaiah 14:14*

Those are the words of Satan. And, as we pointed out yesterday, this is the exact thrust of legalism. Legalism is an attempt to ascend to be like the Most High. But this is also the exact thrust of the New Age Movement. As we said, there is **nothing** new in the New Age deception. It is dangerous. It is the spirit of antichrist. It is dead wrong. It leads to the pit. That is how God responded to Satan's attempt to make himself like the Most High: In the next verse, verse 15, God addressed Satan:

> "Nevertheless you will be thrust down to Sheol,
> To the recesses of the pit."

Satan's attempt to be **like** the Most High was in fact an attempt TO BE the Most High. As we said yesterday, the same is true of **all** legalistic attempts to be like the Most High. Legalism tries to obligate God, which is in fact nothing short of a veiled attempt to munipulate God or to rule God and therefore to **be** God.

The proponents of the New Age Movement are generally quite out front with their deception. Most New Age proponents come right out and say that you (and all of us) are God!

The New Age Movement is rife with all kinds of "pathways," for "ascending" (mostly appropriated from Hinduism and Buddhism), for raising so-called "levels of consciousness," consciousness, that is, of the "divinity" of one's own self.

In the United States, most New Age proponents are claiming that their beliefs and disciplines will, in fact, also increase an individual's awareness of personhood and identity. This is a flat-out lie. Anyone who knows anything about all these Eastern pathways knows that their ultimate objective is to **escape** from personhood and finite identity: The individual, the person, actually attempts to dissolve into the infinite. The aim is in fact a total loss of identity, a total annihilation of personhood, not at all an increase in definition of personhood or of finite identity. Take note: Since Satan hates the image of God, he is committed to the destruction of personhood.

It is all a deception, even if the experience of divinity seems real. There will be no escape from finite identity or from moral responsibility:

> ...it is appointed for men to die once, and after this comes judgement...
>
> *Hebrews 9:27*

The Lord's rebuke against Babylon (where the New Age had its esoteric beginnings) stands:

> "...For you have said in your heart,
> 'I am, and there is no one besides me.'
> "But evil will come on you
> Which you will not know how to charm away;
> And disaster will fall on you
> For which you cannot atone,
> And destruction about which you do not know
> Will come on you suddenly."
>
> *Isaiah 47:10c, 11*

Like the New Agers, the Babylonian priesthood thought they were the "I am." Today, the Babylonian priesthood is dead, and under the judgement of God. **All** New Agers who do not repent will ultimately join the Babylonian priesthood under death and judgment.

Any attempt to ascend to be like the Most High is dangerous, and obviously impossible. So, when Nicodemus asked Jesus how he could be born again, the first thing Jesus answered (after rebuking

107

Nicodemus) was:

> "And no one has ascended into heaven, but He who descended from heaven, *even* the Son of Man.
>
> *John 3:13*

So, #1, if you want to be born again, you must understand that, "no one has ascended into heaven," and you must quit trying to ascend.

Then, in John 3:14-16, Jesus went on to explain to Nicodemus **how** new birth would occur. His answer to Nicodemus is the exact opposite of New Age teaching. Check it out for yourself.

If grace is emphasized, then the distinctions between the Gospel and the New Age teachings are clear. New Agers attempt to ascend to be like the Most High. That is the exact opposite of grace.

Let me add this note of caution: Paranoic fear among Christians concerning the New Age Movement is totally unwarranted even though New Age deception is undoubtedly prerequisite to the rise of Antichrist. When we walk in grace, demonic powers are scared to death of us. Let us walk in the authority of our God, not paranoia. **Please!** Jesus Christ is not trembling before the New Age Movement. Why should Christians tremble? Let us be led by the Spirit rather than driven and divided by fears of the New Age Movement. Let us be informed concerning the devil's tactics, but let us take our direction from the Holy Spirit (rather than reacting to satanic teaching).

Obedience Is Better Than Sacrifice

Here is a Scripture which the enemy can twist and use against you so that you cannot appropriate God's grace: "to obey is better than sacrifice." (I Samuel 15:22 KJV)

The scenario goes something like this: This verse is often misinterpreted (torn out of context) to imply that God disdains Christians who often need forgiveness (that is, those who need Jesus' sacrifice). Instead, it is thought that good Christians should seldom need forgiveness (because "obedience" is better than sacrifice). In other words, Christians who need to appropriate Jesus' blood sacrifice on a daily basis are seen as inferior to a somewhat mythical group of Christians who are somehow so obedient that they seldom need forgiveness! This **seems** both logical and scriptural. But it leads to frustration and hopelessness for many sincere believers.

First of all, it is the ability to appropriate grace on a daily basis that leads to true obedience! Paul's emphasis throughout Romans is that to believe God and therefore to be reckoned righteous **is a way of life**. It is God's way. It is the way of faith! It is not inferior. It is the **only** way to reign in life with Jesus. So how should we interpret I Samuel 15:22? Well, for one thing, the prophet Samuel was not rebuking salvation by grace when he rebuked King Saul by telling him that obedience is better than sacrifice. Let's examine I Samuel 15:22 more closely.

The prophet Samuel rebuked King Saul for not slaughtering the Amalekites' sheep. The Lord had commanded King Saul to keep nothing for himself from the victory God had given him over the Amalekites. King Saul was instructed by the Lord to slaughter all the animals. But instead the King kept the best animals for himself and gave the prophet Samuel the excuse that he had kept them in order to sacrifice them to God. So Samuel rebuked Saul, and Saul lost his Kingship. Read the story yourself and see. One thing you will see is that the prophet Samuel did **not** rebuke Saul for any sincere desire on Saul's part to repent and to appropriate grace to atone for his sin. Saul had no such sincere desire! Saul merely begged not to lose his

Kingdom, after getting caught. Yet this verse is often used incorrectly against Christians who **do** have a sincere ongoing desire to repent. As a result, many repentant Christians are made to feel bad and second-rate because they need grace.

Do you see what I'm saying? Yes, obedience is better than sacrifice, clearly, yet Samuel did not rebuke Saul for sincerely wanting to appropriate atonement for his sin. Something perverse and insidious was at work here: King Saul was trying to pass off his disobedience (in keeping the animals) as obedience (to sacrifice to God). He literally wanted to make his sin **itself** (the animals) into his sin offering! He tried to make his sin **itself** into obedience, which is exactly opposite to God's grace, which calls sin sin. Obviously, Saul was unrepentant. He was in rebellion. This verse **cannot** be used legitimately to discourage sincere but imperfect Christians from appropriating daily forgiveness and cleansing. Saul did not even admit that he had sinned until **after** Samuel announced that Saul had lost his kingship as a result of his sin. Furthermore, Saul tried to blame others for his sin (see verses 15 and 24) and, as we now know, such behavior is not repentance.

Have I explained the difference between Saul's rebellion and daily grace enough ways to clarify it? I certainly hope so.

Even if we agree that obedience is better than sacrifice (and I do), we must still joyfully accept the Lord's way, that true obedience develops **through** appropriating the sacrifice of Jesus, not apart from it. Since the Holy Spirit works as we respond to the blood, and since the fruit of the Spirit, such as love and self-control (and all obedience, for that matter), is born in response to grace, perhaps it would be best to teach that obedience **is born** through Jesus' sacrifice, rather than to harp on obedience being better than sacrifice.

You are not a second-class citizen if you appropriate grace. You are a right-on, New Testament Christian.

No Shotgun Wedding

Thy people will volunteer freely in the day of Thy power...

Psalm 110:3a

Here is an important concept. God is looking for **volunteers**. When the Lord moves in His "power," He gets volunteers. Thus, when God moves in His power, there is no need to beat or coerce His people into His service. Thus, wherever God's people are being beaten, or manipulated through guilt, or otherwise coerced into submission, even by sincere preachers and teachers, it is obvious that God's power is not there! Even if an occasional miracle occurs, God is not moving powerfully there.

Such tactics do work. People can be beaten, manipulated by guilt, and otherwise coerced into submission. This may appear to be the correct approach because it gets "results." It may look spiritual. It may raise large amounts of money. But coercive or manipulative tactics are not needed when God moves in His power.

Jesus doesn't want a shotgun wedding! That is, He doesn't want a bride who is forced into marrying Him with the proverbial gun to her head. Why should someone as magnificent as Jesus need this? He would be the laughingstock of all creation.

In our country the term "shotgun wedding" has, of course, always meant something quite different from the way I'm using it here, but the reason I think the term shotgun wedding is appropriate the way I'm using it here is that it has always meant that one or both marriage partners had to be forced to the altar. I want to graphically illustrate and to emphasize what a reproach it would be to Jesus if His bride had to be forced to the altar. The shotgun wedding has always been a reproach.

The Lord's people volunteer freely in the day of His power. That is the only wedding Jesus will accept. It is true that Jesus' bride is being chosen and drawn to Him by His Father. But this neither limits nor eliminates volition on the part of His bride. In fact, my point is that when God draws powerfully the bride volunteers.

A bride with a gun to her head does not glorify Jesus. Therefore, I want to encourage all true servants of the Lord to avoid coercion and manipulation of His bride. Allow the Holy Spirit to convict and to draw people to Jesus. Preach convicting messages, yes, seasoned with grace. And **do** give strong leadership. The Bride of Christ needs strong leadership. But please do not try to lord yourself over God's people. Allow God's program to function. If you do not have confidence in God's power to transform people without your constant coercion, then you had better go find out why. The problem is in you, not in Jesus.

Then again, on the other hand, perhaps the problem is not in you at all. Perhaps it is in your listeners. Perhaps you need to preach elsewhere. If your listeners submit only under duress when beaten, you need to ask yourself, "Am I feeding sheep or merely beating goats?" Understand that, among goats, even if you manage to beat them into submission, it can't last. They never become sheep. Nothing has been added to the Kingdom. My advice is, find another flock! Good preachers know that, even among sheep, a good "goat clubber" sermon is needed from time to time, but not every Sunday. No way. There will be no shotgun wedding for Jesus Christ and His bride.

Here is some more food for thought: There are many spiritually hungry Christians in the United States, but, just in case you can't find a hungry flock here, please consider an alternative. Perhaps the Lord wants to send you overseas. Let me tell you that there are millions of hungry Christians overseas who have no qualified pastors at all. Not only is this situation inequitable, it is dangerous. If you are sick of goats (and hopefully we all are), believe me, there are many of God's sheep scattered all over the world without shepherds. Perhaps the Lord is sending you to them. Ask Him.

In the United States these days pastors are practically stepping on each other's toes; and they are constantly invading each other's territory. There is much competition. This situation makes no sense at all. It is time for many frustrated pastors to go cross-cultural. At least that's my view of things. Ask the Lord for yourself.

Strange Fire

Aaron, Moses' brother, was the first High Priest in Israel. Aaron had four sons. Two of them were killed during the performance of their priestly duties because they knowingly offered "strange fire" before the Lord. The story of their deaths is repeated **three** times in the Old Testament: Leviticus 10:1-4, Numbers 3:4 and 26:61. Any time the Lord repeats Himself, there's something important He wants us to know.

The question here: What does strange fire symbolize? God's Law said that all fire used in His service and worship in the Tabernacle (for instance, for the burning of incense) must be taken from the perpetual fire of the Bronze Altar. This was God's fire. See Leviticus 16:12 for example. Fire supplied from any other source was forbidden on penalty of death. Obviously there were many sources of fire, but only God's fire from God's altar was acceptable for God's service and worship.

We know that the Holy Spirit has actually manifested Himself as fire (Acts 2:3), but for our purposes here, it is the **symbolism** of fire which we need to focus upon. It is common knowledge that fire is an important symbol of the Holy Spirit in the Bible. Logically, therefore, the "strange fire" which God forbid for Tabernacle worship was intended by God to symbolize some spirit **other than** the Holy Spirit (for example, an evil spirit, or the human spirit) being utilized in the service and worship of God. And the use of strange fire in the service and worship of God inevitably brought death to those who tried it.

So two of Aaron's sons died offering strange fire. Then the Bible says,

> Then Moses said to Aaron, "It is what the Lord spoke, saying,
> 'By those who come near Me I will be treated as holy,
> And before all the people I will be honored.'"

> So Aaron, therefore, kept silent.
>
> *Leviticus 10:3*

So, any offering of strange fire before God dishonors God.

You and I were born again through the Holy Spirit, not the human spirit. John 1:13: "who were born not of blood, nor of the will of the flesh, nor of the will of man, but of God."

This is one of the main reasons I am writing this book on grace: To help us all learn to live by grace in the power of the Holy Spirit, rather than by strange fire.

Therefore, as I did yesterday, I wish to encourage all servants of the Lord to avoid coercion and manipulation of His bride. And, to-day, I must expand our understanding to include all appeals to fleshly desires and motives. The use of all such devices in the service and worship of God amounts to strange fire. Thus, Jesus Himself was **never** noted for His flesh appeal. (See especially Isaiah 53:2) The use of strange fire in God's service is every bit as deadly now as it was in Moses' and Aaron's time. Outpourings of the Holy Spirit have been killed by it. In addition to high-pressure tactics and flesh tactics, denominational walls fit into this category of strange fire; not denominations, per se, but denominational **walls**. No true work of God needs walls to keep people from escaping.

Conversely, anti-denominationalism (supposedly the opposite of denominationalism) often erects similar walls by teaching that the Lord won't work within denominations. What bologna! God works wherever He wants.

Above all, however, and beyond addressing this admonition to preachers, I want **you** to apprehend the personal application concerning strange fire to your own life: Live by grace in the Holy Spirit, without strange fire. Whatever everyone else is doing, you are learning to discern when you are walking in strange fire, and when strange fire is being used to manipulate you. Walking in God's fire, and avoiding strange fire, does **not**, repeat, does **not** mean that effort on your part is unnecessary. No, sometimes walking in God's fire can necessitate great personal effort and sacrifice. Strange fire in your personal life means legalism, works righteousness, and the fleshly striving which inevitably manifests. It means responding to guilt instead of responding to God.

Oh, and one more thing: Sometimes there is a fine line between **manipulation** and **persuasion**. Throughout the Scriptures, servants of God can be observed working to **persuade** people to turn to God. The Lord anoints such persuasion. God helping us, we must persuade people. We must powerfully persuade **our** generation to turn to Christ.

We can do this without crossing that fine line into strange fire. It's a simple matter. We must become keenly aware that Jesus promised that **He** would build His Church (Matthew 16:18); so that, although we are co-laborers together with Him, **He** is the One Who gives the increase (I Corinthians 3:6-9). Thus, if we are doing **His** thing, not doing our thing, strange fire is both unnecessary and counterproductive. If we are building **His** Kingdom, not our own kingdom, then discernment is readily available to us, so that we know His fire, and strange fire is repulsive to us.

Which fire are you trusting? This question is crucial today, even as in the days of Moses.

Clay Pots

Let us not be too hard on our preachers and teachers, even if they make mistakes from time to time. I say this in defense of all true men and women of God in His service. I say it also on my own behalf. I feel that, in more than one respect, I am the product of 47 years of mistakes, all of which God has used! Paul said an extremely important thing in this regard:

> But we have this treasure in earthen vessels [clay pots,
> if you will], that the surpassing greatness of the power
> may be of God and not from ourselves;
> *II Corinthians 4:7*

Every man and every woman of God is trapped in a clay pot: Their bodies and brains and natural functions are from the dust, and return to the dust. This means that, though soul and spirit are immortal, every man and every woman of God has imperfect memory, imperfect knowledge, and other obvious shortcomings. Everybody knows this, right? Then, why are unrealistic expectations and picky criticisms of men and women of God rampant in the United States today? Paul said; "We know in part, and we prophesy in part." (I Corinthians 13:9) He said "we," including himself, even though he was able to declare the whole council of God (Acts 20:27). Paul wasn't perfect!

I have heard so many comments and questions, "Why do all these famous men and women of God have such **obvious** flaws?" The answer should also be **obvious**: So that, when the Lord moves powerfully through them, it remains **obvious** that the power is from God and not from them. Otherwise people are tempted to worship the men and women of God themselves! This tendency is frightfully strong. Thus, the clay pots in which we live are essential.

God chose Israel to conquer the Promised Land, not because she was the most powerful or most impressive nation available, but rather because she was the **least** likely to succeed. Thus, the other nations of the earth would be forced to marvel at the greatness of Israel's God, rather than at the greatness of Israel herself. (See, for example, Deuteronomy 7:7, 8, 16-21; 8:17, 18; 9:1-7.)

It works the same way for Christians:

> ...but God has chosen the foolish things of the world to shame the wise, and God has chosen the weak things of the world to shame the things which are strong, and the base things of the world and the despised, God has chosen, the things that are not, that He might nullify the things that are, that no man should boast before God.
>
> *I Corinthians 1:27-29*

Thus, you need **not** expect even famous men and women of God to live up to all of your expectations. They are clay pots, and God has anointed them. Their clay pots are visible in order to remind everyone to worship God.

I'll never forget the first time I saw Kathryn Kuhlman. I was sitting near the stage in an audience of 5,000 or so in the Shrine Auditorium in Los Angeles. Kathryn came floating and dancing out on stage with a giant smile on her face, in a flowing white gown, like some fairy godmother! I thought it was all an act, showmanship for the audience. Inside I said: "Oh God, what flesh!" I was terribly offended. **And** I was terribly wrong. Truth is, her outward appearance had absolutely no flesh appeal.

She began teaching, and then, it wasn't long before she began speaking specific words of healing to people all over the auditorium. People started forward, testifying of their healings. She had doctors right there on stage with her. It was no fraud. She had a powerful anointing from God!

But her clay pot offended me terribly! Therefore, though I came to a place of deep respect for Kathryn, she never became an idol or a superstar to me. There is only one Superstar, Jesus Himself.

I'll never forget the first time I heard that Billy Graham had (it seemed) made a public mistake. It was nothing serious, and it helped me to see him as an anointed but normal human being. I have more respect for him now than before. But we must glorify **God** for Billy Graham's accomplishments. Billy certainly does!

I hope you see the lasting benefit of this. It is God's design for now. **But**, now, I had best hasten to qualify what I've said: I AM NOT

EXCUSING ANY PREACHERS WHO GET INTO IMMORALITY. OBVIOUSLY, THEY MUST BE DISCIPLINED AND BEAR THE SHAME. We cannot accept or validate such behavior. Anyway, with this qualification, my objective in this article has been to emphasize the **benefits** of our clay pots rather than to lament the liabilities: Everyone is well aware of the liabilities! The Lord certainly doesn't command us to agree with everything we see or hear from clay pots, but He certainly does call us to love and respect all genuine servants of God. Their ministries are eternally valuable even though their clay pots are temporarily necessary. We must accept this. It is God in His wisdom who has ordained it.

Conviction vs. Condemnation

It helped me a lot when I finally understood the difference between conviction and condemnation.

The Holy Spirit **convicts** to expose **real** sin in us, to draw us to Christ. Whenever He does this, He **draws us to Christ** through the Gospel, which provides us with God's immediate answer to our sin problem. So we receive forgiveness and hope and reconciliation to God.

The Devil **condemns** us, producing exactly the opposite result: He skillfully points out our sin, but of course with no reminder of the Gospel, so that we are left feeling hopeless and alienated from God. We feel pushed away from the Lord, or we feel much too dirty to get close to Him. Condemnation makes us want to quit, or it makes us mad at God for not changing us.

This is the difference between the conviction of the Holy Spirit and the condemnation of Satan: Are you being drawn **to** the Lord with mercy made available, or are you being driven **away** from the Lord in guilt?

God calls Satan, "the accuser of our brethren...who accuses them before our God day and night." (Revelation 12:10b) Satan and our sin are the source of our condemnation. Jesus and His righteousness are the source of our freedom. Let's look more closely at Revelation 12:10,11:

> And I heard a loud voice in heaven, saying, "Now the salvation, and the power, and the kingdom of our God and the authority of His Christ have come, for the accuser of our brethren has been thrown down, who accuses them before our God day and night.
>
> "And they overcame him because of the blood of the Lamb and because of the word of their testimony, and they did not love their life even to death."

See how the accuser is overcome? Always, "**because** of the blood of the Lamb." **And**, you need to **speak out** against all condemnation. This is "the word of your testimony" dealing with condemnation: That Jesus plus nothing is your righteousness, and you claim no other righteousness. Satan can accuse your imperfect righteousness all day long, but not a demon in hell can accuse **Christ's** righteousness.

The conviction of the Holy Spirit may cause you to weep, and even to travail, over your sin. You may feel cut to the very heart as did thousands of people in Acts 2:37 as the Apostle Peter preached to them concerning the crucifixion of Jesus. But you will feel drawn to the Lord, and to God's cure, Calvary. And all of this will be immediately available to you, as it was when Peter preached.

I think, for most Christians, the most common source of both conviction and condemnation is preaching. Of course, some preaching is so watered down or so academic that it carries neither conviction nor condemnation, but that is another issue, perhaps for another book. Ignoring that problem for now, suffice it to say that there is preaching available which is powerfully convicting when needed, and such preachers always know how to make grace available to their listeners whenever sin is exposed. Unfortunately, there is also a lot of preaching available which is primarily condemning, and not at all seasoned with grace. Such preaching may contain truth, it may sound spiritual, it may produce frequent large altar calls, but, except for the fact that God may work **in spite** of it, it produces little permanent transformation or fruit.

Learn to discern what you are hearing. You don't have to respond to every preacher or to every message, only to the genuine conviction of the Holy Spirit.

And one more thing: I have heard it taught that the Holy Spirit never convicts the Church because Jesus said that the Holy Spirit would "convict the world," (John 16:8) and, therefore, any preaching which convicts the Church is inappropriate. My answer to that is this: The Holy spirit will convict worldliness, i.e. sin, even in His Church. That is, whatever is left **of the world** in the Church is a legitimate and scriptural target for the conviction of the Holy Spirit. Thus, the Holy Spirit can "convict the world" **in** the Church, when necessary.

If you know grace, you will learn to embrace the conviction of the Holy Spirit as a dear friend. AND you will learn to reject condemnation.

The Law Is Mercy

It is very difficult to see that the Law is mercy until you've learned to live in grace: The Law of God is good; the problem is in us:

> So then, the Law is holy, and the commandment is holy and righteous and good.
> Therefore did that which is good become *a cause of* death for me? May it never be! Rather it was sin...
> *Romans 7:12,13a*

No doubt you'll recall from a previous article in **Celebration of Grace** what the Bible says: "the letter [law] kills." (II Corinthians 3:6) But you must understand **why** this is true. It is not a problem with God's Law, but rather, it is a problem with **our** sin.

The Lord's intent in giving us the Law was to bring us to His mercy. (Recall Romans 11:32 and Galatians 3:23:24) But we must also bear in mind that the Law itself is good. Once we see this, the Ten Commandments themselves can become our dear friends.

Here is an example of how the Law itself, under grace, became my friend. Back in 1967, my counselor used to tell me, "Jeff, if you ever want to be a well-adjusted person, and enjoy your life, you have to quit comparing yourself with other people." I knew he was right, and I tried to stop. I was in great pain. I was always comparing my muscles, or my face, or my car, or my apartment with the few people who were more successful than me. And I was angry because I wasn't where they were. Time passed. I couldn't change.

Years later, when I had learned the grace of God, I was **still** comparing myself with others; I even compared myself with better pastors. What pain. One day, as I was reading the Ten Commandments, one of them came alive to me:

> "You shall not covet your neighbor's house; you shall not covet your neighbor's wife or his male servant or

> his female servant or his ox or his donkey or anything
> that belongs to your neighbor.''
>
> *Exodus 20:17*

Suddenly, the Lord spoke this word of freedom right into me. It was His rhema to me, in this case a creative word which set me free from comparing myself and my possessions with others. In other words, He freed me from coveting. He showed me (through the Law) that I had been coveting, and He gave me real repentance, and He forgave and cleansed me, and He did a creative work in my mind and emotions that day.

I still covet sometimes, but now escape is quite easy. Mostly now I can spend my days praising and thanking God for my face, and my body, and my family, and my house, etc. What freedom! I don't even have to compare myself with other Christians! Truly, the Law is mercy, now that I have found mercy.

May the Lord do the same in you.

Please note also that, in recommending the Law in this way, I am speaking mainly in terms of the Ten Commandments themselves rather than in terms of the numerous sacrificial or ceremonial aspects of the Law. Likewise, I am not arguing for church meetings on Saturday or for circumcision (though, hygienically, the latter is often a good idea).

With these qualifications, under grace, the Law may well become one of the best friends you've ever had, as the Lord applies it to you. Christianity is about **supernatural transformation** from the inside out, as the Word and the Spirit work together in you.

Of course, bear in mind that the entire Law of God comes down to love:

> ...love therefore is the fulfillment of *the* law.
>
> *Romans 13:10b*

Why The Father Doesn't Always Explain Why

God often explains to us why we should obey Him. But there are times when He doesn't. There are times when He can't! — because we couldn't understand, even if He did explain. He wants us to learn to trust Him that He knows what He's doing.

Here is a good example. In our study yesterday we saw that the Law is good. But, in that Law, the Lord required lots of things of the Israelites which they could not have understood at that point in time, 1450 BC. As you read this example, you may wish I had chosen something less graphic, especially if you're eating lunch, but it's in the Book! So here it is.

In Deuteronomy 23:12,13 the Lord commanded the Israelites,

> "You shall also have a place outside the camp and go
> out there, and you shall have a spade among your tools,
> and it shall be when you sit down outside, you shall dig
> with it and shall turn to cover up your excrement."

You see what I mean. I apologize if you are eating lunch. But you can probably agree that, to many Israelites, this must have seemed like a stupid law. It meant they had to go to **a lot more trouble** to relieve themselves under the Law of God than when they were in Egypt without the Law! This law made it very inconvenient to obey God. The camp of Israel was gigantic — there were about three million Israelites. Going outside the camp could mean a long walk in a very hot sun. Imagine the possible objections: "Man, what a waste of time … We have to go for this **long** walk, clear outside the camp, and go to all this trouble… It was a lot easier in Egypt. **There** we could just allow sewage to flow down the streets! **Why** can't we just dig holes for ourselves **inside** our camp, next to our tents?"

These days we understand that the Lord was saving Israel from the horrors of typhoid, cholera and dysentery, diseases which have often ravaged civilizations, killing millions. The Lord promised Israel in Deut. 7:15, "And the Lord will remove from you all sickness..." But Israel could not have understood how Deut. 23:12,13 related to Deut. 7:15. They had no science to explain it. They had to trust God.

The Lord never says anything just for the fun of it. And He never sets up arbitrary standards. And His motive is always merciful towards us.

Sometimes we spend too much time asking the Lord, "Why?" As we learn to trust Him, we learn instead to ask Him, "**What** do You want, Lord?" More "**what**," less "**why**." He is good. He can be trusted.

The Law As A Diagnostician

What would you think of a doctor who knows that you have a deadly (but curable) disease, but who refuses to tell you, so that you ultimately die? A dastardly, dangerous person, right? So then, I wonder why everybody gets mad at God when He diagnoses our sin problem for us?

One of the important tools which God uses to diagnose sin is the Law. This is the primary reason the Lord gave the Law: To help us diagnose our sin problem. Paul says,

> I would not have come to know sin except through the Law; for I would not have known about coveting if the Law had not said, "YOU SHALL NOT COVET."
> ...for through the Law *comes* the knowledge of sin.
> *Romans 7:7b and 3:20b*

There is no reason to get upset. The Lord is an excellent physician. He is a perfect diagnostician. And He has the perfect cure.

> Therefore the Law has become our tutor *to lead us* to Christ, that we may be justified by faith.
> *Galatians 3:24*

"If"

Matthew, Mark and Luke all record the temptation of Jesus by Satan in the wilderness. Satan tempted Jesus to turn the stones into bread, to cast Himself off the pinnacle of the temple, and to bow down and worship Satan in exchange for the world. Three temptations — right?

Yes, and no. There is a very real sense in which Jesus was tempted **five** times in the wilderness, not just three. This is because in two of the temptations Satan stuck in a double whammy:

> ..."If you are the Son of God, command that these stones become bread.
> ..."If you are the Son of God throw Yourself down..."
> *Matthew 4:3 & 6*

The double whammy was the "if."

Two times. That's it — probably the most sinister and subtle part of the whole excruciating trial. If Satan could get Jesus to doubt who He was, to accept the "if," Jesus would be beaten.

Just before the temptation in the wilderness, Jesus had been baptized. When He came up out of the water of baptism the Holy Spirit descended upon Him as a dove and the Father spoke from heaven saying, "This is my beloved Son, in whom I am well pleased." (Matthew 3:16,17)

God said, "This is my beloved Son." Satan said, "**If** you are the Son of God..." Twice!

Satan does the same thing to you. The Lord reckons you righteous, He grants you right standing before Him by grace. You are a son or a daughter of God. Satan knows however that if he can get you to doubt who you are in Christ, then he can pressure you either into legalism or into some other sin.

A second subtle weapon inherent in these **ifs** is this: If you are the Son of God, **prove it**, turn these stones into bread, or do something spectacular. In other words, prove to **Satan** that you are spiritual.

Really weird! Jesus didn't buy it, but Christians fall for this trick all the time, without knowing it. They get tricked into trying to **prove** they are spiritual, rather than just standing in justification by faith. They fear the big "if" and respond accordingly.

Martin Luther had a powerful definition of hope, but I think his definition applies better to faith, so I have appropriated it and changed it into my definition of saving faith: Faith is living, daring confidence in the grace of God, so sure and certain that a man would stake his life on it a thousand times.

Standing in grace makes you less vulnerable to temptation, not more, because Satan can't hit you with the "if." You'll need to stake your life on the grace of God daily in order to avoid trying to defend yourself to the accuser.

So stand! Put on the whole armor of God, which is finalized and completed by the "helmet of salvation and the sword of the Spirit." (Ephesians 6:17) You put on your helmet of salvation through living, daring confidence in the grace of God.

"In"

Many Christians get up in the morning and, without realizing what they are doing, they renew their struggle to get ''in'' with God. They do not realize that they are already ''in'' because the Lord has put them in. (Review I Corinthians 1:30) Often they do not **feel** in. They do not **feel** spiritual. They do not **feel** God's presence. So they **feel** out! Yet, they are not out, they are in.

Concerning this struggle, I believe (if my memory serves me correctly) it was Watchman Nee who asked, "Can you imagine the frustration of trying to get into a room that you are already in?" Ridiculous? Yes. Comical? Yes. But a fact of life for many Christians.

In and **if** seem like little words, hardly worth serious or extensive study. But in fact, **in** and **if** are giants. **If** is central to Satan's warfare on the Church (as we saw in yesterday's article). **In** is central to understanding and experiencing salvation.

In is one word which must be understood in order to understand the letters of Paul: Paul used this word **in** repeatedly, with extreme significance:

> For as in Adam all die, so also in Christ all shall be made alive.
>
> *I Corinthians 15:22*

See: Who you are **in** makes all the difference. You came to be **in** Adam through birth. And the Bible teaches that you came to be **in** Christ through birth; born again, from above. Who you are **in** makes all the difference. Look how this little word **in** impacts upon your understanding of your relationship to the Lord:

> ...and in Him you have been made complete, and He is the head over all rule and authority; and in Him you were also circumcised with a circumcision made without hands...
>
> *Colossians 2:10,11a*

128

For He delivered us from the domain of darkness, and transferred us to the kingdom of His beloved Son, in whom we have redemption, the forgiveness of sins.
Colossians 1:13,14

If you will take time to read Ephesians 1:3-14 you'll discover that it is **in** Christ, **in** the Beloved, **in** Him, that you are seated in heavenly places; that it is **in** Him that you are chosen; that it is **in** Him that you are predestined to the adoption as a son (or a daughter) of God. It is **in** Him that you have redemption and the forgiveness of sins: It is **in** Him that you have an inheritance with the rest of the saints. And it is **in** Him that you have been sealed by the Holy Spirit of promise.

If you have been **born in** you must cease striving to **get in**!

For all the promises of God in Him *are* yea, and in Him Amen, unto the glory of God by us.
II Corinthians 1:20 KJV

In Christ all the promises of God are yea and amen. You can quit destroying your faith by trying to get into a room that you're already in. Rather, abide, respond, rejoice and proclaim: You are "in" with the ultimate in-crowd, you are "in" with the Creator of the universe and with His bride. You are "in" with all the right people!

"Abide"

Jesus said,

> "Abide in Me, and I in you. As the branch cannot bear
> fruit of itself, unless it abides in the vine, so neither *can*
> you, unless you abide in Me."
>
> *John 15:4*

The branch need not strive to get in the vine, it is in. It need not
strive to bear fruit. Everyone knows this. Therefore, Jesus' point is
crystal clear. All the branch does is abide.

To abide is simply to stay in Him. It means to rest in Him and all
that He is for you. That's the crux of the matter. The place of abiding
is rest, it is peace, it is faith in Jesus, not in ourselves.

Then you can begin to allow His Word to build in you without being threatened by it. So that,

> "If you abide in Me, and my Words [rhemata] abide
> in you, ask whatever you wish, and it shall be done for
> you."
>
> *John 15:7*

Once you know how you got in Jesus, you also know how to stay
in. Therefore you already know how to abide.

> As you therefore have received Christ Jesus the Lord,
> *so* walk in Him,
>
> *Colossians 2:6*

Who Is Jesus?

If your savior is inadequate then he cannot save you. Logically, then, you would have to save yourself. That is precisely the problem with every cult and false teaching: Their saviors are inadequate. Therefore every cult must have works righteousness or works salvation, in one form or another, to save themselves, **or** they must deny either sin or hell, **or both**, in order to eliminate the need for a savior.

In the case of cults which claim to "believe" in Jesus, in every case they err concerning **who** He is: One cult may err concerning Jesus' humanity while another may err concerning His divinity. In either case, their "Jesus" cannot fully save them. Many so-called "Christian cults" err concerning the Godhead itself. Typically they either deny that the Father, the Son, and the Holy Spirit are fully God, and fully One. Or they blur all three into one, denying the Personhood of each. There are hundreds of variations of error concerning Jesus and the Trinity. But in every case, without exception, cults demonstrate that a distorted concept of God leads to some form of works righteousness. And you will also discover that there is **always** some distortion concerning Jesus Himself. It is, therefore, crucial that every Christian be well-taught concerning **Who** Jesus is.

Satan's primary attack is always against Jesus Himself.

Jesus Himself is **both** FULLY MAN and FULLY GOD. He is NOT a little less than God because man is mixed in, and He is not a little more than man because God is mixed in. Did you get that? This understanding is essential because Jesus is NOT some sort of "new species" as some have erroneously taught. That is, Jesus is not some God-man mutant!

Do you know why this understanding is essential? Because a "new species" can not die for the sin of the old species. Jesus could not be "more than man" because only man could die for the sin of man. God said that if **man** sins, **man** must die. (Genesis 2:16,17) Therefore, only one who is FULLY MAN could die for the sin of man. Jesus was born FULLY MAN through Mary, and it makes sense that He **had to** remain FULLY MAN on the cross.

Some say that Jesus, in becoming sin for us (II Cor. 5:21), obliterated both His humanity and His Divinity at Calvary. If that is the case, then our sins remain unatoned, **because a new species cannot die for the sin of the old species**.

Interestingly, many who teach that Jesus' identity was obliterated by sin at Calvary also teach a new form of works righteousness, turning faith into works. Such conclusions result logically from an inadequate Jesus.

The Bible is full of the revelation that Jesus is fully man. For example:

> Since then the children share in flesh and blood, He Himself likewise also partook of the same, that through death He might render powerless him who had the power of death, that is, the devil...
>
> Therefore, He had to be made like His brethren in all things...
>
> ...*yet* without sin.
>
> *Hebrews 2:14, 17a; 4:15c*

Remember, **He had to be made like us in all things**, yet without sin, because a "new species" could never atone for our sin.

This incredible act of God is called the INCARNATION:

> And the Word became flesh, and dwelt among us, and we beheld His glory, glory as of the only begotten from the Father, full of grace and truth.
>
> *John 1:14*

Jesus is FULLY MAN, but He is also FULLY GOD. No savior who is **only** fully man can save us, because the Bible consistently maintains that mankind cannot save itself, but only God can save us. Thus, Jesus **had to** be FULLY GOD as well as FULLY MAN:

> For in Him all the fullness of Deity [i.e., God] dwells in bodily form.
>
> *Colossians 2:9*

See, **all the fullness of God**. Jesus could never be "less than God."

And if you still doubt He is fully God, look:

> And He is the image of the invisible God, the first-born of all creation.
>
> For by Him all things were created, *both* in the heavens and on earth, visible and invisible, whether thrones or dominions or rulers or authorities — all things have been created through Him and for Him.
>
> And He is before all things, and in Him all things hold together.
>
> *Colossians 1:15-17*

Many have said that the "doctrine" of the virgin birth of Jesus is not essential to our faith. But the virgin birth is central to the **identity** of Jesus Christ, both the Son of Man through Mary, and the Son of God, conceived through the Holy Spirit (See Luke 1:26-35). The virgin birth has direct bearing upon **who** Jesus Christ is. The virgin birth is taught clearly in the Bible. The virgin birth explains the completeness, both the humanity and the divinity, of Jesus.

How did God do this? That is, how can Jesus be FULLY GOD and FULLY MAN without being less than God and more than man? And how can Jesus be FULLY GOD and FULLY MAN and yet not have a split personality? I don't know, but such is the biblical reality of the Incarnation.

I cannot fully **explain** Him, but I can fully receive Him. The fact that I, in my puny brain, cannot fully comprehend the how of the Incarnation does not in any way invalidate the Incarnation, nor does it provide any legitimate excuse to play theological games with the Person of Jesus Christ. Theologians who demand that Jesus be reduced to our puny intellects risk not only their own souls, but also the souls of all who revere them. Jesus can be comprehended as our Savior and Lord, but He cannot be reduced to a test tube. I, for one, rejoice.

Your Savior is totally adequate and complete. Therefore you can be complete in Him (Colossians 2:9,10). He never emptied Himself of His divinity to become man (some have asserted that He did, based on Philippians 2:7). Jesus consistently spoke of His own divinity and of His own Sonship. He said, "He who has seen Me has seen the Father." (John 14:9) Yes, He emptied Himself of His glorious abode in heaven, and perhaps He emptied Himself of some of His **prerogatives** as God, in order to be made like us in all things, but

He never abdicated or lost His divinity.

Therefore, your Savior is totally adequate. The world is full of inadequate saviors, but you need not serve any of these.

The story is told (perhaps you've heard it) of a soldier in Viet Nam during the war there, who observed hundreds of refugees fleeing from their village to escape the Viet Cong. Most were either carrying or dragging as many of their worldly possessions as they could take along. Many villagers were observed to be carrying their household idols. The soldier inquired of one refugee, "Why are you carrying these idols while you have left behind so many essential items?" The refugee responded, "This is my god and I'm saving it."

Here is the utter heartbreak and the wicked irony of inadequate saviors, and it is certainly not limited to idolatrous cultures. Rather it is typical whenever and wherever Jesus Christ is not known. People must not only save themselves, but they must also save their saviors!

Thank God! Your Savior is totally adequate. Therefore trust Him fully.

Eternal Security?
Eternal Insecurity?
Or The Security Of The Believer?

Another way to say this might be, Calvinists? Arminians? or Sons and Daughters of God?

Can you lose your salvation? That is a scary question. Calvinists have generally taught that you can't. Arminians (not Armenians), named after Arminius, have generally taught that you can.

There are, even today, extreme Arminians who live in such fear of losing their salvation that they "get saved" thousands of times during their lifetimes, and they hope and pray to God that they don't die on a down day! They are always striving to get in. There is little or no grace in this.

The other extreme, as I mentioned in my Introduction to this book, is cheap grace. People who are into cheap grace are in effect trying to use God for fire insurance. The fact is, it is impossible to abuse grace in this way because God knows the hearts of all men, and God is not mocked. (Galatians 6:7)

However, this book is dedicated to all Christians who meant business with God when they gave their lives to Christ, trusting **Him** with their destinies. I.e., I am writing to true believers (as imperfect as they are). I am not writing to people who are merely trying to play God for a fool.

I received much of my early Christian training under Calvinists, then I went to an Arminian Bible school. Talk about confusion! Wow! I found that each camp has lots of Scripture to support their positions. It's true, they do. And they flatly contradict each other. For many years I could not resolve the contradiction. My faith was severely shaken because I took the Bible seriously.

Needless to say, I do not expect to satisfy either the Calvinists or the Arminians with my book. My first pastor, Owen Onsum, taught me something which he called "the security of the believer," and this has proven to be the correct view. I didn't comprehend it at the time.

Now I do. Thanks, Owen.

My confusion wasn't from God, He doesn't contradict Himself. So the Bible couldn't be contradicting itself!

The whole contradiction resolves itself, not in a **doctrine**, but in a **relationship**. God is now our Father. We were born into His family, in Christ, when we trusted Christ.

Now get this: YOU CAN CHANGE YOUR NAME, BUT YOU CAN NOT CHANGE YOUR BLOOD! That is, your earthly father is still your father even if you change your name! Or even if you change your behavior! So it is in Christ. Your new Father will always be your Father. You are born in a new bloodline. You can try to change your name, but you cannot change your (His) blood! His shed blood is now your bloodline.

I quit my Christian life for five years once. (Five years **wasted** I hasten to add.) I "changed my name" and no longer identified with Christians. I was mad at God because I felt He had not kept His promise to transform my life. I did not understand grace or imputed righteousness. So I quit. But guess what! God never quit on me. My Father remained my Father.

Quitting **cost** me, and I do not recommend it, but I could not change my blood. Here's the thing: I meant business with God when I asked Him to take over my life. I have never been more sincere about anything in my life than when I made my decision to trust Christ. And the Lord took me seriously: He **never** backed out on me even though I tried to back out on Him. He loved me and He disciplined me until I came back. He is my Father and my Savior.

Look at what the Apostle Paul taught concerning the security of the believer:

> For I am convinced that neither death, nor life, nor angels, nor principalities, nor things present, nor things to come, nor powers, nor height, nor depth, nor any other created thing [Since you are a created thing, this must include you!], shall be able to separate us from the love of God, which is in Christ Jesus our Lord.
>
> *Romans 8:38, 39*

Look at what Jesus taught concerning the security of the believer:

> "I am the good shepherd; and I know My own, and
> My own know Me, even as the Father knows Me and
> I know the Father; and I lay down My life for the sheep...
>
> "My sheep hear My voice, and I know them, and they
> follow Me; and I give eternal life to them, and they shall
> never perish, and no one shall snatch them out of my
> hand.
>
> "My Father, who has given *them* to Me, is greater than
> all; and no one is able to snatch *them* out of the Father's
> hand.
>
> "I and the Father are one."
>
> *John 10:14, 15, 27-30*

Furthermore, Jesus defined "eternal life" not primarily as a span
of time, but as a relationship:

> And this is life eternal, that they might know thee the
> only true God, and Jesus Christ, whom thou hast sent.
>
> *John 17:3 KJV*

See, eternal life (and therefore eternal security) is defined **primarily** in terms of relationship. Eternal security for believers is simply a
logical function and a logical necessity of eternal life because we know
that eternal life also means to live forever. It is nonsense to believe
that eternal life can end, then begin, then end, then begin. That's
why, in John 10:28, Jesus said, "They shall never perish." Never!
He has **already** given to us eternal life. Therefore, it cannot end!
I John 5:13 also declares this, in no uncertain terms:

> These things I have written to you who believe in the
> name of the Son of God, in order that you may know
> that you have [present tense] eternal life.

God wants you to **know** and not doubt that you **now have** eternal
life. Eternal means eternal! True believers have eternal security. But,
you see, it is "the security of the believer," not just some cheap fire
insurance for fakes who never really meant business with God.

In this context it is quite easy to deal with Scriptures such as
Hebrews 6 and 10 which **seem** to say that true believers can go to
hell. Neither passage teaches this simply because neither passage con-

tradicts other Scripture. Careful study is needed. It turns out that, in fact, Hebrews 10 is perhaps the strongest warning in Scripture **against** legalism and **against** abandonment of grace righteousness.

Your God says,

"I WILL NEVER DESERT YOU, NOR WILL I EVER FORSAKE YOU..."

Hebrews 13:5b

Let this promise sink into you today, and refuse to give it up for anyone.

How Grace Works:
Worst Possible Scenario

Rejoice not against me, O mine enemy: when I fall,
I shall arise; when I sit in darkness, the Lord *shall be*
a light unto me.

I will bear the indignation of the Lord, because I have
sinned against Him, until He plead my cause, and execute judgement for me: he will bring me forth to the
light, *and* I shall behold His righteousness.

Then *she that is* mine enemy shall see it, and shame
shall cover her which said unto me, Where is the Lord
thy God?

Micah 7:8-10a KJV

Here is a worst possible scenario! I include it for obvious reasons.
It illustrates perfectly, from the Scripture, how grace works for God's
people, even under the worst possible circumstances and performance.

This passage is marked with certainty that the Lord will ultimately
intercede and save all who hope in Him, even though they may have
sinned grievously.

First, these people were obviously the Lord's people, under His
chastening. The chastening itself proves sonship (Hebrews 12:5-13).

Yet the chastening itself is not the primary focus of this passage.
You see, when believers have fallen and are being disciplined, the
enemy is right there accusing, ''Where is your God now? He has forsaken you, of course, because you are such a sinner, such a failure!''

This Scripture says plainly that the Lord Himself will turn this horri-
ble shame which the believer feels back against the Accuser himself.
And the Accuser, not the believer, will be covered with shame. Praise
God!

This passage says that the Lord Himself will plead our cause, even
under such circumstances. It says plainly that the Lord Himself will

execute judgement for us. He did this, of course, at Calvary.

Jesus pleads our cause constantly:

> Who *is* he that condemneth? *It is* Christ that died, yea rather, that is risen again, who is even at the right hand of God, who also maketh intercession for us.
>
> *Romans 8:34 KJV*

In Micah 7:8-10, don't fail to notice WHO shall bring us forth to the light, and WHO shall cause us to behold His righteousness. Note again: His righteousness.

Don't fail to notice WHO will be light to us even in the midst of such deep personal darkness.

Because of all this which the Lord does when we fall, we shall arise! That's what it says.

"Don't laugh Satan, our God will never forsake us."

Now think about this: If this is our worst possible scenario, can you imagine the best? The best must be incredible! And you'll get there some day, too. You're already on your way. Just keep trusting Jesus plus nothing.

If this passage describes the bare minimum, the bottom line, the low point, imagine what the maximum must be.

If this is what the Lord will do in the midst of disobedience, imagine what He will do in the midst of obedience!

The Lord will get you there, perhaps soon. Don't give up hope. His maximum, His best, is His will for you, in this present life. You are called to reign with Him. Just keep trusting Jesus plus nothing.

How To Let Jesus Be Your Righteousness

"In His days Judah will be saved,
And Israel will dwell securely;
And this is His name by which He will be called,
'The Lord our righteousness'..."

Jeremiah 23:6

Theologians often argue over what this means, "The Lord our righteousness," and over what Paul meant by "the righteousness of God." But, for me, the argument is over.

And I hope that the Lord is giving you understanding of this truth so central to the Gospel. You know first of all that God's righteousness has been **imputed** to you through faith in Christ. And secondly, His righteousness has come to dwell in you through the Person of the Holy Spirit. Essentially, you are to exchange your sin for His righteousness.

We have covered several important applications of this truth already. Here is another example of how you can let Jesus be your righteousness. Let's say that your faith is weak. Most Christians experience this frequently. We have already observed that you **must** begin to solve this problem by dealing with the sin of unbelief and by getting forgiven and cleansed. Then, of course, there is much teaching available on building faith through Scripture, so much, in fact, that little can be added to it.

But, beyond that, here's a crucial truth which is seldom grasped: You can learn to live on Jesus' faith. Jesus lives in you through the Holy Spirit, and He has perfect faith. Right? He has no unbelief whatsoever. He is the, "author and perfecter of faith." (Hebrews 12:2) You can learn to access, and to live in, His faith, rather than your own faith. In Jeremiah 23:6 and 33:16 the Bible calls the Lord our righteousness. You can learn to let Him be your righteousness, literally!

This happens as you learn to trust **His** presence with you and **His** faith in you. This means trusting not only in His imputed righteousness, but also in His literal presence with you; not only that He is there, but also that He is there with perfect faith. And **you** can appropriate His faith exactly as you have learned to appropriate His blood.

Once, when I was learning this, I was preaching at a large church, and I preached until I preached myself out, so to speak. I didn't **feel** up to doing more ministry after the meeting, but I had to, because so many people responded to the preaching. I felt drained rather than empowered at that point.

One young lady, a nurse, needed healing for a serious back problem and, of course, she asked me for prayer. Instantly I knew that I didn't have the faith for her healing. But I was learning to allow Jesus to be my righteousness, and therefore I could minister from Jesus' faith. I was learning to rely upon **His** presence and upon **His** faith. So I simply brought her to Him. I prayed, "Jesus, I know that you are here with us right now, and I know that you know what the problem is, and I know that you have perfect faith. We don't try to tell you how to heal this back, we just trust your presence and your faith right now to accomplish this miracle." And so on. The prayer was very brief. **My** faith was shot, so I couldn't put any faith in my faith. BUT I COULD STILL MINISTER EFFECTIVELY. Why? Because I put my hope in Jesus' faith. She called me a few days later to say that she had been healed. And, of course, her healing **was** medically verifiable.

Healing does not always work this way for me, believe me. Therefore, this testimony is not intended to provide an ironclad formula for healing, since there can be several other important ingredients in healing. But this girl's healing is intended as an example of how to allow Jesus to be your righteousness. I'm sure you can see that **His** righteousness has very broad application, touching any and every area of need. He is not only the author and finisher of faith, but He is the source of all other true righteousness as well. And He is there with you right now. That is **how** and that is **where** you find lasting stability as a Christian: His righteousness and His faith are as stable as a rock. You have ups and downs; He does not.

Once I asked a friend of mine, Dan Adams, "How are you doing today Dan?" He responded, "I'm not doing so well today…" He paused, then he exclaimed, "But Jesus is doing fine!" Dan was learning to live in Jesus' righteousness.

Once you learn this, you become much more dangerous to the devil because you can witness or minister at any time, whether you feel "spiritual" or not. It's great fun! Try it. If you need faith or discerning of spirits or joy or love: Okay, Jesus is there with you, with ample supply for both of you. Thus, you can become as stable as Jesus, because Jesus becomes your stability.

Suppose "the accuser of the brethren" comes at you with accusations concerning some of your past sins, or suppose he is pointing his finger at some of your motives which aren't perfect yet. Okay, Jesus is your righteousness, not you. Speak your word of testimony concerning the blood, concerning the fact that Jesus is your righteousness. Aim your words right at Satan, and don't bother to justify yourself. You can become impossible to stop.

This insight should shed new light on Peter's assertion that,

> ...his divine power hath given [past perfect tense] unto us all things that *pertain* unto life and godliness, through the knowledge of him that hath called us to glory and virtue.
>
> *II Peter 1:3 KJV*

And here's what will happen: As you learn to walk in all that He is **for** you, these new qualities begin to become part of your character: **Your** faith will grow, because it is faith in Christ. As He is, you become, as you live in Him.

This is God's way to bring about true obedience in your life. Anything less is mere striving, human and inadequate. The Holy Spirit wants to empower you through the righteousness of Jesus Himself. Thus, God's **imputed** righteousness becomes His **imparted** righteousness.

The Bathtub Revival or
Putting On The Lord's Righteousness

As I said before, in 1968 I almost died. I was 28 years old. After I was released from the hospital (I had been in there for over three months) I had to spend three hours per day soaking in my bath tub to help heal an incision which had abscessed and was open. I weighed about 112 lbs. (My normal weight was 165 lbs.) I couldn't work and the future looked very dark. It was the darkest period of my entire life.

Yet it was during that very period that God was revealing His grace to me, and I was learning that He is my righteousness. I spoke of this period earlier in this book.

One day, sitting in the tub, bored to tears and open to God, the Lord suddenly took over. I was thinking about His Name, "I AM." (John 8:58 and Exodus 3:14) An interesting question came to my mind, so I asked Him, "Since Your Name is I AM, what **are** You, Lord?" His answer to my question, "What are you, Lord?" began to flow instantly (in my mind, not audibly). And He made it clear to me that He was going to reveal His nature to me, specifically in terms of His righteousness **for** me: His list of all that He is **for me** lasted a **minimum** of five minutes, and in all my years of study I have never been able to duplicate it with a list of my own which lasts even three minutes. That's how I know it was God. Not only that, I was also greatly strengthened and encouraged. That's how I know it wasn't Satan!

So this is only a partial list: He said, "I am your friend, your Savior, your Lord, your healer, your Comforter, your righteousness, your supply, your next job, your finances, your dwelling-place, your peace, your joy, your direction, your love, your faith, your self-control, your mental stability, your physical strength, your mercy seat, your intercessor, your High Priest; I am the door, the way, the truth, the life, the Good Shepherd, the Son of God, the Son of Man, the Creator, the sustainer, the Everlasting Father, the Mighty God, Immanuel, the

God of Abraham, Isaac, and Jacob, the Husband of the Church, the true vine, the root and the offspring of David, the Holy One of God; I am your teacher, your companion, your enjoyment, your future, your eyesight (I had an incurable eye disease which doctors told me would render me legally blind in a few years); I am your hearing, all of your senses, your I.Q., your clean conscience, your voice of praise, your Baptizer, your glorious King; I am Faithful and True; I am your salvation, I am your hope."

Like I say, that is a very partial (2 minute) list. I'm sure I could think of more if I took the time but I could never duplicate His list. You name it, it was on His list of all that He is **for** me.

Many of the things He said I had never thought of before. That's another way I know it was God. These days I refer to this experience as my "Bathtub Revival."

Not long after my bathtub revival, I had to get out of bed and get outdoors. I had to try to get back into the mainstream of life again, so I enrolled full-time at the University of California at Santa Barbara. As the day approached to begin school, I became afraid. I had been in bed most of the time for many months. I was literally having to learn to walk all over again. My muscles were atrophied. I didn't think I could walk to school, let alone sit erect for hours in classes. I didn't have any padding left on my "seat," if you know what I mean: I was skin and bones, and I had been a pin-cushion for months, punctured by countless hypodermic needles. I was very sore in some areas, and numb in others.

I prayed. I said, "Lord, you are literally going to have to hold me on my feet, or I'll be falling down at school." "Oh," He said, "that's the way it has **always** been in reality, but you just didn't know it. Now you do. I am the strength of all mankind." Thus, I learned that He is my strength, literally. At school, though I moved slowly, I never faltered or fell. Not once!

He **is** our life, totally. We are not self-sustaining. We are clay pots. It's much easier if you just accept that, and let Him reign! Let Him be your righteousness, and grow from there. Proceed in all that He is for you, and in His literal strength.

The place of rest for Christians is to rest and to work in all that Jesus is for us. To move outside of Him is all striving and vanity and vexation of spirit.

145

Jesus Himself Is The Armor Of God

Finally, be strong in the Lord, and in the strength of
His might.

Put on the full armor of God, that you may be able
to stand firm against the schemes of the devil...

Stand firm therefore, HAVING GIRDED YOUR LOINS
WITH TRUTH, and HAVING PUT ON THE BREAST-
PLATE OF RIGHTEOUSNESS, and having shod YOUR
FEET WITH THE PREPARATION OF THE GOSPEL OF
PEACE; in addition to all, taking up the shield of faith
with which you will be able to extinguish all the flam-
ing missiles of the evil *one*.

And take the helmet of salvation, and the sword of
the Spirit, which is the word of God.

Ephesians 6:10-11, 14-17

So Stand! Put on the whole armor of God, which is finalized and
completed by the "helmet of salvation and the sword of the Spirit."
(Ephesians 6:17) And let me hasten to remind you that the helmet
of salvation is fundamentally living, daring confidence in the grace
of God.

You are probably beginning to understand that, ultimately, your
salvation is Jesus Himself. (See Colossians 1:13, 14) In fact, you will
find that **every piece** of the armor of God **is** ultimately Jesus Christ
Himself: Jesus is the Truth — John 14:6, Jesus is our Righteousness
— I Corinthians 1:30 and Jereimah 23:5,6; He Himself is the Gospel
of Peace — Ephesians 2:13-18 and John 1:17; He is the Author and
Finisher of Faith — Hebrews 12:2; He is our Salvation — Colossians
1, 13-14 and Acts 4:12.

Paul himself confirmed for us that each piece of our armor is primarily a Person, Jesus, in that Paul also told us to put on the Lord Jesus
Christ:

But put on the Lord Jesus Christ, and make no provision for the flesh in regard to *its* lusts.

Romans 13:14

Therefore, stand in who you are in Him. Stand in all that He is for you.

How You Can Be
Smarter Than The Devil

"Be as wise as serpents," is how Jesus put it. It is not so hard to be smarter than the devil: You just have to be plugged into grace!

Spiritual warfare is a reality. (Ephesians 6:10-18 and I Peter 5:8-9) Therefore it behooves each of us to be aware of as many of Satan's subtle, crafty devices as we possibly can. In this article I want to expose a couple of Satan's favorite tricks which seem to beset many Christians repeatedly, yet Satan seems to be going undetected.

Here's one that probably happens to you frequently: Satan loves to tempt you, putting plenty of pressure on you to commit sin. **Then**, if you don't sin, if his temptation doesn't work, he simply shifts his approach and begins condemning you for being tempted! That way, even when you haven't sinned, you feel bad because you were tempted. You feel like you lost, even though you won. You feel like you sinned, even though you didn't. Next, if you've bought that defeated feeling, Satan tries to bury you. He says, "You've sinned in your thought-life. And if you've **thought** it, you might as well **do** it. [The Bible doesn't say that!] Being tempted is the same as sinning. [The Bible doesn't say that!] Therefore you might as well go out and put your thoughts into action."

No way. It isn't a sin to be tempted. The temptation is not the sin! Jesus was tempted. If, like Jesus, you did not yield to the temptation, praise God! If you **did** sin in your mind, confess it and repent. And that's it; you're free and clear.

Here's another of Satan's favorite tricks: You're getting right with God; you are confessing your sin to God. Suddenly, right in the midst of your repentance, this thought pops into you mind: "Your confession is not valid because you aren't genuinely sorry for your sin." Well, don't you have to be sorry for sin in order to be forgiven? And suppose in this case that this accusation is true, that, for some stupid reason, you really **aren't** sorry for your sin. Since you aren't sorry, you can't defend yourself. Right? Right!

And that's the answer: Don't defend yourself! If it **is** true that you aren't sorry, then you have nothing to defend.

So, confess that! Treat it just like any other sin. Get an even deeper cleansing than you had expected. Confess your sin if you sinned. And confess that you're not sorry if you're not sorry. Push it as far as necessary. Ask the Lord to grant you true repentance.

I have a little saying: As often as God makes you able, as often as you get the opportunity, cram Satan's garbage right back down his filthy throat! Perhaps he will leave you alone next time.

Sin is always dealt with the same way, whether the Lord is convicting you or whether Satan's accusing finger is pointing at you.

Thus, you can **always** be reconciled to God, and Satan can **always** be defeated.

Majoring In The Majors

If we want to see people redeemed, we have to preach the Gospel itself. That seems to be obvious enough. One thing you'll notice in the book of Acts, along with many miracles, is that the Apostles preached the Gospel. The miracles served, among other things, to draw people to the Word preached and/or to confirm the Word preached. How many miracles do you suppose would have occurred had they not preached the Gospel? Jesus said,

> "And I, if I be lifted up from the earth, will draw all
> men to Myself."
>
> *John 12:32*

I usually hear this verse quoted out of context. We sing songs such as, "Lift Jesus Higher," by which we mean to lift Him higher in worship. Such songs are valid because true worship means to exalt Him. But that **isn't** the specific context in John 12:32, and that isn't the kind of "lifting up" which Jesus was referring to here. We know exactly what sort of lifting up Jesus was referring to in verse 32 from verse 33:

> But He was saying this to indicate the kind of death
> by which He was to die.

Thus, according to Jesus Christ, it is His "lifting up" ON THE CROSS which has the power to draw all men unto Him. The Gospel itself must be preached in order to draw mankind to Him.

We have to keep in mind that, though the United States is called a "Christian Nation," the majority of our citizens are either unchurched or liberal churched, and they **really** do not understand the Gospel. They are secularized.

This secularization has accelerated rapidly in the past twenty years. During this same period, the Body of Christ has been experiencing a broadened emphasis in its teaching to include subjects such as Body life, emotional healing, faith, prayer, family life, demonology, creationism, and so on. All of this expanded emphasis has been essential, but, understandably, as our emphasis has increased on all these other important subjects, our emphasis on the Gospel itself has diminished. Thus, the gap between the Body of Christ and the secular world has been **increasing** in terms of our ability to draw unbelievers to Christ.

Jesus said that men would be drawn to Him specifically through His death for sin at Calvary.

We are now witnesses to Christ in a culture where most of our citizens have no concept of the uniqueness of Jesus. Most of our citizens have no idea that His death and resurrection actually CAN wipe out **real** guilt, and actually CAN reconcile them to God. These days, almost no one in our country understands that sin is **the** problem. In the 1970's many Christians had bumper stickers which read, ''Christ is the Answer.'' But then, in response to that bumper sticker, someone came out with a bumper sticker which read, ''What Is The Question?'' This is a perfect example of an unchurched society: Not only are they blind to the **answer**, they don't even know the question.

Jesus said that His work at the cross would draw all men unto Him. Cultures change, but mankind doesn't. Sin and death remain ubiquitous realities. Likewise, the cross and the resurrection and the grace of God remain totally relevant. The Gospel is as central and as necessary and as powerful as ever. Without the Gospel, the Church has no unique message. All it can do is moralize, exactly like so many non-Christians do. Teaching Positive Mental Attitude may be popular, and even important, but, like secular psychology, without the blood of Jesus PMA is a pea shooter against an H bomb!

Nothing has changed. Therefore, while not neglecting God's truth on all other important subjects, and while expressing the compassion of the Lord through signs and wonders, let us get back to preaching the pure, simple, powerful Gospel itself. Preaching miracles or prosperity is **not** revival. Miracles followed the preaching of the Gospel itself. And prosperity appeals to the flesh! I submit that both miracles and prosperity will ultimately cease if they continue to be preached more or less in isolation from the Gospel.

A tendency has developed in the body of Christ to define success in ministry in terms of pulling **Christians** from one church to another, depending on what's ''hot'' at the time. Books have been written on how to produce such "Church Growth." But the migration of Christians from one church to another is not church growth.

Do you understand that not all "church growth" is **actual** Church growth? Church growth means non-Christians becoming Christians. No other kind of "church growth" has much significance, even though the migration of Christians from one church to another may be necessary from time to time.

I pray that this book has helped you to understand the Gospel itself. And I hope that the ultimate impact of this book will be to move the Body of Christ back toward majoring in the majors.

Forgiving Others

It's pretty tough for us to receive forgiveness from God for all of our sins against Him, and then to withhold forgiveness from others who have sinned against us. Nevertheless, you may hit some major roadblocks when you begin trying to forgive the sins of others against you.

One of the most common roadblocks to forgiving others is the misconception that in order to **do** forgiving you must first **feel** forgiving. This problem is especially acute if you have experienced major injuries from others, because your injuries themselves will block your **feelings** of forgiveness and love. You may want to forgive, but **feelings** of hurt and unforgiveness will constantly agitate against the very people you are trying to forgive.

Solution: Forgiveness is **not** primarily a feeling. Forgiveness is primarily a choice, a DECISION which **you** can make to **cancel** someone else's legitimate **debt**, debt which they owe you. You can **do** this whether you feel forgiving or not. Forgiving feelings will come later.

Let's review Jesus' concise definition of forgiveness. We found this definition in Matthew 18: In Jesus' definition, a slave owed his lord millions and millions of dollars and his lord cancelled the entire debt. First the slave owed millions; then he owed nothing. The primary definition of forgiveness, according to Jesus, is the cancellation of debt. Pure and simple.

Now, even if you feel nothing, you can nevertheless make A DECISION to forgive someone else's sin against you by cancelling their debt. You can CHOOSE to cancel their debt whether you feel like it or not. Thus, you don't have to **feel** forgiving in order to **do** forgiving.

A simple method to facilitate this cancelation of debt, which I learned years ago from Derek Prince, is as follows: **Verbalize** your forgiveness, whether you feel it or not, something like this: "In Jesus' Name, because He forgives me, I CHOOSE to forgive so-and-so [plug in the name of the individual or group]. I hereby cancel their debt. Henceforth they owe me nothing. They never have to apologize; they never have to admit they were wrong. They never have to admit I was right. I let them off the hook. I cancel their debt. They owe me nothing.''

Repeat: You can do this whether you **feel** like it or not, just like punching buttons on a bank computer to cancel debt. You have made a decision. No need to **feel** it to do it. In some cases you might have to do it many times for the same person (through a period of weeks or months) to get rid of your recurring feelings of unforgiveness toward them. This is normal, especially if the injury was a deep one. I once spent three weeks letting the Holy Spirit remind me of people I had hated. The list went on and on; there were hundreds of people. When I began this process, I did not **feel** forgiving. But by the time it was over, I **felt** forgiving, I **felt** loving, I **felt** good, I **felt** lighter than air. And somewhere in that process the Lord told me to forgive myself, along with everybody else. What a relief to forgive myself! I had punished myself for many years.

Since then I have counseled with many Christians who knew that they were "saved," who knew that they would go to heaven when they died, yet they had no personal **experience** of God's forgiveness, and no joy. They did not **feel** forgiven or saved.

First, in every case, they did not believe grace. And second, in every case, they had been unable or unwilling to forgive themselves and others. Often they were willing, but they did not know how, because they thought they had to **feel** it before they could do it.

Unforgiveness, with its bedfellow guilt, is the root cause of much psychological pain and spiritual torment. The parable which Jesus taught defining forgiveness in Matthew 18 explains why: Basically, unforgiveness itself opens us up to torment and pain. The Lord designed us so that we feel pain when something is wrong. Pain signals us that something is wrong. Since most of us cannot ignore pain, seeking relief leads to health.

Let's trace the inevitable progression from unforgiveness to torment in Jesus' story of the unforgiving slave who had been forgiven millions in Matthew 18. This slave,

> "...went out and found one of his fellow-slaves who owed him a hundred denarii [about $18]; and he seized him and *began* to choke *him*, saying, 'Pay back what you owe.'
>
> "So his fellow-slave fell down and *began* to entreat him, saying, 'Have patience with me and I will repay

you.'

"He was unwilling however, but went and threw him in prison until he should pay back what was owed.
Matthew 18:28-30

Thus, the slave who had been forgiven a debt which would have been impossible for him to repay refused to forgive a debt which could have been repaid quite easily by his fellow-slave. He unfairly put his fellow-slave into prison, creating a situation where repayment would be impossible, a "Catch 22" situation where the imprisoned debtor was unable to repay the debt because he was in prison, yet he couldn't be released from prison without repaying the debt.

When the lord of the forgiven but unforgiving slave heard what had happened he was, "moved with anger," and, "handed him over to the torturers until he should repay all that was owed him." (verse 34) Then, Jesus said a shocking thing,

"So shall My heavenly Father also do to you, if each of you does not forgive his brother from your heart."
(verse 35)

Please notice, this verse does not refer to hell. It refers to now! There **is**, of course, a real, eternal hell. But **this verse** refers not to hell but to being turned over to the torturers...**now**! Many, many "torturers" are common in people who harbor unforgiveness: guilt, fear, self-punishment, fear of rejection, outbursts of anger, infidelity — all of these are packed with torture and pain. As you know, even Christians can be severely oppressed by these things. Such tortures are often labeled "psychological problems," but actually they are seldom "psychological" in origin. The list of tormenters is a very long one, as some of us can aptly testify. Nevertheless, if you can receive it, all such pain and torment is our friend, to let us know that something is seriously wrong, so that we can repent, forgive, and be healed.

You may need to confront a person who has wronged you. This is according to Matthew 18:11-17. I'm not saying that forgiveness would always make confrontation unnecessary. But the **only** biblical way to confront another person is with forgiveness **already** working in your heart. Thus, your aim will be the redemption of the other person rather than merely (and self-righteously) aiming to win an argument.

So, let the process begin today. You have nothing to lose but torture and pride.

Still Having Trouble Forgiving?

Here's one other important consideration if you're still having trouble forgiving: You will tend to have ongoing bitterness against people who, one way or another, maintain manipulative control over you. In fact, the Holy Spirit Himself will agitate against such slavery because He wants Jesus Himself, not someone else, to be Lord of your life.

All of us have had to learn to forsake rebellion and to obey others, at work, for example. This is normal. But if someone is somehow supplanting the Lordship of Christ in your life, watch out: It is going to produce some rotten fruit.

Actually, there are a few people who can live comfortably under the manipulative control of others, but their growth is always stunted. Most of us can't live that way. Most of us find it nearly impossible to love or to forgive someone who constantly manipulates us.

Perhaps there is no one in your life who is presently trying to control you, yet you find it very difficult to love people, even as a Christian. Do you know the most common reason for this? Caring too much what other people think of you! (Also known as fear of rejection!) If you care **too much** what other people think of you, then you have, in fact, made other people your lord. Then, you will automatically begin to hate them, because you have given them a sort of manipulative control over you. What if they reject you? Talk about pain — Wow!

And, if you succeed in pleasing the multitudes for a season, you will probably wind up not pleasing the Lord.

Is popularity your God? Watch out. You are on very thin ice, under which lies unforgiveness, disillusionment and rebellion.

The way out is through turning the Lordship of your life over to Jesus Christ. You'll find that Jesus is much more accepting than the multitudes.

It takes courage to grow up and to reject manipulation by others. But this is one important key to loving.

You have to be free to love, not forced to love. As long as someone manipulates you, you are not **free** to love them! And you will therefore experience bitterness.

Accept your acceptance in Jesus, and take your stand.

Reconciliation and Restitution

One of the beautiful and crucial things about the forgiveness of grace and the obedience of faith is that it enables us to fix a lot of things we broke before we were Christians. Sometimes broken marriages can be restored. Parents can be reconciled to children; children can be reconciled to parents. All kinds of broken relationships can be healed.

Sometimes it is possible to repay old debts, to return stolen money or goods, to go to those we've injured and apologize, or even to do some time in prison if necessary, because God gives us grace to get straight with our past, to stop running, and to face the music.

Hey, whatever it takes, the Lord can help you to do what needs to be done, in **response** to grace.

If some of your past is still hanging over your head, you are going to need to deal with it. **But**, you need God's wisdom and God's timing.

Sometimes there is nothing you **can** do. Other times there is nothing you **should** do.

But don't pass up legitimate opportunities at reconciliation and restitution. Such response to grace can bring you more joy than you would believe.

One of the best examples of this in the New Testament is little Zaccheus, who climbed the sycamore tree trying to see Jesus. Much to Zaccheus' surprise, Jesus invited Himself to Zaccheus' house for dinner.

Zaccheus, you'll recall, was a hated tax-gatherer, and he was very rich, and Jesus was severely criticized for visiting him.

Zaccheus was overwhelmed that Jesus cared for him and that Jesus apparently accepted him. In that culture, Jesus' visit was an expression of friendship and trust.

Zaccheus was filled with joy because of this, and the Bible records Zaccheus' response to Christ's amazing love to him:

> And Zaccheus stood and said to the Lord, "Behold,
> Lord, half of my possessions I will give to the poor, and

if I have defrauded anyone of anything, I will give back four times as much.''

And Jesus said to him, ''Today salvation has come to this house, because he, too, is a son of Abraham.

''For the Son of Man has come to seek and to save that which was lost.''

Luke 19:8-10

Reconciliation and restitution: Each provides another way to unload the heavy burden of our past. What joy! What relief!

I Shall Not Want

"The Lord is my shepherd. I shall not want." This is **the** most well-known statement in Scripture, probably even ahead of Genesis 1:1 and John 3:16.

The Lord said it. I believe it. It's Psalm 23:1. If the Lord is my Shepherd, I shall not be in want. ("Want" here refers primarily to legitimate need.) Therefore, everyone should be a Christian. Right? The entire world is **full** of people who "want." According to the Word of God, if everyone will turn their lives over to the Lord as their Shepherd they will not want.

Absolutely right! They will have whatever they need. It doesn't take extensive theological training for this verse to go to work in our lives. Here are two or three of the basics of Psalm 23:1:

"The Lord is my shepherd." He is my personal shepherd. That means I unreservedly, trustingly, follow Him. He knows where the green pastures and quiet waters are. He knows who I am a lot better than I do, and so He knows what I need. Thus, fulfillment will result from utter submission to Him. This submission is not merely one singular event, but a process of growth as grace works obedience in me. All this is true for you as well. The Lord wants to show you how all of your needs can be provided, as you are gainfully employed, and as you are willing to work to your potential. Submission to the Shepherd is basic to the fulfillment of Psalm 23:1.

There is one more crucial issue. Many Christians quote Psalm 23:1, and demand the provisions, but they have a subtle problem which thwarts their fulfillment: They covet. Therefore they feel in "want" no matter what their circumstance. To covet means to want what someone else has, and to be dissatisfied with what we have. Someone once told me, "Jeff, if all the stones on the ground were turned into gold, there wouldn't be enough out there to satisfy the lusts of your flesh." This means that the natural man cannot be satisfied. A lustful or covetous person cannot be satisfied, even when satiated. This is the second principle which is basic to the fulfillment of Psalm 23:1.

There are some Christians who need to understand Psalm 23:1 this way: "The Lord is my shepherd. He makes me to be satisfied with who I am and with what I have. He sets me free from habitually comparing myself with others and from being jealous. He sets me free from coveting. Thus, I find His green pastures and quiet waters. Thus, I do not want."

This doesn't mean we cease to believe God for greater things in the future. It doesn't mean we cease aspirations and ambitions. It doesn't mean we cease to plan for growth.

It means we are full of thanksgiving **now**! Thank you Lord for **my** face, for **my** skills and abilities, for **my** wife, and for **my** car, and so on! Right now. Thank you Lord for Calvary. Thank you Lord that you can take all the bad things that have happened to me and use them to my advantage!

There is a big difference between a shepherd and vending machine. Our Lord is not a vending machine. Before the Lord, may you be truly satisfied. Covetousness, like all sin, is dealt with at the cross. Real cleansing is available to you each day so that you can experience the power, the provisions, and the truth of Psalm 23:1.

Deeds Worthy of Death

We know that, "the wages of sin is death." (Romans 6:23a) Well, the Apostle Paul has given us sort of a synopsis of sin, i.e., deeds worthy of death:

> But realize this, that in the last days difficult times will come. For men will be lovers of self, lovers of money, boastful, arrogant, revilers, disobedient to parents, ungrateful, unholy, unloving, irreconcilable, malicious gossips, without self-control, brutal, haters of good, treacherous, reckless, conceited, lovers of pleasure rather than lovers of God; holding to a form of godliness, although they have denied its power; and avoid such men as these.
>
> *II Timothy 3:1-5*

Avoid such men as these? Many of us are, or were, such men as these. **This** is what sin looks like. **This** is why Jesus had to die. This is what Jesus is calling us to repent of.

We don't have to read very far in this Scripture to find ourselves: "men will be lovers of self, lovers of money...."

For example, a friend of mine recently visited his son's first grade class. The scene was exactly what we would expect to find in practically every first grade classroom in America. For one thing, the teacher had displayed lots of art work and papers from her class on the walls of her room. In one assignment she had asked the children this question: "If you could have three wishes, what would they be?" My friend said that, in virtually every case, the children had wished for riches: "I wish I was rich." Or, "I wish my family was rich." Usually they listed both of the above!

All the **first graders** were desiring to be rich. I assert that their craving for riches reflects the spirit and the moral climate of our entire nation. This is what we have come to. I constantly fight this in myself. Don't you? Who can deny that the body of Christ itself in our nation contains the same climate, there is widespread craving for riches. Many Christians have practically forgotten eternity; they are living primarily for now!

We need Christ. We need grace. We need repentance. We need deliverance. We need transformation. We need to return to our First Love! And, yes, we need to learn to love ourselves... but according to GOD'S definition, which begins with worshipping Him rather than riches. See Matthew 22:35-39.

The Real Danger or
How Much Is Enough?

Let us see just how far the grace of God can go, shall we? Can this grace reach as far as the curse is found? Can it touch the very core of our sin? And deliver us? Let us again confront the **real** danger:

> But realize this, that in the last days difficult times will come. [KJV reads "perilous times"]
> For men will be lovers of self, lovers of money, boastful, arrogant, revilers, disobedient to parents, ungrateful, unholy....
> ....holding to a form of godliness, although they have denied its power; and avoid such men as these.
>
> *II Timothy 3:1, 2, 5*

Note that Paul did **not** warn that the greatest peril in the last days would be persecution. But he warned that our "perilous times," our "difficult times" would be because of love of self, love of money, boastfulness and arrogance.

We are already painfully aware that the entire spiritual/moral climate of our nation is becoming greed, love of money. But now it seems like much of the Body of Christ has joined right in, quoting Scripture all the way. Many Christians love money deeply and many Christians who have suceeded in getting money are quite boastful about their faith, and they are often quite arrogant (usually without realizing that they are arrogant). They are **sure** that their values are God's values.

And Christians who **fail** to make lots of money are often very "ungrateful." (Again, II Timothy 3:2!)

Love of money is at the root of the cocaine drug cartel. Right? Yes. Fact is, the greed of the drug lords is no different than Christian greed, only more blatant. Different products, same motives. Can we demand that drug lords repent without Christ, whereas we have not repented even with Christ? You had best begin listening to God, not greed.

Listen to the Bible:

> But godliness *actually* is a means of great gain, when accompanied by contentment.
>
> For we have brought nothing into the world, so we cannot take anything out of it either.
>
> And if we have food and covering, with these we shall be content.
>
> But those who want to get rich fall into temptation and a snare and many foolish and harmful desires which plunge men into ruin and destruction.
>
> For the love of money is a root of all sorts of evil, and some by longing for it have wandered away from the faith, and pierced themselves with many a pang.
>
> But flee from these things, you man of God....
>
> *I Timothy 6:6-11a*

What does God say here? Has the body of Christ **forgotten** that all prophecy and teaching must be judged by the Scripture? Too many prophets and teachers keep teaching Christians how to want and get more possessions, rather than how to repent and be content. This is a **form** of godliness! The power of godliness would be deliverance from the world system and its values.

And another thing: The Apostle Paul seemed to feel that there would be **plenty** of money available for the work of God even if Christians are content with what they have. But, in the body of Christ in our nation today it is quite popular to teach or to imply, "Make all the money you can because this will make more money available for God's work." This is often an attempt (in ignorance) to turn the sin of greed into righteousness! My experience has taught me (and I believe that statistics will support this) that even when Christians become so rich that they can live quite comfortably on 50% or less of their income, they seldom give more than 15% or 20% of their income to God's work.

Have you been listening to the wrong prophets and teachers? Can you admit that you have been gripped by greed? Would you be willing to listen to the Lord and repent if He shows you sin in your heart and enables you to repent? Or, are you willing to be made willing? Well then, that's a beginning. Don't put this off. Seek the Lord today. Continue to claim His mercy; such a transformation in values could take some time.

Question: Doesn't the Lord entrust some Christians with great wealth? Yes! Clearly, this is a biblical fact. But you see, the issue in this article is not so much wealth as it is greed. And if you'll reread I Timothy 6:6-11, you'll see that the Lord's concern is that you not maim yourself with greed. **This** is the context in which the Body of Christ must understand Scripture such as III John 2:

> Beloved, I pray that in all respects you may prosper
> and be in good health, just as your soul prospers.

Psalm 1 also provides strong confirmation of what I have said here. It is best to allow THE LORD to define "prosperity" for you. HIS definition may well include a wonderful job, a decent house, adequate financial planning and a good retirement program. Greed, on the other hand, would destroy all of that through stupid, get-rich-quick investments, excessive indebtedness, and workaholism. (Review I Timothy 6:10 concerning injuring ourselves.)

Do you see what I'm trying to sort out here? I don't know that I've done an adequate job, but I do know the Lord Himself will help you sort this out. I also know that, for many of us who are prospering, the Lord has raised one not-so-simple question: "How much is enough?"

Laughter: An Ultimate Weapon

Satan cannot stand ridicule. He cannot stand to be scorned or laughed at. Why? Pride. Pride is at the heart of his evil: Pride in his beauty and power. (See Isaiah 14:4,12-15 and Ezekiel 28:11-18, especially verse 17). Satan wants to be feared and respected, not ridiculed. He probably prefers confrontation and rebuke to being laughed at, for the former appeals to his "macho" and gives him a chance to try a power play, while the latter merely scorns him.

Satan doesn't mind being laughed at by those in our culture who consider him mere superstition, because he has **them** deceived into believing that there is no Satan. Thus, with them, he has won. They never even see the enemy who destroys them. "Laugh on," says Satan!

The scorn the Devil can't stand comes from those of us who know he is real. We do not deny that he has impressive power, and that he is crafty and potentially dangerous. We have all felt his deadly sting. We know he is no joke, yet we can laugh at him as if he is a joke. We do not fear him because we fear our God. (And, if we fear God, we need fear nothing else.)

Many Christians do not understand that Satan can't stand to be laughed at. They cower before his accusations and threats, and they are discouraged. What **he** says is the reality they frequently live with. They do not know how to rest in the righteousness of the Lamb Who was slain, and to **laugh**, and to make melody in their hearts unto the King of Kings. (Ephesians 5:18-20)

What could be more disconcerting to an army than to hear their enemies singing and laughing while marching toward the battlefield?

Psalm 2:1-4 says,

> Why are the nations in an uproar,
> And the peoples devising a vain thing?
> The kings of the earth take their stand,
> And the rulers take counsel together

Against the Lord and against His Anointed:
"Let us tear their fetters apart,
And cast away their cords from us!"
He who sits in the heavens laughs,
The Lord scoffs at them.

The Infinite is not threatened by the finite. Lucifer decided he would be God. How stupid! So also, many earthly rulers, in their days of power, thought to virtually dethrone the Almighty. There are nations attempting this even now. But the Lord is not trembling! To challenge the Eternal, Infinite, All-Knowing, Almighty God is laughable, like Mickey Mouse attacking the U.S. Marines.

So learn to laugh, you who belong to the Lord. It's so healthy for you. And Satan's great pride is shattered by your laughter.

I do not care to go into detail in this book, but let me tell you that I have seen demonic powers literally put to flite by laughter. Not only that, but I've seen this work for baby Christians who knew next to nothing about authority over demons.

What horrible thing has the Devil threatened you with lately? What has he accused you of today? Perhaps you should stop defending yourself and start laughing. Imagine what a giant roar of belly-laughter might do to some of your most wretched moods and to some of your biggest fears.

The most important thing about laughter as an ultimate weapon is that such laughter **expresses faith**, sometimes a great deal of faith! And such faith is not only devastating to Satan, but it is also very pleasing to God. Thus, you win both ways when you laugh!

Would you like to see more laughter in the Scriptures? It's there, but you may not have noticed. Begin with Psalm 126:1-3, then, get out your own concordance and look up laughter, and study it for yourself.

You Don't Need A Thorn In The Flesh

It's possible that the body of Christ has had nearly as many arguments over Paul's thorn in the flesh as they've had over far more serious theological issues. Arguments over Paul's thorn in the flesh usually center on **what** it was. A physical problem? An emotional problem? Persecution?

Personally, I don't care **what** Paul's thorn in the flesh was. The problem, as I see it, is that so many Christians think that they have a thorn in the flesh! There is cause for great amazement in this. There is cause for great amazement in the fact that so many Bible-believing Christians think that they **need** a thorn in the flesh. Why? Here is what Paul said concerning his thorn in the flesh:

> ...but I will go on to visions and revelations of the Lord.
>
> I know a man in Christ who fourteen years ago — whether in the body I do not know, or out of the body I do not know, God knows —such a man was caught up to the third heaven. And I know how such a man — whether in the body or apart from the body I do not know, God knows — was caught up into Paradise, and heard inexpressible words, which a man is not permitted to speak.
>
> ...And because of the surpassing greatness of the revelations, for this reason, to keep me from exalting myself, there was given me a thorn in the flesh, a messenger of Satan to buffet me — to keep me from exalting myself!
>
> *II Corinthians 12:1b, 2-4, 7*

I used to think I had a thorn in the flesh until I understood **why** Paul had his thorn in the flesh. Paul had his thorn in the flesh specifically to keep him from exalting himself because of the massive revelations the Lord had given him. I believe it was Kenneth Hagin who asked the most relevant question I've ever heard concerning the thorn in the flesh: "To what great heights of God's revelations have you risen that you should **need** a thorn in the flesh?"

It is important, of course, to recognize that the Lord **does** allow us to encounter various forms of resistance in order to help keep us dependent on His grace and power. But such resistance seldom falls into the category of a permanent thorn in the flesh!

I doubt that any Christian can tolerate a constant stream of success without some intermittent resistance to help maintain dependence on the Lord. But I have observed that, most often, it is Christians who are **least** likely to **need** thorns in the flesh who seem to believe that they have them. Or, said another way: Christians who are **most** likely to claim thorns in the flesh are not those with massive revelation, but rather those who are suffering. Yet a thorn in the flesh is not merely **suffering**. Unbelievers often suffer as much as believers.

My observation is that this thorn in the flesh thing is usually a deception which accommodates and rationalizes suffering.

Our real need usually is **not** for any thorn in the flesh, but rather for roots deep in grace, and for power from the Holy Spirit. Therefore, unless you have revelation like Paul, you don't need a thorn in the flesh.

The Suffering Approach
To Spiritual Maturity

An unsaved husband. An alcoholic husband. Chronic illness. Unemployment. A wayward teen-ager. Being misunderstood or judged by in-laws. Pressures at work. Emotional problems. All of these may be situations and problems which allow no easy or immediate solutions.

How often have you heard such things spoken of as "crosses" we must bear?

The Bible says that God is good. (Matthew 19:17 and James 1:17) Yet, there is a satanic concept of God (prevalent even among some Christians) that the Lord allows and/or causes suffering as a **primary** vehicle to produce spiritual growth in His people.

The fact is that even horrible continual suffering cannot transform anyone. Such suffering can, and often does, cause people to turn to God (at least temporarily), but, just as often, it causes people to hate God.

There is no "magic" in suffering, in and of itself. If suffering transforms people, then all humanity should be transformed by now! No, it is the Holy Spirit working with the Gospel that transforms people.

In my own life I know that suffering and torment **did** bring me to the point where I would finally open up to the Gospel and to the Holy Spirit. And, thus, during my years of suffering I came very close to the Lord, I became more and more dependent on Him and I learned much of Him through the vulnerability and brokenness which suffering produced in me. But such experiences do not prove that the Lord **prefers** to work that way. I believe He **prefers** that we simply believe His Word and respond appropriately.

Suffering itself does **not** lead to spiritual maturity. But satan would love to have all Christians believe that suffering is the cross that God has for us. What deception!

171

What is the believer's "cross" to bear? Jesus said that believers do indeed have a cross to bear. But it is not suffering, since the entire world suffers. Does the entire world bear the cross of Jesus? Certainly not. Therefore, suffering is not our cross.

> And He [Jesus] was saying to *them* all, "If anyone wishes to come after Me, let him deny himself, and take up his cross daily, and follow Me."
>
> *Luke 9:23*

The believer's cross which Jesus spoke of here is unique to all who would follow Him, and it is not shared by the world. Very simply, it is OBEDIENCE to Him. Jesus clearly related the believer's cross to self-denial and to following Him, **not** to sickness and disaster.

Obedience in love is what caused Jesus to take up His own cross:

> And being found in appearance as a man, He humbled Himself by becoming obedient to the point of death, even death on a cross.
>
> *Philippians 2:8*

See, **obedience** put Him there!

In response to His amazing love, He calls each of us to deny ourselves, i.e., to deny our flesh, and to follow him. Therefore, **our** "cross" of obedience is a reasonable response to **His** cross of obedience.

Do you see that? We are called to reckon ourselves dead unto sin (Romans 6:11), and we are called to live in the new man in Christ. (Romans 6:11-14)

Now consider this: Far from being identified with the world's kind of suffering, our cross of obedience frequently provides deliverance for us from the world's kind of suffering. For example, clean living usually leads to healthy living. Remember that EVIL spelled backwards is LIVE, and Jesus promised us abundant life. Life is the opposite of evil.

Thus, you can joyfully embrace your cross of obedience as a cross of deliverence. You can reject the satanic concept that God wants His people suffering. You can reject the idea that Jesus' agony on the cross was intended by God as a model for us to emulate. You know better than that now. You know why Jesus died: Not primarily as our model, but as our sin offering. Salvation is not in suffering: It is in receiving Him. Praise God!

Pray Effectively

In effect, **Celebration of Grace** is a manual on how to pray effectively. Our first step has been to help you to **stop** praying because of any kind of fear that God will reject you if you fail to pray. Now you know that right standing before God is a gift of His grace which you can never **earn** no matter how much you pray. Now you know God's acceptance.

Second, now you are learning what it means to pray in Jesus' righteousness rather than in your own righteousness. I submit that this is primarily what it means to pray "in Jesus' Name." You cease praying as a means of making points with God, i.e., you cease striving through prayer to **obtain** right standing before God. Now you can pray effectively because **you already have** right standing before God "in **Jesus**' Name," in **Jesus**' righteousness. You cease striving in prayer to **obtain** God's favor, and you begin praying because **you are the object of God's favor**.

Imagine what can happen through prayer if you learn to pray this way. No, you won't be able to turn the Lord into a vending machine. The grace message itself tends to stop us from trying to manipulate God, and grace certainly causes us to realize that He does not owe us anything. Legalists are always trying to put the Lord in debt to them.

But now, in this grace context, it is time to understand prayer as Jesus would have us do it:

> "Truly, truly, I say to you, he who believes in Me, the works that I do shall he do also; and greater *works* than these shall he do; because I go to the Father.
> "And whatever you ask in My name, that will I do, that the Father may be glorified in the Son.
> "If you ask Me anything in My name, I will do *it.*"
> *John 14:12-14*

This is the power of prayer **in** Jesus' name. And notice: This passage of Scripture is crucial to effective prayer not only because in it we see the power of prayer in Jesus' name, but also because in this passage Jesus explained **why** He would answer prayer in His name: "that the Father may be glorified in the Son." You must understand that God will **always** answer prayer in accord with His own glory.

Grace and the glory of God: These are the foundations for effective prayer.

Question: Can the Body of Christ be taught to pray effectively and fervently without the employment of legalistic coercion? Absolutely! One area, for example, in which the vital nature of prayer can be understood is spiritual warfare:

> ... for the weapons of our warfare are not of the flesh,
> but divinely powerful for the destruction of fortresses.
> *II Corinthians 10:4*

Prayer in Jesus' name is an unequaled, divinely powerful weapon of our warfare. Evil spiritual powers which dominate the people and the values of this world must be broken if the Gospel is to gain entrance to all nations. Thank God for teaching which is now coming forth concerning how to do this. I believe that the day is upon us when the Body of Christ, praying corporately, will break "spiritual **forces** of wickedness," (study Ephesians 6:10-20) and thus release entire cities and even countries for outpourings of the Holy Spirit.

Here, then, is one strong motivation (among many) to become a praying person. Such motivation flows from devotion to the cause of Christ rather than from coercion.

Praying Boldly

You can't pray boldly if you aren't 100% sure where you stand with God. Thus, bold prayer must rest in grace:

> For we do not have a high priest who cannot sympathize with our weaknesses, but one who has been tempted in all things as *we are, yet* without sin.
> Let us therefore draw near with confidence to the throne of grace, that we may receive mercy and may find grace to help in time of need.
>
> *Hebrews 4:15,16*

KJV says, "Let us therefore come boldly unto the throne of grace..." I like that wording.

What this Scripture emphasizes is exactly what I'm teaching on effective prayer: Grace is both the cause and the effect of confident prayer. Bold praying is confident praying. You get a personal audience with the Lord, and receive the same hearing as the Son Himself receives from the Father. No teaching on prayer, no matter how current, no matter how timely, no matter how important, can supercede Jesus as "the way," nor can it supercede praying in grace. Jesus is not a new formula, He is the "new and living way" into the throne room. (See Hebrews 10:20)

Thus, the only sort of bold prayer which is effective is that which is rooted in grace. There are Christians who pray boldly because they are self-righteous, or because they've been taught that they should assert their "rights." Often that is pride, pure and simple. God's people do in fact have rights, but it is both advisable and effective to forsake all prideful approaches to God.

The Lord has **always** found people, in touch with His heart (grace people), who have learned to pray boldly. His design is a living partnership with His people through prayer, advancing His Kingdom.

Many Christians, not all, have actual intercessory prayer ministries.

176

I myself have seasons when I have a deep intercessory prayer ministry, during which I know that, together with the Holy Spirit, in accord with the Word, and in accord with His direction, I am literally birthing something important. This book is a product of such a season.

Whether you ever experience this or not, I have no doubt that your prayer life will grow and prosper through the years. Ask the Lord to make you 100% part of what He is doing in the earth today. He will.

There is so much more I wish I had space to say concerning your prayer life, but this book could really get out of hand if I did. And besides, there is **so much** good teaching on prayer already available. My mandate from the Lord for this book is to expose works righteousness so that grace can become your only foundation for praying boldly. Then, as holiness develops in your life, you will develop greater and greater "leverage" in prayer, because you will pray more and more according to the mind of the Lord. (I Corinthians 2:16 and John 15:7) Thus, you will pray more and more boldly and effectively. But, because holiness guides you, you will continue to pray on a grace basis and you will never return to any attempt to put the Lord in debt to you through self-righteousness.

Grace people are bold, but not arrogant. You will find this to be according to the nature and character of God.

"Lord, If You Loved Me You Would..."

I used to say those exact words often when I prayed, but, once I came to know grace, I couldn't say them anymore. Now I pray exactly the opposite: "Lord, if you never do another thing I ask, you've already done more than I deserve in dying for me. I demand no further proof of your love, and you owe me nothing. Calvary is more than enough. Thank you."

Of course, the Lord **loves** to continue to answer prayer, as you well know. He exhorted us many times to continue to pray. He works hand in hand with prayer. But He certainly doesn't need to answer our prayer in order to **prove** His love, because He has already proved His love for us in a more radical way than He can ever do it again. Incredibly, He continues to prove His love for us again and again. But He doesn't **have** to do that.

Nothing that the Lord could do for you **now** could ever prove His love as thoroughly as He has **already proved it**. Keep that in mind when you pray.

> But God demonstrates [proves] His own love toward
> us, in that while we were yet sinners, Christ died for us.
> *Romans 5:8*

The Father Loves You As Much As He Loves Jesus

This whole grace thing seems too good to be true. I'm convinced that this is the reason why many Christians don't trust grace. They **hear** it, but they can't believe it. They automatically think, "That **couldn't** be true. It's too good to be true. There must be a catch somewhere."

"The catch" was paid by Jesus! If you think that grace is too good to be true, here is the actual basis for it. In John 17, Jesus, just before He climbed Golgotha and died for you, prayed for you,

> "I do not ask in behalf of these [the Apostles] alone,
> but for those also who believe in Me through their word
> [that's us!]
> "...that the world may know that Thou didst send Me,
> and didst love them, even as Thou didst love Me."
>
> *John 17:20,23b*

See, it says here, in black and white, that THE FATHER LOVES YOU AS MUCH AS HE LOVES JESUS: "Thou didst love them, even as Thou didst love me." A great preacher named Hobart Vann pointed this Scripture out to me. He said it was the most important sermon he had. Thanks, Hobart!

Now, reread what Jesus prayed. Note carefully: He didn't just pray that **we** would know that the Father loves us as much as He loves Jesus, but He prayed that **the whole world** would know that the Father loves us as much as He loves Jesus.

What if you begin to live your life as if the Father loves you as much as He loves Jesus? What if you begin to pray as if the Father loves you as much as He loves Jesus?

The primary way in which grace produces obedience is as **a response** to love. "We love, because He first loves us." (I John 4:19) It makes sense that the Father loves you as much as He loves Jesus, since He exchanged Jesus, His Beloved Unique Son, for **you**. That's a fact of history.

For many years I Corinthians 13, "The Love Chapter," was, in fact, a threat to me. It describes love graphically:

> Love is patient, love is kind, *and* is not jealous; love does not brag *and* is not arrogant, does not act unbecomingly; it does not seek its own, is not provoked, does not take into account a wrong *suffered...*
>
> *(verses 4 and 5)*

I say that this Scripture was a threat to me. It was a threat because I couldn't **do** it acceptably. I got to where I couldn't even read I Corinthians 13 because I couldn't **do** it, at least nowhere near perfection. **My** love was hopelessly flawed.

Then, one day, the lights came on: "God is love." (I John 4:8,16) Therefore, I Corinthians 13 is not, first of all, what God expects of me, but rather, first of all, I Corinthians 13 describes all that God is **towards** me.

So, God is patient with me, and with you! God is kind... God is not arrogant... God is not selfish... God does not take into account a wrong suffered... "bears all things, believes all things, hopes all things, endures all things." (verse 7) That's how He is towards me, and towards you.

"Love never fails..." (verse 8a) You could read this, "Love never quits." This means God never quits on us.

Yes, God also intends that you and I never quit on Him. But He knows that we are not the source of that kind of love. Therefore, Jesus prayed that we could know HIS incredible, never-quit, too-good-to-be-true, love. He is the source of this love.

Knowing Him is the only route to true love in you. You **will** love as you come to know and accept His unconditional love wherein the Father loves you as much as He loves Jesus. In this context you are enabled to heed the books and teaching currently available on love being a decision, a choice, a commitment. VERY IMPORTANT! But always remember that God's kind of love is the power of the Spirit working with applied grace. Mere self-help love is like a Band-Aid on a hemorrhage. Self-help therapies alone cannot redeem mankind.

"If . . . Then" or "Yea and Amen"

The Bible says, "For all the promises of God in him *are* yea, and in him Amen, unto the glory of God by us." (II Corinthians 1:20 KJV) Clearly, this verse says that all of the promises of God are fulfilled, they are yea and amen, in Jesus Christ. Let's discuss the significance of this truth.

The old covenant (the Law given at Sinai) was full of "if...then" promises. An "if...then" promise means that God was saying, "If you will do this, then I will do that." The people had to fulfill the ifs before God would fulfill the thens. The new covenant in Christ has many ifs and thens also, but under this new covenant, the ifs have been fulfilled and completed in Jesus Christ so that the thens can be fulfilled and completed in us. Thus, and only thus, can the "if...then" become "yea and amen." Jesus is the "yea and amen," having fulfilled the "if...then," to all the promises of God.

Where have you placed your faith and hope? In your performance (the if...then)? Or in the grace of God (the yea and amen) in Jesus Christ?

My observation is that many of the most committed believers in the Body of Christ are under heavy piles of "if...then" teaching.

Are you being vexed by the ever-growing list of ifs which you are being taught you must perform in order to obtain the blessings of God upon your life? The vexation is there to bring you back to simple grace. The Holy Spirit is allowing you to feel vexed in order to tell you something is wrong. Ultimately, of course, the Lord works His ifs and thens into you. This is sanctification. But sanctification happens **because** Jesus has **already** fulfilled all of the ifs and thens **for you**. (Recall I Corinthians 1:30 in this context)

Allow your list of ifs and thens to be a very short one. And let it begin with, "If Jesus...then fulfillment."

Let's review something: The primary purpose for the Law (the "if...then") is to show you your sin when you fail (Romans 3:20) and, through this, to bring you to Christ so that you can be saved by faith in Him:

> Wherefore the law was our schoolmaster *to bring us* unto Christ, that we might be justified by faith.
> But after that faith is come, we are no longer under a schoolmaster.
>
> *Galatians 3:24,25 KJV*

Your failure at the "if...then" is to bring you to grace, "the yea and Amen."

> "For through the Law I died to the Law, that I might live to God...
> "I do not nullify the grace of God; for if righteousness *comes* through the Law, then Christ died needlessly."
>
> *Galatians 2:19,21*

How God Our Father Disciplines Us

You have probably discovered that even though you are saved by grace, sin still has terrible consequences in your life.

That is of God. You see, Jesus didn't die to justify sin. He died to justify sinners.

A sister wrote me once and said, "For the grace of God that brings us salvation teaches us to say 'no' to sin, and to live self-controlled lives, upright and Godly." (I don't know if she knew that she was nearly quoting Titus 2:11,12.) If the Lord loves us, then He will see to it that we learn to live Godly lives. It makes sense.

He will do this through His Word, through the Holy Spirit, through Christian friends who are not afraid to speak the truth in love, through non-authoritarian accountability in the Body of Christ, and through "tough love" whenever necessary.

Tough love means, for one thing, that the Lord will make sure that our sin causes us enough pain so that we walk in the Spirit rather than in the flesh:

> "Your own wickedness will correct you,
> And your apostasies will reprove you."
> *Jeremiah 2:19a*

Some sins I did early in my Christian life burned me so badly that I know better than to do them again. This is not cruelty. It is a Father's true love. It ultimately **internalizes** self-control! What a gift! What love! Now I **do** discipline myself in these areas that previously had power over me.

There are lots of parents who could help their children greatly by allowing them, as it becomes appropriate, to take the consequences of their own decisions and sins. Some parents bail their children out much too often.

Discipline in love (the only kind of discipline God uses on His children) is not to kill, but to heal. It must **hurt** in order to save us from the power of sin. In knowing grace we also come to know the Fatherhood of God. He **reparents** us. Thus, in grace, a relational, reverential fear (respect) for the Lord grows. Sin is **never** cheap even though it can be forgiven. He prefers that we simply respond to His Word, but if not:

> ...and you have forgotten the exhortation which is addressed to you as sons,
> "MY SON, DO NOT REGARD LIGHTLY THE DISCIPLINE OF THE LORD,
> NOR FAINT WHEN YOU ARE REPROVED BY HIM;
> FOR THOSE WHOM THE LORD LOVES HE DISCIPLINES, AND HE SCOURGES EVERY SON WHOM HE RECEIVES."
> It is for discipline that you endure; God deals with you as with sons; for what son is there whom *his* father does not discipline?
> But if you are without discipline, of which all have become partakers, then you are illegitimate children and not sons.
> Furthermore, we had earthly fathers to discipline us, and we respected them; shall we not much rather be subject to the Father of spirits, and live?
> For they disciplined us for a short time as seemed best to them, but He disciplines us for *our* good, that we may share His holiness.
> All discipline for the moment seems not to be joyful, but sorrowful; yet to those who have been trained by it, afterwards it yields the peaceful fruit of righteousness.
> *Hebrews 12:5-11*

Thus, you see, the Lord has corrected us **without** rejecting us. In fact, He has corrected us **because** He has not rejected us.

He has not rejected you. Therefore He will correct you. This is His promise. This too is His grace.

You Can't Drive Your Car To Hawaii

Obedience to the Lord makes perfect sense. And disobedience is stupid. It is insane. It is **always** a losing proposition. Why?

Because you can't drive your car to Hawaii. It isn't designed to float. Nobody in his right mind would suggest that you try.

Similarly, you wouldn't put water in the gas tank of your car because your car was designed to run on gasoline. Yet, practically the entire world insists on trying to run their lives on sin without God, which totally contradicts God's design for us. Those who are apparently successful in sin are often highly respected; they are thought of as sophisticated and wise, and millions envy and emulate them. Yet they all die, and many die broken and hopeless.

Surely you realize that, like your car, you are carefully designed. Just as you know that your car was not created by accident, you also know that you were not created by some cosmic accident four billion years ago. You realize that accidents wreck your car...always. This fact is scientifically observable. So, how could accidents create order and life? They don't. You are no accident: You are an ingenious design.

You are **designed** for God, and your body is designed for obedience to Him.

> Food is for the stomach, and the stomach is for food; but God will do away with both of them. Yet the body is not for immorality, but for the Lord; and the Lord is for the body.
>
> *I Corinthians 6:13*

> For in Him all things were created, *both* in the heavens and on earth, visible and invisible, whether thrones or dominions or rulers or authorities — all things have been created through Him and for Him.
>
> *Colossians 1:16*

Therefore, you were created **for** Him, and your body was not designed for immorality, but for the Lord. However, everyone is trying to live on sin. That is why everyone is dying. Everyone is trying to drive their cars to Hawaii, so to speak.

You were designed by and for the Lord. You run best on love and forgiveness and prayer and the Word and self-control.

The whole "trip" in our society today is "finding yourself" and "expressing yourself" and "fulfilling yourself." But, who ARE you? This question has become practically a national crisis.

Only one solution makes sense: The best way to "find yourself" is to follow the One who designed you, because He is the only One who knows who you are, **and** only He accepts you like you are. Logically, the best way to "fulfill yourself" is to dump the world's philosophy, and all immorality, and trust Christ.

Don't confuse grace with "sloppy agape." Grace or no grace, sin is still brutal. Grace doesn't make sin "work." Just the opposite! Now that you are under grace, the Lord will see to it that sin doesn't work for you. You are designed for Him, and His mind is made up, and He is **committed** to you. He will win any argument, so you might as well reconcile yourself to that. Reconcile yourself to God's design.

You are accepted and forgiven, and this works for you daily. But say, for example, that, in anger, you toss a thirty pound flower pot off the roof of a twenty story building. And say, for example, that as the flower pot is falling you change your mind and repent and ask the Lord to forgive you. **He will do that**. But the flower pot will still be destroyed at the bottom. So it is with all sin. Forgiveness is readily available, but the **consequences** of sin are not always easily reversed.

I have seen the Lord deliver repentant drug addicts from withdrawals and repentant convicts from prison: **Sometimes**! This has proven to be especially true for first-offenders and first-time withdrawers. What He does in your case will depend on one thing: What will help you the most? Don't forget that, while Jesus died to justify sinners, He did not die to justify sin. He did not die to make sin successful. Obviously the Lord has delivered many of us from many of the consequences of our sins, or we wouldn't be here to talk about it. Yet, it would be absolutely wrong to assume that grace means no consequences.

God causes **all** things to work together for your good to conform you to the image of His Son. (Romans 8:28,29) Thus, the Lord can cause even your sin (because Romans 8:28 says "all things") to work together for your good, to conform you to the image of His Son.

The way He usually does this, if you do not respond to His Word, is simply to allow sin's power and its consequences to work trouble and pain into your life until you come to your senses, flee the hog slop, and return to your Father. And **that** is grace. Rejoice,

> FOR THOSE WHOM THE LORD LOVES HE DISCIPLINES.
>
> *Hebrews 12:6a*

I am not saying that any Christian is perpetually doomed to live under the consequences of former sins. No way. God is not into perpetual suffering. The discipline is not perpetual; it decreases as you respond. Only **rejoice** that God won't let sin continue to work **for** you the same way it seems to work (temporarily) for many unregenerate sinners. Thus, you will not die in your sin. This is mercy.

It is great to be in the family, and to learn to cooperate with our Father's design.

Count The "I's"

For the past two days we have spoken of the discipline of the Lord and the consequences of sin. But remember, God **knows** when you are trying to respond to His discipline, and He **knows** that you will not achieve sinless perfection in this life. He knows when discipline is **not** needed, and He is the only one who can evaluate your progress objectively.

His discipline is to bring you to where you will totally trust His Word and His grace and the power of the Holy Spirit.

The Apostle Paul confronted false teachers in Galatia who were trying to persuade the Galatian Christians to trust works righteousness as equal in importance to the shed blood of Jesus and the power of the Holy Spirit. So Paul wrote to his Galatian converts and asked,

> This is the only thing I want to find out from you: Did you receive the Spirit by the works of the Law, or by hearing with faith?
>
> Are you so foolish? Having begun by the Spirit, are you now being perfected by the flesh?
>
> Did you suffer so many things in vain — if indeed it was in vain?
>
> Does He then who provides you with the Spirit and works miracles among you, do it by the works of the Law, or by hearing with faith?
>
> *Galatians 3:2-5*

This is precisely the point of **Celebration of Grace**. Having begun by the Spirit in grace, we cannot now be perfected by the flesh in legalism. Like the rest of us, Paul learned these things the hard way. In Romans 7 he described the personal agony which he had suffered trying to fix his flesh through the power of the flesh:

For we know that the Law is spiritual; but **I** am of flesh, sold into bondage to sin.

For that which **I** am doing, **I** do not understand; for **I** am not practicing what **I** *would* like to *do*, but **I** am doing the very thing **I** hate.

But if **I** do the very thing **I** do not wish *to do*, **I** agree with the Law, *confessing* that it is good.

...For the good that **I** wish, **I** do not do; but **I** practice the very evil that **I** do not wish.

Romans 7:14, 15, 16, 19
Note: **Bold type is mine**.

Years ago the Lord helped me to understand the failure which Paul described in this passage.[1] One way to understand the failure described in Romans 7 is to count the I's. Paul well remembered when he had tried to fix Paul. He described his efforts: I this and I that and I this and I that.

This passage moves on through despair in verse 24 to victory and hope in verse 25: "Thanks be to God through Jesus Christ our Lord!" Logically, the next chapter, Chapter 8, is all about the power of the Holy Spirit working through the power of grace. Thus Paul's miserable failure to fix himself led him through total hopelessness into total dependence on the shed blood and the power of God.

One thing hits you square between the eyes here in Romans 7 and 8: The vivid, radical, eternal contrast between the frustration of legal righteousness and the power of Jesus' righteousness.

I want to describe to you how I used to feel as a legalist. Picture a guy standing in the middle of a room wearing a very unusual belt: Wires are coming out of this belt, about 100 of them, evenly spaced all the way around the man's waist. The room he stands in is also very unusual in that the walls are lined with electrical outlets. He is surrounded by four walls with twenty five typical electrical outlets on each wall. This guy thinks the Lord wants him to plug all 100 wires from his waist into all 100 outlets around the wall, in order that awesome power can reach his body through the wires. He has completed one wall and thus he has 25 wires plugged in. He is feeling some power.

The problem is that most of the wires are shortened because of sin,

---

[1] I do not remember that this particular truth came to me through Nee, but it may have: See *The Normal Christian Life*, p.158.

but the poor man doesn't realize this. He scrambles to plug in more wires. But, as he nears the opposite wall to begin plugging, he automatically jerks out all the wires from the wall he just completed, because his wires are short.

He is surprised. He doesn't really understand what happened. But he scrambles and completes this second wall, then he turns and runs for the opposite wall to replug all the loose wires. But, just as he reaches that wall to begin replugging, bang! Everything pulls out of the wall he just plugged. Now, imagine that he continues thrashing about like this for years, not learning anything from his experience. That's what I did!

And that is exactly how many Christians thrash about: It is a Romans 7 experience.

It is time for the Body of Christ to get beyond this. It is time to count the I's and to understand the failure. Amazingly, many Christians who emphasize the power of the Holy Spirit seem to be scrambling and thrashing as frantically as everyone else.

Want deliverance? First you must see Jesus and realize that He has all **His** wires plugged in, **no short wires**! Now, **you** plug into Him! The focus must shift from all the lose wires to Jesus Himself, from all the I's to Him. You cannot plug into more power than that. Now it's only a question of what He wants you to do with His power. That's all.

Lucifer fell when he said, "I will make myself like the Most High." (Count all Lucifer's I's in Isaiah 14: 12-15.)

But when God described our salvation in Ezekial 36:22-38 virtually all of the I's refer to Him and to all that He does for us. Please, study this for yourself.

You Can't Have It Both Ways — Or Can You?

At this point, several questions have probably occurred to you. Such as, "Does God sanctify me, or do I sanctify myself?" This question is totally appropriate since, on the one hand, I have emphasized that the Father will discipline you in order to cause **you** to choose to obey Him. Then, on the other hand, in practically the same breath, in the article we completed yesterday, I also emphasized that the I's explain the failure in Romans 7. You probably doubt that I can have it both ways. How can it be that God does it, yet I do it? This seems to be a paradox. How can it be that the I's in Romans 7 explain the failure while at the same time I must learn obedience and self-control?

Even though you ask the question, you probably already understand the answer: The Lord grants us right standing before Him, and we wind up participating completely! It may **seem** something of a paradox, but not really. It is not a logical contradiction. It is rather to be expected that His grace, His acceptance, His Fatherhood, and His Holy Spirit working in us will ultimately produce the best obedience (fruit) from the purest motives.

I am not suggesting any form of synergism. That is, I am not suggesting that any part of our salvation **originates** in us. No, the whole package originates in God. I am not suggesting that either justification or sanctification **originates** in us as well as in God. No, both originate in God. But we are responders: Not originators, not the Source, but responders.

Thus it turns out that sanctification has its source in God, but simultaneously it is something which **we** do in response to grace, in the power of the Holy Spirit. See what I mean? So Paul said,

> Even so consider yourselves to be dead to sin, but alive
> to God in Christ Jesus.
> Therefore do not let sin reign in your mortal body that

you should obey its lusts, and do not go on presenting the members of your body to sin *as* instruments of unrighteousness; but present yourselves to God as those alive from the dead, and your members *as* instruments of righteousness to God.

Romans 6:11-13

And then, literally in the same breath, Paul said,

For sin shall not be master over you, for you are not under law, but under grace.

Romans 6:14

See how **you** do it, yet not under law. He reckons you righteous, and you respond by reckoning yourself dead to sin, and alive unto Him. Real grace ultimately produces real obedience. Stay under grace no matter how you think you are performing. It makes sense. Only grace releases you from the power of sin. Romans 6:14 proves this.

Yes, sanctification takes commitment and self-control. Sanctification involves many decisions against strong fleshly desires. Sanctification is much more of a process than it is an event because growth is involved rather than instant maturity. There is no magic pill or short-cut to maturity. You'll find you often must **decide** to love and to forgive, whether you feel like it or not.

I think the following Scriptures clearly express (better than I can) the essentials of the relationship between what God does and what we do in sanctification:

So then, my beloved, just as you have always obeyed, not as in my presence only, but now much more in my absence, works out your salvation with fear and trembling; for it is God who is at work in you, both to will and to work for *His* good pleasure.

Philippians 2:12,13

For by grace you have been saved through faith; and that not of yourselves, *it is* the gift of God; not as a result of works, that no one should boast.

For we are His workmanship, created in Christ Jesus for good works, which God prepared beforehand, that we should walk in them.

Ephesians 2:8-10

Hand In Hand, Not Hand In Glove

There is an old heresy which taught that victory in Jesus happens as we become like gloves, and God fills each of us as a hand fills a glove. Thus, we move only when He moves, like a glove depends on a hand for movement.

Beware: Such experiences happen in occult practice to mediums who yield to evil spirits. But this is not what grace does. It is clear in the Bible that the Lord is a person and He created us in His image. Thus we are persons, not mere empty shells. Thus, the grace of God does not obliterate us as we obey Him. Rather, grace restores us, and restores our personhood.

Grace means that, while our salvation is totally of God (no synergism), yet, we end up participating totally, and not as robots. Incredibly, and this is the miracle of grace, it turns out that we walk **in partnership** with God, hand in hand, not hand in glove. Listen to what the Bible says,

> ...and the spirits of the prophets are subject to prophets...
>
> *I Corinthians 14:32*

No robots here! In the Body of Christ, prophetic utterances do not take control of the prophets, but rather the prophets are responsible to examine and to judge the prophetic utterances which they receive in order to determine whether or not they are from God. It is a partnership; the prophets are to work together with God, hand in hand with Him. The Lord does not turn His prophets into robots since, "the spirits of the prophets are subject to the prophets."

Concerning Spirit-empowered ministry Paul said,

> For we are God's fellow-workers...
>
> *I Corinthians 3:9a*

Co-workers with the Lord, no less! This is no hand in glove thing. Obviously it is hand in hand.

Therefore, you need not commit intellectual suicide in order to walk in the Spirit. Rather, the Lord wants you to love Him with all your mind. (Matthew 22:35-38) Nor does the Lord call you to disappear as a person so that people, "only see Jesus when they look at you," or so that the Father "only sees Jesus when He looks at you." (I'm quoting from unscriptural teachings which I've heard many times among Christians.)

Such teachings may **sound** spiritual, but they are unbiblical false religion, even if taught by Christians.

God doesn't want mere robots or gloves. There is nothing fulfilling or meaningful in being "loved" by a robot or a glove. The miracle is that, through grace, the Lord transforms **you**, and His finished product is still **you**, more a person than you were before!

I can't repeat this enough: God's grace means the redemption, not the obliteration, of the whole person: body, soul and spirit.

> Now may the God of peace Himself sanctify you entirely; and may your spirit and soul and body be preserved complete, without blame at the coming of our Lord Jesus Christ.
>
> *I Thessalonians 5:23*

Clearly, God Himself sanctifies you, He changes you, yet somehow He also preserves your identity and makes you totally whole. He wants to save you, spirit, soul, and body. He does not obliterate you, but instead He wipes out everything that obliterated you. Sin obliterates, Satan obliterates, but the Lord preserves and restores.

Naturally Supernatural

I know of a pastor who once said, "I'm so much in the Spirit these days that I really have to get into the flesh in order to make love to my wife." No doubt you can understand why such "spirituality" inevitably led to problems in both his marriage and his church. It did. He is not in the ministry today. He was part of a hyperspiritual, "God's elite," type movement. Everyone was trying to be super-spiritual. And they got weird! In contrast to such wierd spirituality, think about this: The Lord Himself doesn't need to **try** to be spiritual! Or supernatural! He already is. He is "naturally supernatural."

Sometimes, the harder Christians **try** to be spiritual, the less they accurately reflect the nature and character of God. Radical hunger for the Lord is a terrific thing. Would that all Christians had it. Yet Satan often causes such beautiful hunger to misfire into many wierd hyperspiritual manifestations which effectively block spiritual growth and fruitful evangelism. Hyperspirituality, trying too hard to be spiritual, produces counterfeit spirituality. This is because it is merely **the flesh** trying to be spiritual.

Try this: Get a pen and some paper. Next, sign your name, just a normal signature. Now, **very carefully**, **very slowly**, try to copy your own signature. Okay now, once you've done that, just sign your name again, normally.

Which two signatures look authentic? The first and the last, right? The two which required only normal effort. But the middle one, the one upon which you worked the hardest, looks counterfeit, phony!

Walking in the Spirit is sort of like that because the Lord lives in you, and He is **naturally supernatural**. If you get into hyperspirituality, you actually get in the way!

I don't know how you feel about this, but hyperspiritual Christians turn me off! I **bless** their hunger, and I know that God looks on the heart, but they always look down their noses at me. I'm too normal, and I don't fit their preconceptions or their molds. I can't listen to them because they look down their noses at me.

The longer you walk with God, the more naturally supernatural you will become. And some of the most "spiritual" things you will ever do, you won't even notice you've done them, and you certainly won't keep score, because such actions will be so normal.

Jesus illustrated this beautifully when He said,

> "But when you give alms, do not let your left hand know what your right hand is doing; that your alms may be in secret...
>
> *Matthew 6:3,4a*

Can we take this left hand/right hand analogy literally? Jesus was emphasizing secret giving, so perhaps the left hand/right hand analogy is only an illustration. For example, it is true that, right now, as you read this book, your left hand doesn't know what your right hand is doing. Why? Because, whatever your hands are presently doing, it is **so normal** that neither needs to be aware of the other. But it seems impossible that giving money could ever become so natural. Therefore, for many years, I did not take Jesus' left hand/right hand illustration literally.

However, I have gradually discovered that even the giving of money can be normal. This is primarily because under grace we can quit striving to make points with God. We can learn to give money primarily because the Father gave us Jesus Christ. Thus, giving can become so much a part of us, it can become so normal, that we can actually quit keeping score. That is what spiritual maturity looks and feels like: It is not a constant conscious striving to be spiritual or obedient. It becomes more and more like signing our names, because the Lord lives in us and He is naturally supernatural. Our signatures are not effortless, but they are normal.

Right now your left hand probably doesn't know what your right hand is doing. It doesn't need to. Clearly when your giving of money gets to that point — Wow! —that is spectacular! It is supernatural! Yet, and this is exactly my point, when you arrive there, you probably won't notice it. And you certainly won't announce it! You won't go around thinking that you have arrived (Philippians 3:12), and you won't join any groups which exude pride and exclusiveness.

This understanding of spiritual maturity as "naturally supernatural" applies, of course, not only to financial stewardship but also to every other area of righteousness.

Praise the Lord, what freedom! It is cause for celebration.

"Faith Without Works Is Dead"

That is the KJV translation of James 2:20.

Martin Luther thought that this letter from James ought to be cut out of the New Testament because James seemed to Luther to contradict salvation by grace. I can understand why Martin Luther reacted so strongly to James, yet there is no way that James endorsed works righteousness. James knew better. It may be a fact that James wrote his letter **before** the conference at Jerusalem concerning the relationship between the Law of Moses and Gentile Christians (which is chronicled for us in Acts 15). At that conference, James himself, as the leader of the Jerusalem Church, enunciated the unanimous decision of the Apostles and of the Church concerning Gentiles and the Law of Moses, that Gentiles need not be under the Law in order to be saved. Nevertheless, even if James wrote his letter before this, there is no indication in his letter that James rejected salvation by grace. No way. Instead, he illuminated saving faith for us: According to James, saving faith is no mere intellectual assent, no mere intellectual "belief" in the existence of God, but rather it is motivating faith, faith which **responds** in obedience to the Lord. James was saying that we **act** upon what we really believe. Such a statement is true and does not contradict grace. Our lives clearly reflect what we actually believe. Saving faith cannot be separated from obedience any more than grace can be separated from sanctification. If we believe God, we obey Him. This is faith.

And it is this true faith, this desire to obey God, which causes us to call sin sin, which causes us to see how utterly sinful we actually are, and which forces us to grace, so that we will receive His imputed righteousness.

Abraham believed God. We know this mainly because God said so, but we also know this because Abraham obeyed God by leaving his home in Ur to travel to the new land which God would show him. His faith had legs. It is very true that after Abraham arrived in Palestine he had lapses, or periods of disobedience (during which God remained with him, illustrating the strength of God's **imputed** righteousness), but Abraham **never** fled back to Ur. He stayed in Palestine because he believed God. What this says is that, though he did some fleshly things, he had a heart to obey God. He had faith.

James spoke of Abraham's offering of Isaac as an example of Abraham's faith expressing itself in good works. (James 2:20-24) Obviously, this is true. Hebrews says that Abraham's faith went so far as to expect the Lord to raise Isaac from the dead. (See Hebrews 11:17-19.) Abraham knew that Isaac was the child of promise. (Genesis 17:19) Keep in mind that it took the Lord many years to bring Abraham to this point of maturity. The miraculous birth of Isaac itself probably sealed Abraham's radically obedient faith. That is what grace alone can do. God's grace taught this obedience of faith to Abraham.

Did James contradict this? No, he taught it.

But remember, the first, the primary act of faith which God wants from you is to trust Christ for right standing before God, forsaking works righteousness. Keep in mind that this doesn't mean that you should forsake good works which result from believing God. It only means that you will not trust your good works for right standing before God.

Jesus put it best, as usual:

> They said therefore to Him, "What shall we do, that we may work the works of God?"
> Jesus answered and said to them, "This is the work of God, that you believe in Him whom He has sent."
> *John 6:28,29*

This simple faith begins with the atonement and leads to an obedient life. This faith **is** obedience.

Self-Talk

No doubt you talk to yourself. Everyone does. The question is, what do you usually say?

But before we look at that, I had better interject a parenthetical comment here: There are a couple of authors out there insisting that anyone who talks about self-talk is part of the New Age Movement. Certainly New Agers have picked up on the value of self-talk. But they did not invent it! Satan did not invent it! Self-talk is common to all human beings. In its simplest form, it is merely the thinking which you do all day. The Psalmist used it. I have no intention of giving up self-talk, given to us by the Lord, just because false religion has appropriated or perverted it. All false religion attempts to misappropriate truth, and also to counterfeit truth. Are Christians supposed to systematically abandon truth just because false religion appropriates, perverts or counterfeits it? I think not. Satan welcomes all such stupidity. And some Christians are advocating it.

The Bible, not false religion, is our authority. I will not allow demon worship to create guidelines for my worship. The Body of Christ needs a few Christian authors to expose the New Age deception. But Satan laughs when these same authors label Spirit-filled believers and gifts of the Holy Spirit as "New Age."

Think about this: The New Agers have appropriated the rainbow as their symbol, but the rainbow is God's gift **to us**. The rainbow is ours and I for one have no intention of giving it up, **unless the Lord says so! He** must be our authority, not the New Age Movement, lest New Agers drive us from God's inheritance. So much for that.

Self-talk happens to be one of God's simple truths which I'm not willing to relinquish to New Agers. And for good reason! The Psalmist certainly knew how to use self-talk. He said **to himself,**

> Why are you in despair, O my soul?
> And *why* have you become disturbed within me?
> Hope in God, for I shall again praise Him

For the help of His presence.

Psalm 42:5

See, he encouraged his own soul with truth.

Start listening to your own self-talk. What are you usually saying? Is it often negative? "I'll never amount to anything." "I'm such a fool, I can't do anything right." "I could mess up a free lunch." "I'm so ugly." "God hates me."

Do you often kick yourself verbally for your failures and mistakes? The Psalmist used self-talk and rebuked his negative feelings and thoughts and encouraged himself (based on the faithfulness of God) and expected the best. Once the Lord spoke in my thoughts and He said to me, "I don't give you permission to kick yourself, Jeff. I bought you with My blood. You are Mine. Leave yourself alone!"

Let me interject something else here: It would be very helpful if Christians could learn to leave themselves (and other Christians) alone; that is, stop kicking and hitting. Christians who kick themselves have a satanic concept of God. I mean, what would you think of a father who, when his kids disobeyed, handed sticks to his kids and commanded, "Here, go beat yourselves"? Such a man should be arrested. Yet it is a common practice for many Christians to beat themselves because they have failed the Father. It is a perverted, satanic concept of God to think that He would approve or allow such a practice.

Use self-talk to lift your soul, based totally on the grace of God. Whatever you do, reverse your negative self-talk and stop kicking yourself.

Jesus said,

"Let not your heart be troubled; believe in God, believe also in Me."

John 14:1

As the Lord applies grace to your life, self-talk, like the Psalmist used it, is a valuable heart-calming tool. You can learn to use it to speak to your heart and to tell it not to be troubled. You can tell your feelings how to feel, in agreement with God's Word.

Self-talk is going to be there. Your mind is seldom blank. Bring your self-talk into obedience to Christ.

Emotions

Emotions are an important part of being in the image of God. God created us with emotions. But, get this straight: Emotions are wonderful servants, but they are terrible masters!

Emotions are usually manifested as feelings. They are not always rational and they do not always reflect reality.

There is a common misconception concerning emotions today: Many people buy the idea that feelings are total reality. Almost nothing else exists. To feel bad, or even to feel uncomfortable, is the end of the world for these people. Again I say, feelings are wonderful servants, but they are terrible masters.

In Western Civilization today, to quite an extent, feelings have become the proof of truth and reality. "If it feels good, do it!" Or, "If I don't experience it, it isn't true."

Feelings are not total reality! Reality is not essentially a feeling! Feelings are merely one aspect of reality. When God created man, man's feelings were in proper proportion with the rest of his being. Feelings were created to be enjoyed. Or, in the case of painful feelings, to warn us when something is wrong.

When sin entered the world, all kinds of negative feelings swept in like a flood: Fear and guilt and insecurity and inferiority and loneliness, and on and on, you name it, until feelings and emotions became perhaps the darkest and most distorted monarchs to usurp authority over fallen humanity. I don't know what your experience has been, but my feelings often lie to me. They tell me that something is wrong when it isn't. They seem (chronically) to expect the worst. They chronically balloon problems out of proportion. Sometimes my feelings tell me that God doesn't love me, or that He has left me. Hey, it's wonderful to **feel** God, but God isn't a feeling. We all know this, I hope. Why should we be thrown into insecurity or confusion during seasons when we can't **feel** God?

Every week I have to spend one or two days straightening out my feelings. I have to use self-talk. I have to speak to them, sometimes

I have to yell at them. I cannot submit to them or let them control my behavior **when they lie** to me. There has been a long process of growth involved in bringing my feelings into submission to the truth.

These days, one tactic which I find effective is to simply **ignore** lying, negative, or tempting feelings. I often find it better to ignore them than to spend all day trying to feel better; I would rather be Christ-centered. Most feelings ease off when I ignore them.

Men and women of God realize that they must ultimately establish authority over their emotions, or else there can be little stability. And almost anyone realizes that marriages, for example, which are based on feelings alone can't last long. Maturity and successful living depend upon our willingness to postpone short-term gratification in order to attain long-term goals and values.

> Why are you in despair, O my soul?
> And *why* have you become disturbed within me?
> Hope in God, for I shall again praise Him
> *For* the help of His presence.
>
> *Psalm 42:5*

This is the same Scripture as yesterday. I include it today in order to point out that the Psalmist was addressing **feelings** in his soul, such as despair. He was preaching God's truth to his own feelings, to correct them.

It takes years to retrain your emotions, but the only alternative for some of you is to submit to your feelings, and therefore to spend the rest of your lives in agony and instability. There's no use sitting around feeling sorry for yourself if your emotions are out of whack. There are people crippled even worse than you are. With the grace and the power of God on your side, you must make your emotions servants of the truth. Then you can enjoy them.

Facts, faith, feelings: That's how you've got to learn to order your life. This means to insist that the FACTS of the Gospel govern your FAITH and your actions, no matter how you feel. Then your feelings will tend gradually to fall in line with the facts. Feelings, faith, facts can't work. It has to be first facts, then faith, then feelings, in that order. You have to trust Christ a whole lot more than you trust your feelings. The objective, through His Gospel and His power, is to make your emotions servants rather than masters. I know this is not easy, especially if you've been hurt a lot, but rest in grace, and don't quit. It will happen.

A Word Of Balance
On Feelings And Emotions

Yesterday we talked of emotions in a general way. We spoke of how emotions can be a plague when given free reign, especially when they lie to us. We said that for many people in our culture today feelings are total reality. We said that feelings and emotions are wonderful servants, but they are terrible masters.

Nevertheless, emotions rightly understood and properly functioning are an important part of being in the image of God. Emotions were never designed to be our enemies. Without feelings and emotions, we would act very much like computers. In fact, such people do exist.

There is a basic difference between feelings and emotions. A **feeling** can be as simple as touch, taste and smell. An **emotion** is much deeper. The distinction gets blurred because we **feel** emotions. But there is a distinction. Pain from an injury or from a surgery can be powerful. But love or grief or hate are deeper: They involve emotions. For example, grief is painful; we **feel** it. **But** it's deeply emotional rather than sensual in origin. Our feelings are merely our senses. Our emotions, on the other hand, are often in touch with the deepest areas of our being.

There are Christians who teach that Christians should never accept a "negative" emotion, such as grief. The first problem with this analysis of grief is the belief that grief is always a negative emotion, just because grief doesn't feel good. In fact, grief is **not** usually a negative emotion. It is painful, but not negative. This is because grief is often a direct result of love.

For the Christian, grief is neither unscriptural nor unspiritual, so long as it is not accompanied by hopelessness. We may grieve, but we do not lose hope, because we know God, and He holds our eternity.

Thus we do not need to grieve as unbelievers who have no hope over our loved ones who have died in the Lord. (See 1 Thessalonians 4:13-18) We **do** grieve because we miss them every day. We may even have to go through some sort of extensive reorientation, learning to live without them. But we have great hope because we **know** we **will** see them again.

My dad died several years ago and there are some special things I wish I could have said to him. The beautiful thing is that I will be able to say everything some day, because I'm going to see him again. We never spent enough time together, but it's okay, I'm going to see him again, and we'll have all the time we want. Some days I still miss him a lot, and I cry some. I wish he could see my children, Stephen and Joe and Arricka now. He loved them so much. But the other day I read a poem which Dad wrote during his extended illness. He was writing to Stephen and he told Stephen that he wanted to visit him once more but that he would be unable to do so because he had an appointment with Jesus. Soon after he wrote that poem he died. He never got to come visit us at our new home in Illinois, but he did keep his appointment with Jesus Christ. So it's okay.

Imagine the millions of reunions of loved ones which will take place simultaneously and instantaneously at **our** resurrection, when we are gathered up to Him. "O DEATH, WHERE IS YOUR VICTORY?" (1 Corinthians 15:55)

I can no longer imagine how people bear life without God. Everyone loses loved ones — husbands, wives, children, moms, dads. When a person dies without God, hope is gone. It is all over. The loved one is gone. **That** is magnum grief. Once I saw a woman try to throw herself on her husband's casket as it was lowered into the grave. I can understand why now. At the time, I thought she was crazy. But she had been with him for 50 years and she knew she would never see him again. It **is** insanity to exist without the Lord.

Perhaps you have lost someone or something recently. Well, it is not unspiritual to grieve, but there is hope! In fact, if whatever you lost was important to you (perhaps a home or a church or a job), there is a grief process which is quite normal, even cleansing, which you will probably go through. Do not be afraid to **feel** it — your hope in God will keep you from being overwhelmed. Such grief is not dangerous. My grief, which is much less now, helped immeasurably to reconcile me to the facts, **and** to the future as it stands in God.

Thus emotions, even painful ones, are wonderful servants. They need not master you as you stand in Christ. They are a gift from God, part of His divinity (He too can be grieved), and part of your humanity. Your life would be intolerably sterile without your emotions.

Significant Friendships And Sanctification

What can motivate Christians to serve the King and His Kingdom with ongoing zeal and strength? We all know that desperate situations can provide powerful motivation, but desperation is usually only a starting point. We know also that His love and grace are becoming our deepest, most permanent motivations. And we know that the power of the Holy Spirit Himself causes us, "both to will and to work for His good pleasure." (Philippians 2:13b)

Now I want to talk with you about another crucial factor for motivation and sanctification:

> Do not be deceived: "Bad company corrupts good morals."
>
> *I Corinthians 15:33*

Conversely, good company **inspires** good morals! I'm not about to say that you should have **no** non-Christian friends, else how can we reach them? But you need to ask yourself, "**Who** are the major influences in my life?"

This is not just a problem with unbelieving friends. All of us know some **Christians** who do not particularly **inspire** deep devotion to the Lord. They may need our counsel, our love, and our exhortation, but are **they** our best choices as close, influential friends?

There are Christians who spend a lot of time talking about their own problems and hurts. They may be deeply wounded. They may need our counsel, our love and our exhortation, but do we spend the majority of our time listening to these wounded people and constantly repeating the same answers, and constantly giving them sympathy? Most of us must be judicious in our expenditure of time with such people.

If you are a wounded person you must, of course, open up and talk in order to be healed, but you can overdo this with Christian friends who listen, and who mainly give you sympathy. You may be hurting yourself. And you may be hurting your friends also.

All of us need to learn to hear and to feel each other's hurts. But if we are seeking motivation, then we had better seek out one or two people who **inspire** us. We had best get exposed to lots of powerful worship with other believers. We had best let such people be **the** major influence in our lives.

With God's help, you must pick your friends, not people full of mere religiosity and spiritual fronts and cliches, not people who always dump problems on you; not people who mainly give you sympathy either. The major influences in your life need to be friends and a church where you are inspired to grow in God. Find people who love the Lord **and** who know grace: Not legalists, not critical or super-spiritual type people, not people that keep you from being yourself. Find friends who will speak the truth in love, who can argue with you or exhort you without rejecting you, and who are willing and able to give you some healthy accountability if you need it. Find a preacher who isn't afraid to rebuke the congregation when appropriate.

Finding such friends will take time, and some false starts, but it will pay eternal dividends.

Ripe Fruit or No Fruit

In Acts 16 we read that Paul and Silas and Timothy were, "forbidden by the Holy Spirit to speak the word in Asia." (vs. 6) Reading on we discover that, "when they had come to Mysia, they were trying to go into Bithynia, and the Spirit of Jesus did not permit them." From there they went to Troas where Paul had a vision: "a certain man of Macedonia was standing and appealing to him, and saying, 'Come over to Macedonia and help us.'" See, Paul and Silas and Timothy were **forbidden** to preach in Asia, but they were sent to Macedonia instead.

I used to think that God was playing favorites. Why would God send these church planters to one place and not to another? Didn't the people in Asia or Bithynia need the Gospel as much as the Macedonians?

Sure they did. But the people in Macedonia were **ripe**. They were spiritually hungry. They were **asking** for Paul's help. They were recognizing their need. They were ready to listen. Revivals happen among desperate people.

If you pick fruit too soon, it's not edible. It's bitter.

The same thing can happen in the Kingdom of God. Have you ever felt wiped out from trying to get someone to respond to your ministry or your witness? You probably talked your head off and the other person argued and argued, and you got nowhere. The same thing happened to me. Many times. Then I discovered that, as a general rule, I had to stop wasting time arguing with people who weren't ripe yet. Sow some seed, that's necessary; but the object is to find people who are ripe and ready **now**. What God showed Paul in Acts 16 was a Macedonian asking for help, for himself and for his people. In this case the Lord didn't command Paul saying, "Go to Macedonia," but instead He showed Paul the **hunger** of the Macedonians.

One time the Lord showed me that, as a preacher of the Gospel, the most valuable thing I could ever find would be a hungry audience.

Some Christians don't witness or minister much at all, for numerous reasons, and that is heartbreaking. But if you **have** been witnessing and ministering with disappointing results, you are probably beginning to feel like a failure. You might even be tempted to quit. Satan would love that.

Perhaps you have been witnessing indiscriminately. Learn to look for spiritual hunger in people. The Holy Spirit can show you who has it, and who doesn't. Usually you can tell in a few minutes. Look for ripe fruit. Such people **are** out there. But Satan wants to waste your time on unripe, bitter fruit, and thus discourage you. Be Wise: Follow the harvest.

Now Jesus' instructions to His disciples as He sent them forth to preach and to heal make a lot of sense:

> "And whoever does not receive you, nor heed your words, as you go out of that house or that city, shake off the dust of your feet."
>
> *Matthew 10:14*

One important reason for this is that there are so many places where the harvest is ripe. Why waste time where it isn't? I'm not saying that God would **never** have you invest years in someone else's salvation. But it makes sense, if hunger is out there, that you go out and find it. You need not suffer constant humiliation casting your pearls before swine. You can be part of the harvest.

Motives For Evangelism

What if you go witnessing because you are afraid that God won't bless you if you don't, or because you have some evangelistic quota to achieve? And what if, while you are witnessing, the person you are witnessing to asks you WHY you are doing it? If you answer truthfully that you are afraid God won't bless you if you don't, or that your have a quota to achieve, your "target" might respond that he already has enough problems in his life without adding religious compulsion and condemnation. Or he might say that he doesn't want to wind up being just another statistic in somebody's self-glorification program.

On the other hand, in contrast to distorted motives, what if you are living in grace, and the joy of your salvation is bubbling out? In this case you are not merely **doing** witnessing. But instead you **are** a witness.

What if you actually love people so that your motives for witnessing are love, and gratitude to the Lord for your own salvation? Wow! There is no condemnation in you.

This way, when you open your mouth, the Lord is opening His heart through your lips. Nothing mechanical here.

Still, success is not guaranteed. But it certainly is a thousand times more likely.

Blasting

In spite of everything I say to the contrary in this book, there are some people who need to be strongly rebuked (blasted, like opening a gold mine with dynamite) to get them to repent. They **want** God, but they are so thick-skulled and stubborn that they are hard of hearing, and only blasting can get them to turn. The Holy Spirit will lead you to blast when needed (if you aren't putting on religious fronts). You may even get downright angry, and it will do the job! Obviously, this approach is the exception, not the rule. Hopefully you will **never** get into such blasting indiscriminately or habitually.

I must be cautious when I suggest that blasting is sometimes necessary because there is much blasting and rebuking which goes on in the Body of Christ which comes from evil roots. There are some Christians, and even a few preachers, who still have roots of bitterness from old hurts, and these roots of bitterness often burst out as assaults on society in the witnessing and preaching that these people do. They use the Bible in place of a fist or a gun to lash out at society, or at their parents, etc. We don't want to do that.

But there is a place for blasting. Take John the Baptist for example. He wasn't always "nice." Luke quoted him blasting religious leaders who were among the multitudes who were coming out to be baptized: "You brood of vipers, who warned you to flee from the wrath to come?" (Luke 3:7) John could blast when needed, yet keep in mind that he also preached grace. (See John 1:15-17 for example.)

Jesus could, on occasion, be very tough also, such as when He rebuked Peter saying,

> "Get behind Me, Satan! You are a stumbling-block to Me; for you are not setting your mind on God's interests, but man's."
>
> *Matthew 16:23*

He did this whenever necessary. It was tough love, not an expression of inner bitterness (He had none of that).

Accordingly the Bible says,

> Better is open rebuke
> Than love that is concealed.
> Faithful are the wounds of a friend,
> But deceitful are the kisses of an enemy.
>
> *Proverbs 27:5,6*

There are hundreds of thousands of children in this generation who are feeling unloved because no one has had the love to rebuke them and to discipline them. There are multitudes of adults suffering from a similar malady. Thus, blasting has a place sometimes. Don't let this book on grace keep you from appropriate blasting. God didn't create us to be namby-pamby, spineless doormats! Our objective is to love people by **God's** definition of love, not by some sloppy agape definition. Genuine love is radical, and it is not passive.

Power

You can have the most beautifully designed, most adequate, best looking performance car in town, but without gasoline it remains in your driveway. Everybody knows this. No power, no performance.

This analogy transfers beautifully, I think, into Acts 1, where Jesus, just prior to His ascension back to heaven, instructed His seasoned disciples not to begin witnessing, but to wait until they received the power of the Holy Spirit. Think about this: These eleven men were hand-picked by Jesus Christ Himself. They were taught and trained by Him. They were experienced. They were **eyewitnesses** to His ministry, to His crucifixion, and, most importantly, to His resurrection. Eyewitnesses, mind you. They were excited, they were enthusiastic, and they were sold out to God.

Surely, men such as these would be adequate witnesses and effective apostles. But no, Jesus said no. He told them to wait for power. **Even these eyewitnesses were not adequate witnesses**:

> ...He commanded them not to leave Jerusalem, but to wait for what the Father had promised, "Which," *He said,* "you heard of from Me...
> "but you shall receive power when the Holy Spirit has come upon you; and you shall be My witnesses both in Jerusalem, and in all Judea and Samaria, and even to the remotest part of the earth."
> *Acts 1:4,8*

Jesus **commanded** these personally trained eyewitnesses not to witness without the power. No power, no performance.

Earlier in this book I said that I had lost my devotional life through legalism. Legalism is often appropriated by Christians as a substitute for the power of God. Although every Christian has received the Holy Spirit, many have never opened up to His power. I guess they feel safer with legalism.

Many seminary graduates get sent out to ministry without the power. And so they minister year in and year out in their own strength, trusting in their own talents, and only secondarily in the Holy Spirit.

Most Charismatics are **not** full of the power of God most of the time either. This is because the power of God is poured out upon us to accomplish work, to advance the kingdom of God, not just to make us feel blessed! The power of God is power we keep only as we give it away doing the things that Jesus did.

Herein lies freedom from sin. Herein is the fulfillment of the Great Commission in our generation. Herein is life!

At the end of this book I shall assert that, for right standing before God, no Christian doctrine or practice can be raised to the same level of importance as the finished work of Calvary. But right now I assert that, when it comes to sanctification and witness, there is no substitute for the infilling and power of the Holy Spirit. Previously I quoted II Corinthians 3:6b, "for the letter kills." The rest of the verse says, "but the Spirit gives life."

> But I say, walk by the Spirit, and you will not carry out the desire of the flesh.
>
> *Galatians 5:16*

Eternal Hell Exists Because God Is Good

The wrath of God is real:

> "He who believes in the Son has eternal life; but he who does not obey the Son shall not see life, but the wrath of God abides on him."
>
> *John 3:36*

And hell is a real place. It is the permanent abode for all people who will not obey Jesus. Revelation 14:9-11 illustrates this:

> And another angel, a third one, followed them, saying with a loud voice, "If any one worships the beast and his image, and receives a mark on his forehead or upon his hand,
>
> he also will drink of the wine of the wrath of God, which is mixed in full strength in the cup of His anger; and he will be tormented with fire and brimstone in the presence of the holy angels and in the presence of the Lamb.
>
> "And the smoke of their torment goes up forever and ever; and they have no rest day and night, those who worship the beast..."

Most preachers don't talk much about hell these days. We hesitate to talk about what we don't like. Today it is popular to say, "A good God would not condemn any one to an eternal hell." But Revelation 14:9 **does** say "any one" and verse 11 makes it clear that these people's torment is eternal.

Does that seem cruel or unfair? Quite the contrary: If there is no eternal hell for eternal sinners THEN GOD IS NOT GOOD! The reason for this is easy to understand. All human beings have a soul, and that soul is eternal. No one can become nonexistent. Thus, if there is no hell, then the entire universe can become **permanently** filled with eternal, unrepentant sinners. Then, logically, there could be no hope of escape from sin for any of us, even for those of us who will repent. We would **all** be tortured by sin **forever!**

That would be cruel. The reign of sin would be eternal. And God would be cruel. Therefore, hell is inevitable because God is good.

Our God's holy nature is always in active opposition to everything that is evil. To those of us who will repent, hell is a promise and a hope, not a threat. Jesus Christ has purchased our deliverance from hell. But to those who will not repent and turn to Christ, hell is a threat and an inevitability.

Therefore, embrace the **whole** Gospel: The reality of hell is basic to our understanding of the Gospel. Unless we are saved from real peril there is no meaning in salvation. If there is no hell, then grace is meaningless.

> For He delivered us from the domain of darkness, and transferred us to the kingdom of His beloved Son, in whom we have redemption, the forgiveness of sins.
> *Colossians 1:13, 14*

God does not compromise with sin. Therefore His grace means complete redemption and nothing less — ever! His grace means that soon the powers of hell will be unable to touch you — forever and ever and ever. This is because the powers of hell will be incarcerated in hell!

God's Marines

I include this article because there is a tiny, rather elite unit of Christians out there who cannot relate to about 75% of **Celebration of Grace**. These people love the Gospel and are totally committed to Christ, and most of them are magnificent servants of God. But I say they cannot relate to about 75% of this book. This is specifically because they have **always** been healthy, balanced, disciplined people. Discipline and decisiveness and confidence are qualities which they were either born with or raised with. Therefore, these people have experienced comparatively few failures, especially in their own personal discipline. And they manage to stay on top of the world and to stay healthy, even in the midst of setbacks.

The miracle is that they recognize their need for Christ. But they do, and they love the truth. They are people who were not dismantled or destroyed in childhood, either at home or at school. Or, at least, they were able to roll with the punches.

And they have taken their more-or-less together lives and given them to God. I praise God for each and every one of them. They are a distinct minority, truly "a few good men" (and women), the slogan of our U.S. Marines. Therefore I call them God's Marines.

I love them, but many of them can neither understand nor empathize with Christians who are not like them. Their discipline and confidence are such that, with few exceptions, they have been able to change whenever God has told them to change (even when such change was very painful for them). He says, "Go," and they go; He says, "Stop," and they stop. God gives them a formula, they apply it, and it works! Most of them do not understand the rest of us who take many years to get to that place of maturity.

I thank the Lord for His Marines because they accomplish so much important ministry which wouldn't get done without them.

Most of us who love the Lord want to be Marines. I think I've actually become something of a Marine, but it has taken the Lord 27 years to do it. The "born" Marines can't relate to that. It is even a cause of embarrassment among them, that most Christians are not like them.

Although I can't see what could motivate any of you born Marines to read this book, I want to address you none-the-less: You don't realize it, but you are one in a thousand, and you have a wonderful gift. I totally accept you. Will you **please** accept the rest of us who are not like you?

Many of you are preachers. Please understand that, if you do not allow us ordinary people the freedom to fail, then you have denied us the freedom to try. Period! If we do not have the freedom to fail, then we dare not try. Therefore we can never succeed. God **will** allow us the freedom to fail and fail and fail, until we succeed. I say you must agree with God.

Please accept us ordinary people as a different sort of "elite" who glorify God in a very different and unique sort of way:

> For consider your call, brethren, that there were not many wise according to the flesh, not many mighty, not many noble; but God has chosen the foolish things of the world to shame the wise, and God has chosen the weak things of the world to shame the things which are strong, and the base things of the world and the despised, God has chosen, the things that are not, that He might nullify the things that are, that no man should boast before God.
>
> *I Corinthians 1:26-29*

If this Scripture causes you to squirm, then you are probably a Marine. You had best accept the fact that you are the minority and that the overwhelming majority of God's servants fit this Scripture perfectly. You had best understand that God looks at the heart, not at the appearance, and not at the performance. **His preference** is to create the performance Himself, "that no man should boast before God." In God's economy, the weak are preferred before the strong. Thus, you need to learn to agree with God. Knowing you, and knowing your love for the Lord, I'm quite certain that you can do this immediately.

Mobilizing The Unworthy

I remain totally convinced that the Lord wants His Church to complete the Great Commission during our generation, **and** I also remain convinced that God's Marines cannot do this alone. Why? Because there aren't enough Marines, and there never will be. It's going to take all of the rest of us working together to do it.

The longer I teach, the clearer I become on what the Lord has called me to do: He has called me to help mobilize (for the completion of the Great Commission) all Christians who clearly identify with I Corinthians 1:26-29, that is, all the "foolish things of the world," all the "weak things," all the "base things" and "all the things that are not," that is, all Christians who could never become vital links to the completion of the Great Commission without total dependence upon grace plus nothing.

The United States could not have fought effectively in WW II with Marines alone. No, our victory in WW II took tens of thousands of our supposedly less elite (yet every bit as courageous) troops: sailors, airmen, support personnel... and infantrymen, lots and lots of infantrymen, the troops known for traveling on their stomachs, through every sort of mud and filth: These "dogfaces," as they were often called, ate C Rations, dug foxholes, fought blistering heat, mosquitoes, freezing cold, disease and homesickness while simultaneously destroying the Axis powers.

There could have been no victory without our lowly dogfaces. Thus, great dignity must be lavished upon them.

A familiar WW II recruitment poster read: "Uncle Sam Wants You!" Similarly, "The Lord Wants You!" Okay, okay, maybe you and I fit only with the dogfaces, but you must realize that there is great dignity lavished upon our lowly outfit as out of our weaknesses we are made strong (Hebrews 11:34), and thus we glorify God. In the early years of our ministry in California, I developed a motto which I felt exemplified our work then, and it applies no less today:

"We the willing, led by the unqualified, have been doing the unbelievable so long with so little, that we now attempt the impossible with nothing at all!"

Balance: All of this is not to say that we should ignore or disdain training and preparation for whatever our parts may be in God's mission (especially when thinking in terms of cross-cultural missions). But I'm speaking to Christians (including myself) who, even **with** all possible training and preparation, remain painfully aware that they may never qualify as Marines. The grace of God compels me to encourage you: GO FOR IT ANYHOW!

And one more thing: You may be fifty-five or sixty years old and you think your age somehow disqualifies you. I would remind you that, yes, in terms of the values of our society you may seem to be approaching retirement, but in terms of biblical values you are more experienced and qualified than all the rest of us to teach. Your children are raised, perhaps your house is nearly paid off, perhaps your health is still good, and perhaps you feel like your present occupation is sort of a waste of time. Listen, the Lord will accept you and place you in an occupation with eternal impact. Some of the greatest heroes in Scripture accomplished their greatest feats when they were beyond sixty years of age. Our society may not value gray hair, but I tell you that the devil is scared to death of you!

What Is Your Concept Of God?

The way you live as a Christian will reflect your concept of God.

I have a friend who, while in the Army, served as a psychiatric assistant on an Army base in Seoul, Korea. Among his many duties he taught a class of thirteen slightly retarded children, all of whom had similar capabilities. Eleven of his students made steady progress, while two of them regressed. For weeks he puzzled and prayed over the two who were failing because he knew that they were every bit as capable as the eleven who were making progress.

Finally he devised a test. He handed each student a piece of art paper and some pencils and said, "Draw your teacher."

Eleven of the students drew smiling faces. Two of the students drew freakish, almost subhuman faces. You can guess which students drew which pictures. The two who weren't making progress had drawn distorted, ugly pictures of their teacher. In other words, their concept of their teacher had a direct bearing upon their performance.

That is a unique and startling example to demonstrate how important your concept of God can be.

The Bible says that God is good. In fact, the Bible says that God is the **only** one who is good: Jesus said, "No one is good except God alone." (Mark 10:18b)

One time, out in Isla Vista, California, a young lady about 20 years old received Jesus. Later she told me of her horrible childhood. And she said that she had always hated God. Immediately I wondered, since she had always hated God, why she had received Christ. So I asked her. Her answer brings this whole concept of God thing into sharp relief. She said that she began to read the New Testament, mainly the four Gospels. She said that although she continued to hate God, she began to love Jesus and to respond to Jesus because of His love and power toward hurting people. Then, she received Him as her Savior and Lord, not knowing that He is God. I had the privilege of opening the Scriptures with her to show her that Jesus is God, and that her former concept of God was satanic. Jesus said,

"He who has seen Me has seen the Father."

John 14:9b

Do you see how this young girl's life reflected her concept of God? As long as God looked ugly to her she acted accordingly. But seeing Jesus changed her forever.

Avoiding Failure or Seeking Success

Is your daily life primarily a story of avoiding failure, or of seeking success?

Your answer to this crucial question will, first of all, reveal your actual concept of God, and, secondly, it will reveal whether or not your good works spring from the joy of the Lord or from fear. **And**, your daily motivation, either fear or joy, will determine how rapidly you can succeed in your endeavors.

In college, in 1961 or 1962, I read a study on human motivation which had a powerful (though not immediate) impact on my walk in the Spirit. I wish I could remember the source, the authors, of this study, but I can't locate the textbook. Anyhow, in this study, two groups of children having similar aptitudes were tested, one child at a time. All children were asked to perform several tasks: To place round pegs in round holes, square pegs in square holes, and so on. These tasks were achievable, yet challenging to children in that age bracket.

As I said, the children had similar capabilities. But the selection of each child for testing was based upon careful studies of their parents, specifically in terms of how each set of parents **motivated** their particular child.

Parents were selected from one or the other of two basic categories: They exhibited either fear of failure or desire for success in motivating their children. Parents were seldom fully conscious of their own motivational behavior towards their children.

I can never forget the two photographs which illustrated the differences in motivation between the two types of parents: Each picture showed a child on the floor performing a task with his or her parents seated on a couch nearby watching. **But**, in one picture the parents were smiling while in the other picture the parents were frowning, and, of course, the parental facial expressions illustrated the two motivational models. One category of parents wanted their kids to succeed fast in order not to embarrass them, or in order to make them look good, thinking, "We want an intelligent child!" The other category of parents mainly enjoyed their children and sat on the couch thinking, "Isn't he cute. Look how hard he's trying. He's doing just fine." Obviously, this latter category was represented by the smiling parents.

Guess what! The children in the **latter** motivational category (with smiling parents) almost always succeeded first. It was discovered that these children with smiling parents were seeking success (as their primary motivation) and enjoying their tasks, while the other children were under pressure: **Their** primary motivation was to avoid failure.

This study ultimately taught me a crucial difference between Christians under legalism (works righteousness) and Christians under grace (the **gift** of righteousness). Christians under legalism are characteristically avoiding failure, although they may vacillate some between avoiding failure and seeking success. Christians under grace are characteristically seeking success; they are less likely to be motivated by fear of failure. Their motivation generally corresponds to their concept of God. It seems to me that this study is exceedingly revealing concerning the contrasting concepts of God which underlie grace and legalism.

You decide: Which approach builds godly character rather then mere religious activity?

What Is Your Concept of God?
He Alone Is Omnipresent

Today we are moving to consider who and even what our God is. A thousand virtues and perfections can't begin to adequately describe Him or glorify Him. First, it is important to realize that Our God has certain characteristics and attributes which are unique to Him and which we can never share. Of course there are many virtues in Our God (such as love and joy and peace and truthfulness and self-control, and so on) which **all** of His people **can** share together with Him, and many excellent books have been written concerning all of these. But perhaps it is even more important for us to understand those characteristics of our God which are **unique to Him** and which **we can never share**, those characteristics which are **never** true of us, but which are **always** true of Him. You see, if there are no ultimate dissimilarities between us (the Church) and God, then the Church itself could be worshipped as God. Conversely, if we cannot think of what is totally unique to Him, and never true of us, then we cannot think of any good reason to worship Him, unless we think that we ourselves are worthy of worship. We know that we are never worthy of worship. But if we know Him, we do worship Him, because there is no one, and nothing, which can compare with Him. And there never will be.

One such characteristic of God's nature which is unique to Him and not shared by us is His **infinity**. And I want you to think on this with me today. I want you to know: Our Lord is infinite.

When we think of infinity we tend to think, "Oh, yes, infinity, we know what that is." It seems simple enough. But we really do not know. Because we are finite. We have definite limits such as size and shape and knowledge. We cannot see the future and we hardly remember the recent past. We know practically nothing of the distant past. Many of us workaholics have wished we could be everywhere at once, but, alas, we could not do it. The point is that, since we have limits, we really do not **know** infinity. Infinity is that which has no limits in size, and no end, and no beginning. Of course, our Lord **does** have moral limits, but they are internal to Him, and not forced upon Him by anyone or anything outside of Himself.

Meditate with me from Psalm 139:6-12a and b,

> *Such* knowledge is too wonderful for me;
> It is *too* high, I cannot attain to it.
> Where can I go from Thy Spirit?
> Or where can I flee from Thy presence?
> If I ascend to heaven, Thou art there;
> If I make my bed in Sheol, behold, Thou art there.
> If I take the wings of the dawn,
> If I dwell in the remotest part of the sea,
> Even there Thy hand will lead me,
> And Thy right hand will lay hold of me.
> If I say, "Surely darkness will overwhelm me,
> And the light around me will be night,"
> Even the darkness is not dark to Thee,
> And the night is as bright as the day.

This Psalm says two things concerning our God which I want to zero in on with you today: First, even though His infinity is too high and wonderful for us, He tells us about it anyhow. And second, God **is** everywhere. That is, He is omnipresent. The Psalmist says that there is nowhere to flee from His presence. Therefore, His presence has no end and no boundaries. He simply **is**. Furthermore, His **Whole** Being is **Personally** present everywhere because He can **Personally** lay hold of the Psalmist wherever he may be. It is essential for you to realize that, while God is everywhere, He is not scattered out, with one part of Him over here and another part over there. But He is everywhere right now, at each and every point, with His **Whole Person**. In fact, it is only "in Him" that "all things hold together." (Col. 1:17) He is a Person, not a cosmic force, and He is wholly and completely and personally present everywhere at all times.

Most New Agers and pantheists believe that God is everywhere in nature because they believe that nature itself is God, or, at least, part of God. That is, God is spirit, but He is also a tree or a tire or a baby or a lizard. But we know that God is **not** the material world — He is a Person. He is definitely in and with everything, governing all creation, yet He is a Person, not a thing. And His presence continues on beyond all creation into infinity. His presence in and with our universe is only a drop in a giant ocean without shores. Furthermore, the ocean is a terribly feeble analogy simply because part of the ocean is here and part of the ocean is over there, while God, unlike water, is not scattered out, but rather He is personally, wholly present everywhere.

Now try to assimilate this: God is **in** and **with** every Christian in a unique, personal, and abiding **relationship** of love and commitment which makes His presence everywhere else in creation pale by comparison. He is present everywhere, but He is **related** to you, as a father to his children, as a husband to his wife. Do you really believe, even in your wildest imaginings, even with all your faults and failures and sin, that you can get lost?

Now please read verses 13-18 in the same Psalm 139, and seek to understand the unique and personal nature of His presence and commitment to you.

Rest in Him.

His Knowledge Is Infinite

What we want to do in today's article is to continue to focus our attention on those magnificent characteristics of our Lord which belong exclusively to Him and which will never be true of us. "Lord, help me to express this; and, in the expression, reveal Yourself to us, since we are incapable of reaching You through our own intelligence. Speak to us Lord, creating faith, letting us see You, for we know that You have a great heart of mercy towards us, and on that basis alone we boldly approach Your Throne of Grace. Amen."

Yesterday, in the light of Psalm 139:6-12, we began looking at how it is that God is infinitely transcendent. That is, He has absolutely no limits of space or of time. And yet we saw that simultaneously He is not scattered out, but instead He fills infinity with His Whole Personal Being: He is omnipresent. Then we asked the question, "Do you really believe you can get lost?" To that we want to add a second question today: "Do you really believe you can be forgotten?" For He knows when a sparrow falls. Actually He has always known because both past and future are present to Him. It is not as if He becomes informed of the sparrow's falling as a result of seeing it fall. He knows it before it happens — He does not gather information from observation as we do. He is not informed by anything. He already knows. (See Psalm 147:5; 1 Samuel 23:10-13; and Romans 11:33-36) And, of course, it is also true, He is there when it happens. God's knowledge of **any** event is never an impersonal, distant knowledge. No. He is there. Thus, when Jesus said every hair of your head is numbered, He did not mean that your hairs are numbered by some giant, distant intelligence or energy. No. He is there in you and with you right now. And He knows you completely. He can read this sentence right through your eyes if He wants to. In fact, He can see everything exactly the way you see it. How may times have you felt that no one understands you? But He understands you completely: "His understanding is infinite." (Psalm 147:5) And there's that word again: **Infinite**.

Now here is a Scripture that should be easy to understand in light of all we've just studied, Proverbs 21:30,

> There is no wisdom and no understanding
> And no counsel against the Lord.

There is no counsel against the Lord...none. How could there be? Why, the very idea is a joke. God's enemies have no privacy. God sits at their stinking war councils! Yea, He always knew them. He knew them before they existed! That's why, "If God is for us, who is against us? ... Who shall separate us from the love of Christ?" (Romans 8:31, 35)

There may be times when Satan looks very big to you. And, true, he does possess supernatural power. And, true, he does "prowl about. . .seeking someone to devour." (1 Peter 5:8) But that in itself is an extremely important point. God is everywhere, but Satan must "prowl about." In Job, when God asked Satan where he had been, Satan answered, ". . .roaming about on the earth and walking around on it." (Job 1:7.) What does such a statement tell you? Clearly, Satan is **not** omnipresent. First he is here, then he is there, but he is never everywhere! **Satan is finite**. He has to travel from one place to another exactly as you and I have to do. Well, not exactly: He uses different conveyance. But, these days, with so many Christians out and about, even though Satan has a lot of help, he probably scurries from one place to another like a harried business executive, never quite catching up with everything. Satan must be a driven workaholic. What a sorry sight! There was a time when he thought he could be God. It should be obvious to you that Satan himself hardly ever thinks about you personally. He can't; he is too limited. He hasn't got time! But it is the very nature of God that He **always** thinks about you. You cannot be forgotten by Him. His understanding is infinite. It is true that Satan has many demons to attack humanity, but you must realize the **massive** differences between Satan and God.

Perhaps the meaning of God's omnipresence is beginning to dawn on you. And hopefully, so also is the meaning of His all-knowingness (omniscience).

A final illustration: You have no direct personal knowledge of what is happening on the planet Pluto right now. The truth is, you weren't conscious of Pluto at all until I mentioned it. In fact, you don't even know what's happening in your own pancreas right now. Even your doctor can't tell you with certainty. That is, he has only general, not personal knowledge of it, without testing. But of course the Lord has perfect knowledge of all that, from Pluto to your pancreas.

In light of these facts, all this bragging that's going on about how smart man is seems ludicrous. This bragging is both the effect and cause of so little knowledge of the Almighty.

What an incredible God we serve! And here is the most incredible thing about Him: That in the midst of all of His intimate personal involvement in the entire universe, there is a person to whom He pays a unique and special kind of attention, attention far beyond the attention He normally and universally gives to the rest of His creation. Listen to Isaiah 66:1, 2:

> Thus says the Lord,
> "Heaven is My throne, and the earth is My footstool.
> Where then is a house you could build for Me?
> And where is a place that I may rest?
> "For My hand made all these things,
> Thus all these things came into being," declares
> the Lord.
> "But to this one I will look,
> To him who is humble and contrite of spirit, and who
> trembles at My word."

There the Lord shall make His Temple, His abode: in him who is humble and contrite of spirit, and who trembles at His Word. And He shall abide forever, in a new and living way. This is a biblical fact.

Only The Lord Is Self-Existent

Our last two articles focused on our God in His absolute infinity. If you'll remember, we also began to contrast infinite God with finite Satan by pointing out that Satan roams to and fro in the earth: He is **not** omnipresent. My impression is that many Christians think Satan is somehow omnipresent and, worse yet, that he is somehow all-knowing. We tend to attribute God-like characteristics to Satan! Very often Christians have asked me, "Can Satan read my thoughts?" This is what the Bible says:

> "O Lord, the God of Israel, there is no God like Thee
> in heaven above or on earth beneath... Thou alone doest
> know the hearts of all the sons of men."
> *1 Kings 8:23a, 39b*

Therefore we know that Satan cannot read your mind unless you give him open access to it. Only the Lord of heaven and earth is all-knowing. Satanic powers may try to whisper thoughts into your mind, but you can learn to bring your thought-life into captivity to Christ. In fact, it turns out that **you** have access to God's mind (1 Corinthians 2:12, 16), but Satan is incapable of gaining access to **your** mind. Jesus' Bride will be absolutely inviolate.

Infinite, Omnipresent, All-knowing. That is our Lord — exclusively! But we can't stop here because there is so much more that is unique and exclusive and awesome about God. Study these words of Jesus with me:

> "For just as the Father has life in Himself, even so
> He gave to the Son also to have life in Himself."
> *John 5:26*

We serve the Living God, but no one has given Him life. He has life in Himself. He alone is the source of **all** life. He **is** life. In another place Jesus said:

> "No one takes it [My life] away from Me, but I lay it down on My own initiative. I have authority to lay it down, and I have authority to take it up again. This commandment I received from My Father."
>
> *John 10:18*

See, He has life in Himself. He is absolutely **self-existent**. No one else can say that! No one else and nothing else is self- existent. **Only God**! You probably think that you agree with this. You will say, "Of course, nothing else has life in itself. Only God does."

But you are a child of the age of science. And you have been trained by materialists. And, therefore, it is likely, for instance, that you have great faith in the so-called "**laws of nature**." Therefore, without even realizing it, you believe that the universe is like a giant precision machine which has sort of a life of its own. Of course, unlike the materialists, **you** believe the universe was spoken into existence and flung into motion by the Lord, the Creator, but now the universe runs more or less on its own, according to laws which God has fixed. Most Christians accept this world view, and it is the source of much error and confusion.

For example, you probably believe in "instinct." Materialistic scientists have taught all of us that the animal kingdom is governed primarily by wonderful, mysterious "instincts." For materialists, instincts somehow explain almost everything, but in reality they explain nothing. Instinct supposedly explains why most animals automatically do the right things to survive without sufficient intelligence or experience to make such decisions. Instinct supposedly explains why and how salmon swim upstream to spawn, and why and how many birds fly south before winter, and on and on.

Yet, close and critical study of so-called instinct reveals many phenomena which the theory of instincts cannot begin to explain. I quit believing in instinct, per se, years ago because I began to see the Personal Presence and government of My God everywhere:

> And He [Jesus] is the radiance of His [the Father's] glory and the exact representation of His nature, and upholds all things by the word of His power. . .
>
> *Hebrews 1:3a*

232

Could God build a universe that could run on its own, independent of His government? Of course He could. And could He make animals and plants with almost magical instincts? Of course, **but** this is not what the Bible teaches. The Bible teaches something entirely different: That His presence and His word uphold **everything** now, and in an ongoing sense. **Thus**, this Scripture, not instinct, explains how migrating birds navigate unbelievable distances. Do you realize that our scientists can only theorize about how birds accomplish this? The fact is that God continually sustains and maintains the universe or else it wouldn't be here. God's creation is **not** self-sustaining. It has no life in itself. And neither do we. The so-called laws of nature are in fact the manifest government of God. Our universe is **not** a giant, independent, precision machine. If it operates in a predictable way according to stable laws, it is because the Lord is there Personally causing it to do so. His Word is upholding it. Colossians 1:17, "in Him all things hold together." **All** things.

Our science is not entirely wrong. It observes the order of things. But our science is inadequate. Science cannot **see** God! The "binding forces" themselves are not observable. And our science deals with observables. Jesus is the binding forces. (Colossians 1:17)

You may say, if God governs His creation so well, why do innocent whales cast themselves on beaches and die? I say God is not the only force influencing them today. The sin of the world is perverting and torturing creation almost everywhere. God is giving mankind time and space to repent; therefore wierd distortions of His design are allowed to continue. But the distortions are not adequate evidence for the cynic to conclude that God has abdicated. No, for it is as true as ever: "In Him we live, and move, and have our being." (Acts 17:28 KJV) Thank you Lord.

Is our universe self-sustaining? No way! Only our Lord has life in Himself. This fundamental change in world view is essential to your faith.

Our next article discusses WHY this change in world view is so essential to your faith.

Why Valid Formulas And Laws Don't Always Work

Valid laws? Valid principles? Valid formulas? Valid keys? Of course these things exist, by the tens of thousands! From physics to football to the Kingdom of God, there are principles and laws which apply. However, all of these function **only** because God sustains them. As we have seen, none of them are self-sustaining, self-existent entities functioning independently from the Lord. We are **not** in a "mechanical universe." God did not merely wind up the universe like a mechanical wind-up toy, then set it free to run itself.

There are lots of valid keys and formulas and laws which apply to walking in the Spirit, several of which are in this book, such as "How To Let Jesus Be Your Righteousness," and "Laughter, An Ultimate Weapon." Outside this book, I've applied scores of valid formulas, many of which are familiar to you. For example, we all know that praise is a powerful expression of faith, and God honors it. And we know that we receive as we give.

I am well aware that many Bible teachers assert that the biblical principles and laws which they expound operate as automatically and as reliably as any laws of physics, because the Lord created these laws and principles. Okay, but keep in mind that, as with any law of physics, none of these biblical laws and principles is mechanical, independent, or self-sustaining. None of them is self-existent.

Surely, all trustworthy Bible teachers are aware that there have been times when the Lord temporarily **countermanded** His own physical laws, such as the time He walked on water, for example. He can do this **any time** He sees fit. He is God. Is it possible that the Lord might also (for good reasons) countermand some of His other laws and principles from time to time? Impossible you say?

Well, of course, the Lord cannot do anything which is against His own nature and character. For instance, God cannot lie (Numbers 23:19), precisely because His nature and character is grace and truth.

But, my assertion is that His nature and character take priority over lesser laws and principles which He created. For example, concerning one of the Ten Commandments Jesus said,

> "The Sabbath was made for man, not man for the Sabbath.
> "Consequently, the Son of Man is Lord even of the Sabbath."
>
> *Mark 2:27,28*

Note how Jesus put this particular Law in its proper place of service in God's hierarchy of priorities: Jesus said that this Law must **serve us**, and that He rules His Law.

A rather difficult situation has developed for teachers in the Body of Christ, especially in the Charismatic Movement: On the one hand, we want to teach all of God's people to BELIEVE HIM, to believe all of His Word, with all of His laws and principles. On the other hand, we want to teach all of God's people to understand His priorities, and His nature and character, so that God's people do **not** give merely to get, and do **not** praise primarily for power, even though these principles (properly applied) are valid. Many of God's people need to learn to stop trying to play god with God through faith. Such practices don't sit well with the Lord, and they are harmful to all who practice them.

All of which leads to this: Is the Lord, in His love, duty-bound to honor His own principles and laws if by doing so He would injure some of His beloved kids in the process? Does that make sense? Remember, love is the very heart of His nature. ("God is love" —1 John 4:8) Thus, His love has priority over many of His physical and spiritual laws. Thus, God's love may countermand His lesser laws and principles from time to time as necessary. The Lord will not violate His own nature and character. Our God is no mere vending machine. Thus, there may be times when some of His laws and principles do not seem to work immediately or automatically for us.

For example, I do not allow my eleven year old son to drive my car at this time, even though I will encourage him to do so in four years. He can't see over the dashboard right now. That is the situation for many of God's kids in terms of spiritual laws and principles. Growth is a biblical principle too. Many of God's kids are not mature enough to handle large amounts of wealth and power, for example.

Don't be disillusioned if some truth doesn't seem to work right now.

Keep eating and growing. Don't get angry at the Lord. He knows what He's doing. Just continue developing your skills, the way children do. Just continue practicing and growing.

This book is not written to attack **any** biblical principles or physical principles, but rather to set them in motion! Many Christians have been applying various laws and principles as a mechanical means to manipulate God and to establish their own righteousness. I.e., they have been applying the Lord's laws and principles legalistically! I see this as more a problem of ignorance than of rebellion, ignorance of the gift of God's righteousness. So, the Lord has been letting many Christians fail in order to bring them back to grace.

Through grace we understand that the Lord **owes** us nothing, and we stop throwing tantrums to get Him to obey us. Yet, we can continue to believe Him to do great and mighty things for His own glory and for our good. We can believe, because we stand in His righteousness.

Here is what all of this has come down to in my own life. I am no longer scrambling to learn new formulas for success, even for my own walk in the Spirit. I've probably heard and tried most of the formulas. Many of them are working for me now. But it's come down to this: Now I'm just hungry for the Lord Himself. That's all. I just want His presence: the Person Himself, without Whom the principles and laws and formulas are empty! Not that the principles and laws and formulas are unimportant, but I want the Person, then the Program, not just the Program.

I firmly believe that most of you will come to exactly this same place sooner or later. Even success doesn't satisfy. Jesus satisfies!

Can *You* Walk On Water?
Should *You* Walk On Water?

Maybe yes, maybe no.

In Matthew 14:24-32 Jesus came walking on the water toward His disciples, who were in their boat. After He had identified himself to them, Peter called out, "Lord, if it is You, command me to come to You on the water." Jesus did, and Peter began to walk on water.

Imagine what might have happened if Peter had decided that the other disciples in the boat could, **and should**, follow him. And, suppose Peter didn't remind them to get the command from Jesus first, as he himself had done. Suppose he insisted that **his** call was **their** call. Picture the other eleven disciples leaping out of the boat in response to Peter's persuasion. In all probability, the rest of the story would have described eleven disciples gagging and gasping for air and shouting for help amid swirls of bubbles and giant waves, until Jesus intervened to straighten the mess out.

This illustration provides a more or less accurate description of the scene in several of the most zealous segments of the Body of Christ today. Here's what I mean: Strong believers, with legitimate vision from God (concerning their own personal call and gifting), often tend to feel that all Christians should share their vision. Their call, or their specific mission field, or their specific work, seems to them to be the most important of all. Therefore, they spend a lot of time and energy persuading as many Christians as possible to share their burden with them. And since their vision and call is from God, the Lord does lead many other Christians to share the burden with them. But, simultaneously, many Christians are being pulled into projects where God hasn't called them. Thus, figuratively speaking, what worked well for the Apostle Peter is turning out to be a swimming lesson for others!

In 20 years as a pastor, I've had literally hundreds of sincere Christians attempt to persuade me to accept their personal visions and burdens. They all meant well, but I can't do it all. And God never called me to do it all, although it is all important. One of my greatest struggles as a pastor has been to settle the issue, what, specifically, does the Lord want **me** doing?

Of course, **every** Christian is called to repentance, and **every** Christian is called to worship and to walk with the Lord. And, in my view, every Christian is called, in one capacity or another (there is **much** diversity), to be part of fulfilling the Great Commission. The beauty of God's plan is that there is a **Body** of Christ. Thus, none of us has to be able to do everything. Jesus said, "My yoke is easy, and my load is light." (Matthew 11:30) You and I were not designed to carry everyone else's yokes. Jesus' yoke for you will **fit** you, or He will fit you for it. Generally, if you attempt to accept someone else's yoke (and it isn't God's will), pain develops. It won't fit. You will feel like David trying to wear King Saul's armor. If you persist, you may burn out.

One of Satan's favorite devices for breaking God's obedient people is this: If Satan can't get you into ongoing disobedience, he takes the opposite approach: He tries to get you to bury yourself under someone else's heavy armor. He tries to burn you out. In other words, if Satan can't get you to do anything **wrong**, he simply tries to get you to do too many things **right**!

Grace means you don't have to be what everyone else thinks you should be. Grace means the Lord isn't angry if you, "test the spirits," (I John 4:1) and if you, "prove all things," (I Thessalonians 5:21 KJV), to see what God's direction is for you.

It takes courage to do this, and it takes confidence in grace. It takes courage to throw off all the religious weight which you carry, but which you never received from God. One purpose of **Celebration of Grace** is to give you such courage, the courage to trust Jesus Himself to reign in your life.

Don't Sweat It

I've heard it said that work is a curse which Adam brought upon us through his sin. But a careful reading of Genesis 2 and 3 reveals that Adam was given work from the beginning, even before he sinned. (See Genesis 2:15 and 20). Work is not a curse. Rather, here is the curse:

> Cursed is the ground because of you;
> In toil you shall eat of it
> All the days of your life.
> Both thorns and thistles it shall grow for you;
> And you shall eat the plants of the field;
> By the sweat of your face
> You shall eat bread,
> Till you return to the ground...
>
> *Genesis 3:17-19*

See: the curse is in the excessive **toil** and **sweat** which survival now requires because thorns and thistles infest the cursed ground to which we all return at death.

Many of us have had jobs where we sweated profusely, drank gallons of water, and ate lots of salt pills. But most of us have also had jobs where we seldom had to sweat. If you have a job which doesn't make you sweat, does that mean you've escaped this aspect of the curse? Hasn't the industrial revolution delivered millions from the curse of hard, sweaty labor? This seems to be true. On the other hand, perhaps hard, sweaty labor is not actually a curse. Medical science now encourages this. Millions of Americans pay big money to health clubs for the privilege and personal benefit of working up a sweat. Therefore, you might think the Bible is unscientific, since it depicts hard sweaty labor as a curse.

But don't jump to such conclusions without looking at the real implications of these verses. The point is that making a living is tough

239

for most people. There is little real security. There are few guarantees. We can't guarantee our own existence. The poor man worries about making a living, and the rich man worries about keeping it. Worry is a key word here.

Jesus Himself, in His parable of the sower, indicated a clear link between worry and thorns and thistles, and remember that Genesis 3 connected thorns and thistles with sweat. In Jesus' parable, the thorns and thistles which choke the fruit tree are the cares and **worries** of this life:

> "And the one on whom seed was sown among the thorns, this is the man who hears the word, and the worry of the world, and the deceitfulness of riches choke the word, and it becomes unfruitful."
>
> *Matthew 13:22*

These are the thorns: "the worry of the world" linked with "the deceit fullness of riches." These curses attack almost everyone, unless we learn to trust Christ. It is interesting that Genesis 3 connects **sweat** with thorns and thistles, and Jesus connects **worry** with thorns and thistles, because this creates a biblical connection between sweat and worry. It is equally interesting that our society has picked up on this connection between sweat and worry in the expression, "Don't sweat it," meaning, or course, don't worry. One definition of sweating in our dictionary is: "a condition of anxiety." (Webster) Jesus' connection of thorns to worry seems to indicate a link in His mind between the curse of Genesis 3 and worry. The critical thing to remember is that Jesus bore the **entire** curse (of thorns, sweat, worry and death) as our substitute at Calvary. In the garden, praying, facing the cross, He certainly **sweated**, great drops of blood. Then, just before He made that climb up Golgotha to die as a criminal (death being the essence of the curse), the soldiers mashed a cruel crown down upon His brow: The crown of thorns! Without realizing it they had crowned Him with the curse of Genesis 3! God wanted you and me to see the complete connection between Genesis 3 and the cross. The connection is total. Jesus bore the whole curse. The work is complete. The sweat, the thorns and thistles, the shed blood: Jesus paid it all.

Now here's my point: My focus in this article is specifically on the biblical and cultural connection between sweat and worry. At Calvary, the thorns and thistles and the sweat of worry and anxiety have been dealt with.

First of all, worry and anxiety must be removed from our relationship with God. This happens as we come to rest in His grace. Then, beyond that, we can repent and be free from the deceitfulness of security in riches, and from the worries of this world. Thus, the fruit of the Kingdom will not be choked by weeds. Instead love, joy, peace, patience and faith, all the fruit of the Spirit, can flourish.

In Ezekiel 44 important instructions were given to the special priests who were going to minister directly to the Lord:

> "...wool shall not be on them while they are ministering...
>
> "Linen turbans shall be on their heads, and linen undergarments shall be on their loins; they shall not gird themselves with *anything which makes them* sweat."
>
> *Ezekiel 44:17b, 18*

Obviously this Scripture has some very practical implications for your personal worship and relationship with God. You are not to have anxiety in it. The prerequisite is a garment which eliminates sweat. That garment, as we have seen many times now, is the Lord Jesus Christ. It is the righteousness of Jesus. It is the gift of right standing before God. Anxiety is eliminated only by eliminating the necessity of works righteousness and forced worship.

Anxiety and sweat are eliminated only as you learn to put all of your trust and confidence in God's righteousness, in God's power, and in the rivers of living water which He makes available in you.

Today again, it is your joyous privilege to put on the Lord Jesus Christ and thus, and only thus, to make no provision for the flesh to fulfill its lusts (or its worries). Review Romans 13:14.

What Can You Learn From The Size Of Your Bible?

Before you ever open it, the Bible can teach you a big lesson. Sound ridiculous? Okay, the next time you are in a good library, take a look at the shelves which contain books on the history of England. No doubt you'll notice that one of the greatest works on English history is a seven-volume set of books which fills about two feet of library shelf space. It seems quite detailed, yet, if you think about it, a great and old nation like England must have generated a mass of historical documents that could easily fill ten libraries from floor to ceiling. So a seven-volume history is actually extremely selective and, for the most part, quite sketchy.

Now think about the Bible, one volume. How much material do you suppose has been generated in **all** of God's dealings with mankind during thousands of years of world history? Jesus' ministry alone could overwhelm our libraries. Speaking of Jesus' three years of ministry, the Apostle John exclaimed,

> And there are also many other things which Jesus did, which if they were written in detail, I suppose that even the world itself would not contain the books which were written.
>
> *John 21:25*

Talk about a selective Book! How many tough decisions do you think had to be made concerning what material to include and what material to omit from the Bible?

Therefore, the Bible is far and away the most carefully selective book in the world. Our Sovereign Lord governed the process.

An almost automatic conclusion has to hit you at this point: The Bible must be filled with the most important words in the world because, out of the billions of events, illustrations, teachings, and characters which the Lord could have chosen, He chose what He chose.

There is Divine Wisdom in each and every word that's there, right down to the genealogies. It is dangerous to teach or to believe that the Lord was somehow imprecise in the way He allowed those words to be chosen and expressed, because, whether we like it or not, our faith hangs most basically on the Bible, not on subjective experiences. It hangs on the Bible as we, as the Body of Christ, learn to understand it together under the inspiration of the Holy Spirit.

Jesus' personal use of Scripture clearly demonstrates my assertion that each and every word (of original Scripture) was carefully chosen and expressed, by the Lord Himself, working through His anointed authors. For example, on several occasions during His ministry Jesus confronted a sect of Judaism called Sadducees: Sadducees did not believe in the resurrection. One of Jesus' debates with the Sadducees is recorded in Matt. 22:28-33. Jesus had such confidence in the Divine accuracy of each and every word in the Old Testament that He hung His entire argument proving life after death on the tense of a single verb — present tense, "am": "I AM THE GOD OF ABRAHAM, AND THE GOD OF ISAAC, AND THE GOD OF JACOB." These words, quoted by Jesus in Matt. 22:32, originated in Exodus 3:6; they are words which God spoke to Moses hundreds of years **after** the deaths of Abraham, Isaac and Jacob. Therefore, Jesus insisted that Abraham, Isaac and Jacob **must** still be alive (even though they had died) because God had said, "I am their God," and Jesus argued, "God is not *the God* of *the* dead but of *the* living." (Matthew 22:32) You see, the Bible is so accurate that, if there were no life after death, God would have said to Moses, "I was Abraham's God, and I was Isaac's God, and I was Jacob's God." But God said, "I am their God." So how could the Sadducees **not** believe in life after death? Read Matthew 22 and you will realize that the Sadducees were silenced by Jesus through the tense of this one verb from the Old Testament. They were stopped cold. They couldn't answer. The multitudes were astonished at Jesus' teaching.

Therefore, we can have absolute confidence in the total, word by word, Divine inspiration of the Bible as it was originally penned. But what happened to the Bible through the years since it was first written? Is it still accurate? Can we still trust the Bible? The answer is that our ancient manuscripts aren't perfect, but we now have many early manuscripts which we can compare with one another. This ability to compare early manuscripts has resolved all but a few minor questions concerning the original text.

However, as important as our scholarship is, there is one issue which is even more relevant to our Bible's accuracy than our scholarship: The present accuracy of our Bible hinges not so much on human mechanisms and scholarship as it does on the integrity and power of God Himself. Has God been able and willing to bring the Bible intact on down to us? Would it be important to Him to do so? Obviously, the answer to both of these questions is an emphatic YES! God loves us to the radical extreme of giving His Own Son to suffer incredibly to redeem us. Therefore, even common sense tells us that such radical love would be careful to preserve the **only** Book capable of communicating His Gospel accurately. Thus, even the accuracy of our Bible rests on grace.

Keep in mind, however, that some **translations** are better than others. To understand the Bible, you need a scholarly translation (preferably, **several** scholarly translations), in modern English, based on the best available manuscripts, you need fellowship with mature believers, and you need to be full of the Holy Spirit. In America you can have all of the above. We are blessed beyond measure.

Very important: Learn to read your Bible as if each verse (even each rebuke) is somehow related to the grace of God, because it is. Let God's grace, and His way of dealing with sin, always be your context. Then all Scripture can accomplish the Lord's purposes in your life.

How To Get Into The Bible
#1 Read First, Study Later

We all face some major deterrents to really plunging into the Bible. Time constraints, TV, laziness, satanic opposition, poor reading ability. And here's one you might not have thought of: Our desire to critically analyze and understand everything in the Bible **the first time** we read it: This tendency, in itself, is a major deterrent to really plunging into the Bible. Of course, this isn't an entirely bad desire if it flows from our desire to know God. But, for many years, my own desire to critically analyze the Bible verse by verse caused me to bog down in details so that I read only small portions of Scripture. I never really got into the Bible.

Here's what I learned and here's my advice to you: First, get a good easy-reading translation and read! Read **fairly rapidly** — just let the Word begin to flow through you. Don't be continually stopping to look up cross-references, and resist trying to figure out everything you can't understand. You see, even if you spend hours tracing down cross-references, many things won't become clear to you until you've read the **entire Bible** completely through. Till then, be careful not to bog down in curiosity.

Certainly, there will be times to stop reading in order to think about or to respond to a passage of Scripture. But, generally, the Holy Spirit won't stop you on things which you **don't** understand. Rather you'll find that He will stop you on things which you **do** understand, to deal with you concerning some important issue.

A good, easy-reading translation? I used to use the King James Version almost exclusively. Many times, after hours of puzzling over a passage, when I finally came to understand it, I would think I had a great revelation, when actually all I had done was finally manage to figure out what the King James English meant. King James English is a bit like a foreign language to us these days. I still love the KJV and I've quoted from it a lot in this book. But there are new, recent

245

translations on the market which are exciting, easy reading.

Then, just let His Word flow through you. Jesus said, "Now ye are clean through the word which I have spoken unto you." (John 15:3 KJV) He said this to His disciples in spite of the fact that they had not **understood** portions of what He had said to them. Trust God and start reading.

#2, Those Big Little Bites

Begin by taking small, manageable bites of Scripture. Start with the shorter New Testament epistles (4-6 chapters), but treat each one as a letter from a friend — that's really what they are. Read each **at one sitting**, just the way you would read a letter from a friend. You wouldn't read a letter from a friend in piecemeal fashion. You can read Colossians (4 chapters) in about 15 or 20 minutes if you use a good translation and if you don't bog down in analysis. You probably have at least 20 minutes or a half an hour to spare several times during the day, not necessarily in the morning, but perhaps at lunchtime or breaktime.

When you have read all of the short epistles, you will have read Galatians, Ephesians, Philippians, Colossians, I, II Thessalonians, I, II Timothy, Titus, Philemon, James, I, II Peter, I, II, III John and Jude. It will have taken you two weeks at the most, if you have read only one or two of these per day. **And** God will have spoken to you and helped you many times.

Now, go to Matthew and John. **Always** read for 15 or 20 minutes, and try to cover four or five chapters each time. At this rate, you will be through the whole New Testament in two and a half months. You won't even know how or when you did it — you'll have eliminated a great deal of wasted time.

Do you see the second principle? Don't try to bite off the whole Bible in one day. Set a goal that you can hit fairly easily. **But then hit it**. Your relationship with God will change immensely. Last week, **in spare time**, I read Galatians, Ephesians, Philippians, Colossians, I Peter, and Luke 1-10. I have read these many times before, but I was helped tremendously. I used the same principles I just described to you.

In a few months, when you have formed new habits, **you won't need these principles anymore**, but by then you will have realized that man shall not live by bread alone, but by every word that proceedeth out of the mouth of God.

#3, Study Aids Have A Place, But They Are Definitely Second!

You'll want to get some study aids, especially a good concordance (Crudens, Strong's, Anderson's, and there are several others). You'll want to do some subject studies and some word studies: i.e., on the Person and work of the Holy Spirit, or on Who is Jesus?, etc. Ultimately, the Lord will have you looking up all kinds of cross-references. You'll need to read many important Christian authors. But I have seen Christians bogged down **in every one** of these things. **Never** let such things bog you down or keep you out of the Bible. They are meant as supplements. **The Bible First**!

Do all the rest. **But never quit simple Bible reading**. Just reading! You'll find the Word dwelling in you richly in wisdom. From **just reading** you'll find yourself becoming quite familiar with the general contents of every book. God wants such knowledge **in you**, not just in the preacher.

One further suggestion: Switch translations often. This way you won't get hung up in anyone's theology. Every new translation gets criticism for mistakes, etc. They all have a few. Don't be afraid. Use several. God will guide you. Switching translations from time to time also has good **shock effect**. That's because **all** translations **have strong points** where the meaning of the Word will hit you square between the eyes.

Oh, yes, and I must close today with a classic quote from Bob Mumford: "If you have a Bible that's so beautiful and so good that you can't mark in it, **throw it away and get another one!**"

Hope this helps you some. God bless you as you do it.

Join The Body Of Christ

> Not forsaking our own assembling together, as is the habit of some, but encouraging *one another;* and all the more, as you see the day drawing near.
>
> *Hebrews 10:25*

Become part of a church which provides you with a healthy environment for growth, but, whatever you do, don't develop unrealistic expectations for the people there. Everyone is a clay pot, and far from perfect. Instead learn to give more and more grace.

You'll find that you need the Body of Christ and that the Body of Christ needs you. But bear this in mind, as a wise old brother lovingly said to me one time, "Jeff, if you ever do find a **perfect** church, don't **you** go there."

Get the point? It no doubt applies to you as well as it does to me.

Let me interject that many hurting people have discovered the vital importance of support groups for overcoming almost any addiction or problem. Well, God invented the support group! It's called the Church. And even though many churches have departed from God's design, the Body of Christ, with grace and power, can still become the best support group in the universe. I myself have experienced two churches which were healthy, healing support groups. They were fulfilling Christ's ministry of Isaiah 61.

Scars

The Apostle Paul, writing to Timothy:

> I thank Christ Jesus our Lord, who has strengthened
> me, because he considered me faithful, putting me into
> service; even though I was formerly a blasphemer and
> a persecutor and a violent aggressor. And yet I was
> shown mercy, because I acted ignorantly in unbelief; and
> the grace of our Lord was more than abundant, with the
> faith and love which are *found* in Christ Jesus.
> It is a trustworthy statement, deserving full accep-
> tance, that Christ Jesus came into the world to save sin-
> ners, among whom I am foremost *of all.*
>
> *I Timothy 1:12-15*

More than once in his letters Paul spoke of how, while a Pharisee,
he had attacked the Church. In Galatians he said he had been trying
to destroy it. On the Damascus Road Jesus told Paul (Saul) that he
had been persecuting Him.

But, do Paul's rather frequent references to his former manner of
life indicate that he was suffering guilt? Obviously not. This is the great
missionary Apostle who carried the good news of the grace of God
far and wide. This is the Paul who knew by his own freedom from
guilt that,

> There is therefore now no condemnation for those who
> are in Christ Jesus.
>
> *Romans 8:1*

Nevertheless Paul's former manner of life left some sort of a lasting
impression on him. He never forgot where he came from, and he never
ceased to marvel at the extreme mercy of God which had saved him.
More than once Paul seemed to be saying, ''If God can save me, He

can save anybody.''

Then there is the Apostle and Gospel writer Matthew: Whenever he mentioned himself in his Gospel he added, ''the tax-gatherer.'' He had been a self-centered traitor to his own nation, and probably a cheating thief. It's important that he never forgot that. There was no guilt; no open, oozing wound from his past life. But what he was ''before Christ'' left a lasting impression on him.

Then there was Peter who had denied the Lord, and John (the authority on love) who had wanted to call down fire from heaven to wipe out an entire city which had not received Jesus. The Bible hides none of this. It glosses over none of it. Nevertheless, Jesus Christ started a world-wide spiritual revolution with these men.

God Himself seems to remind us regularly where the Apostles came from. Why? Because all that they had ever been, and all that they had ever done, plus all that Jesus Christ had done for them, shaped what they became in Him.

The Apostles were men with many deep scars from their past. These were not open wounds. They had been healed. The Apostles were not plagued by guilt. They had been forgiven. They were not plagued by self-pity. But they all had scars, scars from wounds which they had received from others or scars from wounds which were self-inflicted. God Himself has recorded some of their scars for us. Scars are precious too — under grace. Even scars glorify God. And they are part of our uniqueness. God makes everything glorify Him.

Here's an important truth which I heard years ago on Christian radio. I wish I could remember which preacher said it in order to give credit where credit is due. But I can't remember. Anyhow, here's what He said: ''You never really know a person until you also know his or her scars.'' What a deep truth, and the implications of it are far-reaching and life-changing.

You may have one or two Christian friends who hunger and thirst after righteousness, but who continue to lack stability. The Body of Christ must learn that people didn't all begin at the same starting point. Some people began with three strikes against them; some suffered immense tragedy; some were abused; some had no family life; some were ugly; many felt rejected. Some people have had to come a lot further than others to attain stability and maturity. In other words, some people have more scars. Don't make a bunch of lame excuses for sin. But shooting the wounded is certainly not in the Gospel, either. One problem is, many Christians never bother to touch and know the scars of others. Thus, they tend to judge others based on performance, or other externals.

It all begins with Jesus' scars. We never really know Jesus until we also know His scars. Isn't that true? If Jesus had no scars, He would be no Savior. Period! Thus, if we don't know His scars, we do not know Him. Receiving Jesus **with** His scars brings reconciliation to God. Likewise, much reconciliation in human relationships depends upon receiving one another, scars and all.

It's possible to know lots of doctrine, but never really know the scars. Jesus' nail scars, and the scar on His side, and the scars on His back, tell the whole story: His love, His redemption, His resurrection, and His intention to return to earth to reign with us.

Celebration of Grace is actually a celebration of scars, first His, then ours. What an amazing God we have. Reach out and touch the scars, first in Jesus, then in you, then in others. Embrace the scars. It will transform your attitudes. It will give you love.

Calvary Has No Rivals

No doctrine, no teaching, no principle, no organization, no ritual, no sacrament, (no matter how "biblical") can be raised to the same level of importance as the finished work of the cross for right standing before God. This includes everything: Baptism in water, circumcision, devotional life, Christian service, Christian experiences with gifts of the Spirit, Christian disciplines, and church membership. Several of these things are extremely important, but **none** eclipses Calvary for right standing before God. None! Any teaching which, in effect, raises anything to the same level of importance as the finished work of the cross for right standing before God is error. Period!

What Jesus did in becoming our sin offering is so complete that there is nothing else which you (or anyone else) can ever offer for your sin. The Bible teaches this clearly. Hebrews 10:14-18,

> For by one offering He has perfected for all time those who are being sanctified. [NASB alternate reading]
> And the Holy Spirit also bears witness to us; for after saying,
> "THIS IS THE COVENANT THAT I WILL MAKE WITH THEM AFTER THOSE DAYS, SAYS THE LORD:
> I WILL PUT MY LAWS UPON THEIR HEART, AND UPON THEIR MIND I WILL WRITE THEM,"
> *He then says,*
> "AND THEIR SINS AND THEIR LAWLESS DEEDS I WILL REMEMBER NO MORE."
> Now where there is forgiveness of these things, there is no longer *any* offering for sin.

If there is no longer any offering for sin, then there is no longer any offering for sin. Therefore, nothing any sinner or any saint can do replaces or rivals Calvary as THE means of right standing before God. I realize that I will have to endure much animosity from the religious community for having said this. Yet it must be said plainly and un-equivocally, lest many Christians remain in confusion concerning the biblical grounds for their redemption.

Jesus Christ Himself is your totally adequate sin offering:

> "And there is salvation in no one else; for there is no other name under heaven that has been given among men, by which we must be saved."
>
> *Acts 4:12*

There is no Christian teaching which can eclipse this, and, in fact, all legitimate Christian teaching builds upon it. Let no man or devil rob you of it. It is your firm foundation (I Cor. 3:11), your anchor (Hebrews 6:17-20), and your hope for eternity (I Peter 1:13). It is your rock. To build elsewhere is to build on shifting sand. Forget this and you forget the Gospel. Stand on this and you cannot be shaken.

Calling Sin Sin

Call sin sin, and emphasize God's solution: I have tried to stress these things in as many ways as I can. One thing I hope is settled is that the blood of Jesus atones for real sin. But we must call sin sin and desist from all attempts at self-justification through religious fronts, rationalizations, excuses or blaming others. Freedom from guilt comes only when we come clean.

Therefore, if you have real sin, and you are willing to call it that, Jesus can help you. He will cleanse you.

Now, if this issue is settled, there are a couple of other things that need to be said concerning calling sin sin, and dealing with it God's way, through Calvary.   If we want revival, if we want a genuine outpouring of the Holy Spirit rather than just the constant turnover of "bigger and better" organizations, and if we want to complete the Great Commission in our generation, then we have to preach the Gospel itself.

That means we have to treat sin in all its seriousness, and offer God's only solution: Grace!

Do you know the real reason why grace is not preached extensively? Do you know why many Christians either fail to appropriate grace or fight it with their legalisms? Because there is so little recognition of how serious sin really is: that it goes to the very core of our being; that only God's cure, applied on a daily basis, can overcome it. The result is that, while sin is constantly blasted in Christian preaching throughout the world, all too often the solutions which are offered are along the line of self-discipline and self-help, with little or no emphasis on the blood of Jesus. And millions of Christians apply these disciplines (zealously but imperfectly) as if sin can be corrected so easily. This is humanism, not Christianity. Sin is being constantly underestimated, and not dealt with God's way. So we have large numbers of Christians who **look** okay on the outside, but on the inside they remain tangled and torn and sin-filled, **and** they are not joyful. Many have lost the joy of their salvation. Christian disciplines must be preached in a context where grace is constantly applied against sin. Otherwise, only superficial changes occur, **and** listeners never really focus on Jesus, but only upon themselves and their personal struggle for perfection.

Another reason why simple grace is not preached extensively is pride. The pride of the flesh hates grace specifically because it is so simple that a five-year-old child can understand it and respond to it. Thus, no ego trip can result from grace. Pride makes us want to muscle and combat sin ourselves, and then praise ourselves for our victory. Pride is praise turned manward.

In any case, sin gets blasted regularly, and we hear many powerful and moving exhortations to obedience, or to new systems of obedience, all of which **could be** very pleasing to the Lord if it were done in a context where grace is simultaneously applied against sin. The tragedy occurs when no one except the unbeliever is exhorted to take his sin to Calvary, and believers are merely exhorted to shape up. Is that what we call being **hard** on sin? No, it is being **soft** on it, and it is playing games with it, because Christians are being left with nothing more than self-help solutions. Death is the only true solution, Jesus in our place. (Even if Christians are exhorted to obey ''by the power of the Spirit,'' the Spirit responds to the blood. He works only in league with grace. He works only in conjunction with God's cure.)

If grace is there, then we can apply new systems of obedience, and **then** we can expect the power of the Holy Spirit to transform people.

Most of this problem seems to me to be a product of ignorance rather than of rebellion. We are talking about **sincere** preachers and believers here.

It is time to deal with this ignorance on a massive scale.

Trusting grace means that we are putting our confidence back in God Himself to transform lives (AND NO ONE ELSE CAN). It means that we are again seeing sin for what it really is, and we are again admitting that nothing short of God's cure on a daily basis will work. It means that we are putting our confidence back in the Gospel itself.

I think the Lord wants me to state these things in the strongest terms possible, so that there is understanding. The message must be clear. God wants an increasing outpouring of the Holy Spirit, and it won't happen (even if crowds get bigger) without renewed gutsy preaching of the real Gospel. Real healing and real transformation flow from this and from no other source,

For I am not ashamed of the gospel, for it is the power of God for salvation [a complete package] to everyone who believes, to the Jew first and also to the Greek.

Romans 1:16

Romans is crystal clear concerning what that Gospel is. Let us not be ashamed to preach it, in all its simplicity.

The Fundamentals

I did not say Fundamentalists. I said fundamentals. There are many so-called Fundamentalists who have long since left the fundamentals of grace in order to embrace legalism. Not that Fundamentalists deserve to be singled out as any worse than the rest of us who have done the same thing, but my point is that Christian fundamentals are not necessarily synonymous with Fundamentalists.

Having successfully made this distinction (I hope), here's why I want to talk fundamentals: I know many pastors and preachers who do not emphasize grace much, not because they do not know it, not because they think it is unimportant, not because of pride, but rather because they ASSUME that, like themselves, most of their listeners already know it! They ASSUME that grace has already become a way of life for most of their listeners.

Even if this were true (and experience has shown me that about 75% of the time it isn't) it is important to review the fundamentals regularly. The coaches of professional sports teams go back to the fundamentals regularly even though all of their players are cream-of--the-crop experts. If such review is essential for experts on sports teams, why not for the Body of Christ?

Here is a process for effective teaching which the U.S. Army taught me: You tell them what you are going to tell them. Then you tell them. Then you tell them what you told them. Such repetition seems necessary. It never ceases to amaze me how many Christians are unable to appropriate grace on a daily basis.

Besides, I can hear the "Old, Old Story" a million times. I love it. Tell it to me again.

Teach everything else, the whole council of God if you can, but remember to review the fundamentals. Many Christians can't even lead a friend to the Lord using Scripture. There is no excuse for this. But, thank God, this problem is easily remedied.

Let's do it!

Therefore, I shall always be ready to remind you of these things, even though you *already* know *them*, and have been established in the truth which is present with *you*.

And I consider it right, as long as I am in this *earthly* dwelling, to stir you up by way of reminder...

II Peter 1:12, 13

Preaching Perfection vs. Preaching Redemption

I originally heard this ingenious terminology (that the Body of Christ should be, "preaching redemption rather than perfection," and, as you will read, that the Body of Christ has never "modeled" perfection very well) from some of my friends in Vineyard Ministries International, but I'm about to add some things to this which may be controversial, and I wouldn't want you to "blame" what I say on them! I'll begin here:

> Be ye therefore perfect, even as your Father which
> is in heaven is perfect.
>
> *Matthew 5:48 KJV*

Jesus said this, and I have to believe that He meant what He said.

One of the primary requirements in the Gospel, as you know, is the righteousness of God, and nothing less. By now this requirement of the righteousness of God should be familiar to you, you should be very much at home with it, and as a blood-bought child of God you should not feel threatened by it. You know how to appropriate grace daily, as the Holy Spirit enables you to do so. Therefore you always know where to begin to fulfill Jesus' injunction to be perfect.

Begin with **imputed** perfection. We know that this word "perfect" can be biblically defined as complete and mature, and that it doesn't **necessarily** imply sinless perfection. Yet, in this passage in Matthew 5:48, Jesus was obviously implying sinless perfection because our Father in heaven is sinless and Jesus said we are to be like Him. Acceptance by our Father requires sinlessness.

The Gospel declares such righteousness, and nothing less. Let us not cop out, and rationalize, and redefine perfection, lest we simultaneously nullify the necessity of the blood of Jesus. No, God continues to be perfect, and therefore we continue to need Christ's redemption.

Here's the point I wish to make today: Jesus Christ preached perfection. There is no doubt about that: His very nature is perfection. **However**, Jesus' **primary** message was **not** perfection. His primary message was redemption. It is absolutely accurate to say that Jesus preached perfection **only** in order to preach redemption. Remember that He came, not to moralize, but rather to die for our redemption.

Listen. It is time for the Body of Christ to stop mere moralizing. It is time to cease preaching primarily perfection, and to return to preaching perfection in order to preach redemption. In other words, preach holiness **God's way**!

Otherwise the Lord will allow us to continue to become the laughing-stock of America!

What is our witness right now, today, before a lost and dying world? What is our testimony?

Has the Church of Jesus Christ been a model of perfection? Surely, after 2,000 years, we must concur that the Body of Christ has never modeled perfection very well. And now a 20th century super-critical secular media, with a lot of motivation from Satan, is always quick to condemn us and to laugh at us.

Recently the roar of laughter has become almost deafening, and perhaps rightly so. You may not like this next statement: The Lord has allowed this humiliation of the Body of Christ in America. I do not deny that the sins of some TV preachers have severely damaged the entire Christian mission in the United States and ripples of damage are being felt around the world. Such behavior has roused the suspicion of many unbelievers that Christians are self-righteous phonies. These preachers' humiliation is in fact our humiliation! Don't kid yourself, most non-Christians lump us "born-agains" all into one lump!

Pastors, teachers, and evangelists, and so forth, are to lead by example (I Peter 5:3), and therefore they need to be above reproach.

It remains to be seen if any of these preachers has actually repented. They haven't had time to demonstrate new track records.

Nevertheless, having said all this, the very real possibility exists that this massive humiliation before a super-critical world is being used by God, even as He used Nebuchadnezzar to humble and correct Israel (see Jeremiah 25:1-11). God is restoring **His** message and **His** Gospel. Henceforth, we must preach redemption instead of perfection or we must shut up!

We cannot model perfection, at least not yet, but we can perfectly model Christ's redemption: Admitted sinners, learning to love, but not perfect by a long shot, powerfully forgiven and freed from condemnation, reconciled to God by grace, heirs to all His promises and to heaven, totally through His gift of grace.

Face it: **Every** Christian is capable of the lowest evil apart from the grace of God:

> Wherefore let him that thinketh he standeth take heed lest he fall.
>
> *I Corinthians 10:12 KJV*

> Pride *goeth* before destruction, and a haughty spirit before a fall.
>
> *Proverbs 16:18 KJV*

The only real difference between us and the rest of the world, or between us and these fallen preachers, is the grace of God. Face it! Preach it! You can also celebrate it!

Satan's criticism can be crammed back down his throat. Paul said,

> For we preach not ourselves, but Christ Jesus the Lord; and ourselves your servants for Jesus' sake.
>
> *II Corinthians 4:5 KJV*

We preach not ourselves. We preach Jesus, our Messiah, crucified and risen. We are servants, not accusers. We definitely want to continue to press into sanctification and to aim at perfection, but we dare not brag about our righteousness to a dying world. In fact, the Lord would forbid us to do that. Let us **do good works, but play down our own righteousness. Then**, Satan's criticisms of our imperfections can be turned into illustrations of the Gospel, since we are sinners saved by grace.

Character assassination has become almost a way of life in the United States, especially in the media. Now, more than ever before, the Body of Christ **can** and **should** be an unequalled oasis from all this condemnation through the message of redemption. However, the preaching of perfection without grace condemns, and it constantly humiliates us because we fail so regularly. This is devastating to the cause of Christ. Worse yet, mere moralizing saves no one!

Let's preach the Gospel! **That** we can model.

Jesus had the wonderful ability to set the standard for perfection, yet, simultaneously, sinners followed Him by the tens of thousands. The only way this can be explained is that they felt loved. Jesus gave them hope in the midst of their sin and shame. This is because Jesus preached redemption.

One thing we know: Jesus was not condescending. He hated the sin, but loved all sinners. He **preached**, then **provided** redemption through His cross.

God sent not His Son into the world to condemn the world. (John 3:17) The Body of Christ had best get that straight. Can it happen? I hope so.

Risk Taker

Some people love taking risks and others hate taking risks. I guess I fit in both categories: I love taking risks, and I hate taking risks. I love being in a secure place, yet I'm bored if an element of risk or danger is lacking. Of course, walking as best we can in obedience to God seems quite secure (and it is) because He holds our future. But still, more than once in our lives, He may ask us to "risk" everything on just one thing: His faithfulness. In fact, that is exactly what happens when we stake our lives totally on grace.

The Bible is filled with the histories of men and women of God who were asked to take incredible risks based solely on the promises of God. Like Moses, at 40, probably the #2 man in Egypt, and possible heir to the throne of the wealthiest nation in the world, who "chose rather to suffer affliction with the people of God, than to enjoy the pleasures of sin for a season." (Hebrews 11:25 KJV) He forsook all the wealth and power of Egypt, a **risk** that never really began to pay off until 40 years later. In the end, however, there was no known contemporary of Moses who knew the Lord as Moses knew Him.

The willingness to take risks is an essential characteristic of leadership.

Yet there is one risk taker who risked much more: Jesus Himself. He took what might seem to be a very poor risk indeed, considering the awful history of mankind: For thousands of years the Creator had invested his best in mankind, but not many people responded. Mostly, the Lord got massive rejection. If I were Him, I would have said, "That's enough, I've invested too much already. To do more would be like throwing good money after bad. Let them die — they seem to love it so much!" But instead, in accord with His Father, Jesus left His place of glory and honor way up there, and took the form of a servant, and was born among us. The Son of God was a baby in a very poor family. Thirty-three years later, dying as a criminal, He accepted the massive rejection one more time. Risking everything, investing everything, He allowed Himself to be nailed to a cross on

Golgotha.

Contemplating the history of mankind, and the motley little crew which Jesus had gathered around Himself, most of whom had fled into the night, it seems like He took the most ridiculous risk in the universe! What in the name of all that makes sense was He doing there? The obvious answer to that question is that He was laying down His life for all of our sin. Clearly, that was His purpose. But it should also be clear that He was convinced that His death for us was worth the risk. Why? If you can handle it, He was staking His life on something: That you and I could not ignore or disdain what He did for us there. I can't help but believe that the Lord could see **us** from Golgotha, and He said, "Now they will respond to Me. Now they will take Me seriously. They cannot ignore this. Now they will risk everything for Me as I have risked everything for them. Now, because of Calvary, they will trust Me."

A few days later, resurrected from the grave, Jesus Christ gave His "Great Commission" to His Apostles. Then, soon after that, He ascended back to His Father. Not long after His ascension, He sent His Spirit. He literally poured His Spirit into them, **enabling them** (with grace) to risk everything for Him as He had done for them. And risk they did! Many of them ultimately, joyfully, shed their own blood for their Savior and His people.

This radical response to grace is exactly what happens to any believer who finally sees Calvary and the empty tomb (**especially** if such a one has also become painfully aware of the depth and the hopelessness of his own sinfulness). This is the **danger**, if you can handle it, of knowing grace:

> For the love of Christ controls us, having concluded this, that one died for all, therefore all died; and He died for all, that they who live should no longer live for themselves, but for Him who died and rose again on their behalf.
>
> Therefore, we are ambassadors for Christ, as though God were entreating through us; we beg you on behalf of Christ, be reconciled to God.
>
> *II Corinthians 5:14, 15, 20*

It is a fact of history that the Apostle Paul lost his life to the grace of God. It remains true that the grace of God is a free gift which we could never earn, yet such grace ultimately claims us, and in the best sense imaginable, grace winds up costing us everything. That's the ''danger'' of knowing, really knowing, grace.

Yes, but this radical commitment is what we have longed and prayed for. Grace is the **only** source of ultimate devotion.

Grace: The Tender Trap

Here is a verse which used to puzzle me greatly:

> But *there is* forgiveness with thee, that thou mayest
> be feared.
>
> *Psalm 130:4 KJV*

This verse was puzzling to me because it says that God is to be feared because of His forgiveness. Why should anyone fear God's forgiveness?

One more time, allow me to illustrate the answer to this question from my own life experience:

Back in 1963, when I quit on the Lord, I had magnificent reasons (not just excuses) for doing so. There were still some areas of my thought-life which were nearly as bad as before I got saved. For example, I was constantly pressured by lust and jealously and anger. I didn't want to be a lukewarm Christian. Therefore, I couldn't accept such gross imperfections. I wanted to be a full-on Christian, or no Christian at all: no half-way, no games. I wanted to be holy as He is holy, or I wanted to quit. You need to know that, at that very time, I was teaching and preaching and the Lord was using my testimony mightily. Believe me when I say that I was no slouch. I was trying as hard as I could. But, because I was so far from perfect, I quit. I went back to my old life, and for five years I sat on bar stools again. I concluded that Christianity was only for good people, only for normal, well adjusted, nice people.

But, after five years, when Jesus brought me back, He taught me His grace. Now I know His grace. I know that His grace is greater than all my sin. I **can** purify myself, even as He is pure. I can get up and start over again anytime I fall. I can serve Him without hypocrisy, because He is my righteousness, not me. I used to be able to say, "I'm too weak to be a good servant of God," but now I have to agree with God that my weakness is no excuse to quit. The Lord says,

"...My grace is sufficient for you, for My power is perfected in weakness."

II Corinthians 12:9a (Jeff's translation)

Specifically, of course, the Lord spoke these words to the Apostle Paul. What an amazing and crucial revelation: That God can manifest His power BEST through our weaknesses! Therefore, Paul went on to express the great paradox of Christ-centered ministry:

Most gladly, therefore, I will rather boast about my weaknesses, that the power of Christ may dwell in me...
...for when I am weak, then I am strong.

Verses 9b and 10b

Thus, my personal weaknesses can no longer provide me with excuses to quit. Thus I now understand that the most fearful thing in God is His forgiveness. Why? Because, if I can always be forgiven, and if I will be accepted in spite of my weaknesses, then I'm trapped!

As you finish this book, you need to realize that the most dangerous thing about God is not His judgement and not His wrath, but rather His mercy! Because His mercy wipes out all excuses. Every sinner qualifies for mercy. Thus, the entire world is left without excuses. **That's why** refusal to respond to grace leads to eternal hell, because THERE IS NO EXCUSE NOT TO RESPOND. Thus **you** are trapped by grace!

Understand this: Legalism can never hold you the way grace can. You see, if the legalist falls, he's dead. But the person who is justified by faith has power not only over sin, but also over defeat. The Bible says,

For a just *man* falleth seven times, and riseth up again...

Proverbs 24:16a KJV

So you see how the grace of God is the most dangerous thing in the world. Even if Satan manages to whip you, under grace you can still get up immediately and start over. You have no satisfactory excuse to remain fallen because God will forgive you. You have **one** option: Get up! Over and over and over and over again, until you learn to stand firm. Quitting will never again be a viable option for you. That's why the Bible says that the just man (by God's definition) gets up as often as he falls. In the formation of godly character, **this** is foundational!

Look what the Psalmist said,

> Surely goodness and mercy shall follow me all the days
> of my life: and I will dwell in the house of the Lord for
> ever.
>
> *Psalm 23:6 KJV*

How did the Psalmist learn this? The hard way. **This** is your verse. Take it. What it means is that there is no way of escape from God's love. You are trapped by **infinite** mercy. Mercy will follow you all the days of your life. Legalism can never save you, but grace will never let you go. The tender trap has been sprung, on you!

"Where Do I Go From Here?"

Good question! Once you know grace, what next? Where do you go from here?

Well, you'll find that as you learn to live by grace you will also learn WHO YOU ARE IN CHRIST. And that's probably what's next. Let me put it this way: Learning and growing in all that the Lord Jesus Christ is for you means that you will **also** be learning and growing in all that you are in Him (together with the rest of the body of Christ, of course).

I pray for everyone who reads this book that it will be a springboard (literally) for you, to launch you into your next stage of understanding and growth in who you are in Him. And **that** is where you will find **the Lord's** call and **His** purpose for your life, which is what you really want, or you never would have finished this book.

I'm going to close this book with the last words, THE VERY LAST WORDS, of the Bible. These last words provide strong affirmation that the Lord's **ongoing** will for you is that you CONTINUE IN HIS GRACE AS YOUR WAY OF LIFE:

The grace of the Lord Jesus be with you all. Amen.
Revelation 22:21